Rethinking Strategic Learning

Rethinking Strategic Learning is a thought-provoking and scholarly book that examines learning as both a social and strategic process, invariably linked to emotions and politics that are mobilized by attempts at learning and organizing. It makes a substantial contribution to theories of organizational learning, as well as developing new ideas about critical reflection and collective leadership.

The author outlines a critical perspective on HRD, arguing that staff responsible for learning and change in organizations have put too much effort into the development of individuals and not enough into understanding organizational dynamics that shape individuals' opportunities and abilities to learn and change. HRD is explained as an intervention within a political system as well as a practice of management and leadership, with all the contradictions that attempting to manage and to lead are likely to reveal. This means that the focus of HRD is on action, on developing the capacity to act, on generating credibility through action, and on influencing and working with others in situations loaded with emotion and politics.

The opening chapters of the book develop ideas about strategic learning by using examples from organizations to explore the relationship between emotion and politics. The focus then shifts towards key issues concerning strategic learning in practice, including reflection and leadership.

Rethinking Strategic Learning will be essential reading for students and academics of Management and Organizational Studies, HRD and all those involved in attempts to implement learning and change in organizations.

Russ Vince is Professor of Organizational Learning at the Business School, University of Glamorgan, Wales, where he is Director of the Leadership and Learning Research Unit. He is editor-in-chief of the journal *Management Learning* and he serves on the international advisory boards of the journals *Human Resource Development International*, *Organizational and Social Dynamics* and *Action Learning: Research and Practice*.

Routledge Studies in Human Resource Development
Edited by Monica Lee, Lancaster University, UK

HRD theory is changing rapidly. Recent advances in theory and practice, how we conceive of organizations and of the world of knowledge, have led to the need to reinterpret the field. This series aims to reflect and foster the development of HRD as an emergent discipline. Encompassing a range of different international, organizational, methodological and theoretical perspectives, the series promotes theoretical controversy and reflective practice.

Rethinking Strategic Learning

Russ Vince

Routledge
Taylor & Francis Group

LONDON AND NEW YORK

First published 2004
by Routledge
2 Park Square, Milton Park, Abingdon, Oxon, OX14 4RN

Simultaneously published in the USA and Canada
by Routledge
270 Madison Ave, New York NY 10016

Routledge is an imprint of the Taylor & Francis Group

Transferred to Digital Printing 2010

Typeset in Garamond by
Keystroke, Jacaranda Lodge, Wolverhampton

British Library Cataloguing in Publication Data
A catalogue record for this book is available from the British Library

Library of Congress Cataloging in Publication Data
A catalog record for this book has been requested

ISBN 0–415–30057–6

For Linda, Emilie and Amanda

Contents

Illustrations

Figures

Tables

Acknowledgements

I would like to thank those friends and colleagues who were prepared to read and comment on previous drafts of papers and chapters, who reviewed the first draft of this book, and/or who came to the 'Future Practice of HRD' conference. Collectively, these are: John Burgoyne, Danny Chesterman, Heather Chisholme, Steve Fineman, Yiannis Gabriel, Chris James, Monica Lee, Philip Lenz, Mike Pedler, Julie Reader, Michael Reynolds, John Stevens, Kiran Trehan, Sharon Turnbull and Jean Woodall.

I have had good support throughout from Michael Connolly, Tony Gear and Chris James – all at the University of Glamorgan. Tahir Saleem was a co-author of parts of the chapter on emotion and strategic learning, and I valued his contribution and approach. My thanks go to all the managers in Hyder plc who participated in interviews and reflections. I am appreciative of my father Ron Vince's reading of and comments on the first draft and for his editing skills. I am very grateful to my wife Linda Vince for her reviews and comments particularly on Chapters 1 and 9.

Some of the chapters are variations on academic papers I have already had published. These include: 'The politics of imagined stability: a psychodynamic understanding of change at Hyder plc', *Human Relations* 55/10: 1189–1208, 2002 (material is reprinted here by permission of Sage Publications Ltd, copyright The Tavistock Institute, 2002); 'Organizing reflection', *Management Learning* 33/1: 63–78, 2002 (material is reprinted here by permission of Sage Publications Ltd, copyright Sage Publications, London, Thousand Oaks, New Delhi, 2002); 'The impact of emotion on organizational learning', *Human Resource Development International* 5/1: 73–85, 2002 (http://www.tandf.co.uk/journals/routledge/13678868.html); 'Power and emotion in organizational learning', *Human Relations* 54/10: 1325–1351, 2001 (material is reprinted here by permission of Sage Publications Ltd, copyright The Tavistock Institute, 2001); and 'Learning in public organizations in 2010', *Public Money and Management* 20/1: 39–44, 2000 (material is reprinted here with permission of Blackwell Publishing).

Various permission to publish figures and tables have been granted. Figure 3.1 is reprinted by permission of Sage Publications Ltd, from R. Vince, 'Power and emotion in organizational learning', *Human Relations*, copyright the

Tavistock Institute, 2001. Figure 4.1 is reprinted with permission of the Association for Management Education and Development, R. Vince and L. Martin, 'Inside action learning: an exploration of the psychology and politics of the action learning model', 1993, copyright AMED and the authors. Table 6.1 is reprinted by permission of Sage Publications Ltd, from R. Vince, 'The politics of imagined stability: a psychodynamic understanding of change at Hyder plc', *Human Relations*, copyright the Tavistock Institute, 2002. Table 7.1 is reprinted by permission of Sage Publications Ltd, from R. Vince, 'Organizing reflection', *Management Learning*, copyright Sage Publications Ltd, London, Thousand Oaks, New Delhi, 2002. Figure 8.1 is reprinted by permission of Sage Publications Ltd, from A. A. Gibb, 'The SME transactional and business relationship network', *International Small Business Journal*, copyright Sage Publications Ltd, London, Thousand Oaks, New Delhi, 1997.

1   An introduction

This book is a collection of ideas and interests that have developed over the past five years. The process of researching and writing it started when, in 1998, I took up the Chair in Organizational Learning at the University of Glamorgan. The post was sponsored for three years by Hyder plc, which was at that time the largest private company in Wales, in the United Kingdom. Hyder, which was taken over and ceased to exist in the autumn of 2000, and Hyder managers, figure to a significant extent in this book. The reason why Hyder people wanted to sponsor a Chair at the university was because they thought that a senior academic linked into the organization would be able to provide in-depth and continuous consultancy and inquiry connected to their efforts to promote learning and to manage change. I am not sure that they got exactly what they wanted. As managers and practitioners they had an idea that I would advise and consult on how approaches to learning, managing and organizing could be best applied within the organization 'to add value'. I would help them to further conceptualize learning within the company, and especially help to devise learning strategies for the senior managers.

From my point of view as an academic, I wanted continuous and open access to the company in order to research and to write about the emotional and political dynamics of learning and organizing within Hyder. As I began to develop an action-research approach within the company I realized that here was an organization with a considerable commitment to an idea of organizational learning. Hyder had highly developed internal processes for individual and group learning. The take-up on these processes was mixed, of course, but where individuals wanted to learn they were given the opportunity – whether this was short courses, exchanges, mentoring, or qualification processes. The only explicit proviso or expectation was that such learning would inform practice, helping to create knowledge that could be applied to the benefit of the company. The Human Resource (HR) group in Hyder, alongside colleagues at the University of Glamorgan, had invented 'the learning journey', a flexible structure of learning for Hyder staff.

From the outset, what the HR managers in Hyder wanted me to do was to help them to develop the learning journey for the senior management within the company. They called this the 'strategic level' of learning (set alongside the operational and business levels of learning that were already connected to the company's learning journey idea). They wanted to know: what could or should the learning journey look like for the senior, strategic level of managers in Hyder? This was an important question for the HR managers because senior managers were already replete with formal and informal development, and yet they were also detached from corporate ideas and initiatives to do with learning. An associated and wider issue therefore was that senior managers, if they were detached from the corporate learning journey, would not be leading and encouraging their staff through the lens of continuous, work-based learning. Clearly, they were not. Indeed, why should they when complicated issues of (for example) finance, position, personality and shareholder value dominated their everyday actions and interactions?

I do not have a convincing answer to that question and, despite my enduring personal belief in the value of learning as an organizational metaphor, I am not sure that I ever will. I am convinced that the analysis of the HR group in Hyder was correct: the behaviours and interactions of many senior managers were not strategic in the sense of leading the future direction of the company, nor were they concerned with learning other than in the sense that learning was generally seen to be 'a good thing' for people. Through my research within Hyder I learned that the HR group's intuition about the importance of combining strategy and learning was insightful. In the last five years I have developed (somewhat belatedly from Hyder's point of view!) a perspective on strategic learning that approximates to the hopes expressed for my role within Hyder, particularly by the HR staff. Since I took up the 'Hyder Chair' in 1998 I have written a number of papers that tell parts of the Hyder story. They are incomplete snapshots of the experience of working within complex organizational settings, and they have been revised, combined and developed within this book. Hyder is not the only organization with a role in this book – other organizations I have come into contact with since 1998 are here, but they are not named directly. Together they represent an attempt to better understand one perspective on strategic learning, and particularly to highlight aspects of the relationship between emotion, politics, learning and organizing. While these four concepts are of particular interest to me, I also want to acknowledge that they are all difficult ideas and processes to make sense of, both independently and in relation to each other.

Hyder managers' orientation towards learning could not resolve the emotional and political turmoil that simmered under the surface of managerial relations, nor could it deal with the broader organizational issues that led Hyder towards its demise. This story unfolds throughout the book, and it reflects what I am seeking to understand and to say about the relationship between learning and organizing. One way I express this in the book is by saying that learning is at the same time both desired and avoided within organizations. My interest is in trying to understand the emotions and the politics that construct and are constructed by attempts at learning and organizing. I am also interested in finding a way to bridge academic and practitioner perspectives on learning and organizing.

The fact that the outcome of my academic task is (at least) two years late as far as its impact on the practitioners that sponsored it are concerned seems somewhat typical of the relationship between academics and practitioners. 'They' want quick-fix, put-it-into-action answers to complex questions and 'we' want to complicate answers by continually reframing them in terms of yet more questions, reflections and inquiries. One aim of this book, however, is to explore the interplay and tensions between my academic voice and the meaningfulness and accessibility of this voice in practice. Typically for an academic, I do this more by raising questions, issues and ideas than by providing answers. This is a book that opens up more things than it attempts closure on. I don't have many prescriptions to offer, nor do I advise them, but I have tried to structure the book in a way that keeps issues and examples of practice firmly in mind while advocating critique as the key to strategic learning.

Not so long ago I made a presentation to Human Resource Development (HRD) managers and practitioners from the National Health Service (NHS) in Wales, in which I introduced and argued for several of the ideas in this book. When I had finished my presentation a member of the audience asked the question 'What you have said is very interesting, but what do I have to do to put it into practice?' In response, I said that if there were aspects of what I had been talking about that seemed particularly useful to develop within his organization then he, together with other staff and colleagues, might try to find ways of putting these into practice. 'Yes, but how?', he said. We could have gone round this circle for ever, and in one sense I think that we do. I think that it is a paradox inherent in the lived experience of organizing that 'how-to' prescriptions are and always will be at the same time both useful and unhelpful. But, then, I would say that. These two perspectives on the same story are inseparable. Each enriches the other, and it is clearly part of any journey that seeks to understand the relationship between learning and organizing to explore further the tensions and possibilities apparent between academics and practitioners.

I find that it is as difficult to write about learning as it is to put it into practice. However, as part of this introduction I am going to try to explain what I mean by the various words that make up the title of this book. First and foremost is *learning*. My favourite definition of learning is that it is 'the capacity to doubt those things that seem unquestionably true' (Palmer, 1979). Learning therefore involves the transformation of ideas and actions that have become an integral aspect of current understanding or practice. Learning implies a continuous need to question the knowledge one has gained before it becomes too solid or rigid, thereby affording the possibility of transformation. The things that seem unquestionably true may be facts, attachments, habits, bottom-lines, beliefs, opinions and ways of doing, but there is nothing about them that cannot be transformed. Of course, this does not mean that there is any reason to reinvent the wheel, but it alludes to the idea that there is every reason to reinvent behaviour, relations and ways of organizing. This is not to say that facts, attachments, habits, etc., are unimportant; on the contrary, they may be fundamental to personal and interpersonal health, stability and meaning. However, the pull between stability and transformation that informs learning (and the actions that make learning possible or undermine it) is a key theme of this book. I can emphasize the importance of this definition of learning by saying that it calls into question my certainty that doubt is transformational.

Two particular terms that connect to learning are important to me; these are *experiential learning* and *organizational learning*. In my mind, experiential learning can be explained by a focus on 'here and now' experience within learning groups or 'learning spaces' that have been deliberately created to entertain the possibilities of learning. My experience in such situations is varied, but the most memorable or potent ones usually arise from moments where I feel anxious but also willing to stick around to see what happens; where existing knowledge and expertise is called into question or seems to make little impact; and where others are similarly caught up in exploring what is being mutually created. In addition, there are two consistent issues that arise with experiential learning: first, the determination to make time to reflect on experience is always an integral part of the experience, and second, learning is always situated in social power relations, cultural practices, contexts and artefacts.

I am fond of the following reflection on organizational learning: 'organizational learning is not for the faint of heart' (Crossan, 2003). To my mind, organizational learning is not for the faint of heart because: attempts at organizational learning often mobilize personal and organizational defences against learning, powerful emotions, political strategies, and the questioning of established assumptions. The study of organizational learning is an attempt to engage with some complex and difficult issues associated with organizing. As a result of all this, organizational learning is a fascinating and an enduring metaphor, one that continually yields fresh insights about organization. In addition, however, there are frustrations about the study of organizational learning. There are many theories and perspectives that claim to inform and to represent organizational learning, some of which are poorly thought through; prescriptions for organizational learning in action are at best temporary, but new prescriptions are nevertheless being invented constantly; and almost every senior manager that I have come across has either done that and moved on, is doing it continually, has her or his own way of defining it in practice, or wants to be told how it can be done. One thing that is generally agreed about the meaning of organizational learning is that 'it is a process' that is connected to 'action' (Sun, 2003). This helps to explain why I talk more in this book about approaches to management and organizational learning such as action learning and group relations than (for example) a syllabus to explore theories and case studies of strategic learning.

The academic perspective that I have on organizational learning is connected to some particular parts of the current body of knowledge. I locate myself with other academics who believe that 'learning . . . stems from the participation of individuals in social activities' (Gherardi and Nicolini, 2001; also Elkjaer, 1999) as well as authors who are interested in the politics of organizational learning (Coopey, 1995; Coopey and Burgoyne, 2000) and emotion and organizational learning (Antonacopoulou and Gabriel, 2001; Gherardi, 2003). The contribution to organizational learning in this book is based on both broadening and bringing together political and emotional perspectives on organizational learning. Therefore, for example, I do not focus on organizations as cultures, since the word 'culture' does not sufficiently connote or emphasize the emotions and politics of organizing. Instead I use the word *establishment*. For me this word effectively represents how organization impacts on the internal worlds of individuals to legitimize or suppress emotions (and the actions that are connected to them), and how emotions generate interpersonal politics (particularly around interaction and the avoidance of interaction) that institutionalize into specific ways of structuring, behaving and working within collectives. At its most direct, my argument is that emotion *is* political.

A final reflection on my perspective on organizational learning is that it is connected to and informed by insights from the psychodynamic study of organizations. This theoretical approach recognizes the role of unconscious processes in the construction of both learning and organizing (Brown and Starkey, 2000). The focus within this body of theory is not individual psychology, but system psychodynamics. Individuals' roles are part of a broader system, whatever personal histories and processes are being enacted. To put this another way, the focus is not so much on an understanding of 'the conscious and unconscious processes underlying emotional life in an organization, as their *meaning*: what they have to say about the organization as a system in context' (Armstrong, 2000). In terms of a practice of management learning and management education that relates to these ideas, the psychodynamic perspective is represented here through my discussions of Group Relations (or Institutional Transformation, as it is known in some countries). Group Relations is an approach to learning from experience that has an explicit interest in understanding the institution or establishment that is being created through the various attempts that individuals and collectives make to learn and to organize together.

The word 'strategic' in strategic learning signifies various things. I have already mentioned that my engagement within Hyder was focused on managers with strategic responsibilities. The word serves as a bridge between my interest in the academic theory of organizational learning and my interest in finding ways to engage and communicate with practitioners. It is often difficult to communicate the fascinating interplay between emotion and politics in the construction of organizing processes that both legitimize and inhibit learning, without alienating at least some practitioners. To talk about strategic learning doesn't have the same effect. This is because managers recognize that learning processes are fundamentally related to future knowledge as well as to the decisions and innovations that are connected to this knowledge. The use of the word 'strategic' therefore connects to a more general interest practitioners have in how to try to shape what will be. In addition, linking learning and strategy provides an opportunity within the book to focus on two key organizing processes, reflection and leadership, that have considerable impact on either supporting or undermining learning processes. One further point about strategy: I am using the word 'strategic' to help to modify learning and to link it with organizing, not as a connection into the academic field of strategy or strategic management.

This brings me to the word 'rethinking'. There is a certain connection in this word to previous publications that have explored management and organizational issues from a critical perspective, particularly to 'rethinking management education' (French and Grey, 1996). Rethinking does not claim to be new thinking, but a different take on (or from) existing thinking; it concerns the integration of knowledge/learning and critique. There is another aspect to the word that is important in this book. 'Rethinking' implies that reflection is an integral and continuous aspect of strategic learning both in theory and in practice. There are two particular ways in which this has been explored and expressed in the production and content of this book (in addition to how the subject has been covered). First, as an explicit part of the process of writing the book, I initiated a small conference of ten academics and practitioners who focused, over two days, on 'the future practice of HRD'. This is consistent with what I am arguing here, that reflection is not the individual process of 'looking back', but an active and integral part of organizing reflection (see Vince, 2002; Chapter 7, this volume; and Reynolds and Vince, forthcoming). The results of this collective experience of 'rethinking' are integrated mostly into the next chapter, but also into Chapter 9. Second, after I had completed the first draft of the book, I sent it to six people, including academic colleagues, practitioners and my father, and asked them to review the book and to send me their comments. My thinking here was that there is much to be gained by getting at least some of the reviews of this book before it is published in order to provide me with the opportunity to integrate the various criticisms and suggestions into the book. To an extent this comes from my experience of reading reviews of my previous publications, where I would have liked to be able to integrate some of the reviewers' criticisms and insights into the works. Having done this, I have learned once again the value of 'rethinking' my ideas with the benefit of others' critique.

Finally, although the phase 'human resource development' is not in the title, the book is part of a series that discusses and develops key issues for HRD. The perspective in this book is that, both in theory and in practice, HRD needs to reconstruct itself less as a means for the training and development of people and more as an approach that supports the impact people can have on organizing, as well as being a focal point for understanding the impact of organizing on people. HRD can and should make a distinctive contribution to organizing. It is an intervention within a political system, a practice of management and leadership, with all the difficulties and contradictions that attempting to manage and to lead are likely to contain and reveal. HRD therefore needs to construct itself critically, and as an integral part of continuous learning and change. HRD practitioners have to take a lead in creating the processes, designs and developments for future business – and this means a focus on how learning and change are avoided as well as planned, on the different forms and approaches to leadership required, and on the complexities of organizational learning. The focus of HRD is on action, on developing the capacity to act, on generating credibility through action, and on influencing and working with others in situations loaded with emotion and politics.

Before I provide a summary of the various chapters I have included, there is one more brief reflection I want to include in this introduction, concerning the emotional experience of writing this book. For me, writing is a process that is full of mixed emotions. At times I am swept along with enthusiasm for and belief in what I am writing, at other times I am bogged down in the rearrangement of words and phrases that seem to make sense one minute and then, as soon as I have looked away, regress to being repetitive, obscure or without meaning. At times I cannot imagine what it was I was trying to say, at other times I cannot contain my joy at the attempt.

A brief summary of the chapters

In Chapters 2 to 6 I build and develop my thoughts and ideas about strategic learning by using examples from organizations to explore the relationship between emotion and politics. The examples demonstrate how emotional responses create political responses, which then shape the ways in which emotions are experienced and enacted both by individuals and by collectives. Such underlying emotions contribute to characteristic or habitual ways of organizing. For example, I describe the emotions mobilized through a major change initiative in Hyder. These emotions are shown to be created from and to reinforce habitual organizational responses to change initiatives. In this example, shifts in the emotions associated with a change initiative (from initial enthusiasm to eventual disappointment or cynicism) help to explain the perpetual rise and fall of change initiatives in the organization. I also explore the organizational dynamics created through repeated patterns of caution and blame within a public-sector organization (not Hyder). These dynamics inhibit processes of reflection and communication within the organization, undermining the implementation and development of agreed strategies. I return to Hyder to analyse the experiences of managers involved in the takeover of the company. These experiences reveal insights about the political and emotional relatedness of managers to strategic learning and change.

The remaining chapters shift towards key issues concerning strategic learning in practice. My focus here is initially on reflection and leadership, and reframing these as collective rather than individual processes. My interest is not on what an individual (reflective practitioner) knows or can learn from her or his experience, nor is it on what it might take to be an effective leader, since these are both areas of scholarship that are already well served in existing publications. Instead, I emphasize the potency of public or collective reflection and the importance of understanding leadership as a product of human community. In the final chapter I return to explore the theory and practice of human resource development. I argue for a critical perspective in HRD: one that encourages engagement with the contextual politics, power relations and emotions that shape the possibilities and limitations of learning. This is not a complicated shift of understanding or practice. At present the emphasis is on the relationship between a person and his or her role in an organization, which means learning to be a more effective manager, leader, follower. In this book I emphasize the relationship between role and organization, which means the collective capacity to mobilize learning, and the strategic impact of this capacity. The focus therefore is on collective attempts to alter the ways in which organizing is imagined and implemented in order to transform the constraints on learning within a managerial, leadership or organizational role.

A chapter-by-chapter synopsis

In Chapter 2, I begin with a discussion and critique of HRD, examining academic and practitioner definitions and assumptions. I consider both the foundation knowledge that informs HRD practice and the role of the HRD practitioner. I argue that HRD needs to get more critical and more complicated. This involves a perspective on HRD that is less about training and develop-ment and more about learning and organizing. An important function of HRD will be to engage with the emotions and politics that underpin and inform organizing; to undermine assumptions and approaches that are more habitual than valuable; and to help to transform how we reflect and lead in order to meet the challenges implied in new organizational designs and approaches. There are currently, therefore, some key questions for HRD: what function does HRD have within the political systems of organizing, how does HRD provide mechanisms for the control and manipulation of members of organizations, and what role does fear (or other such powerful emotions) play in defining how HRD is and is not done? The leap of faith that is integral to HRD is that development is less about what is known, or even knowable, and more about what is mutually discoverable. In this chapter I start to develop my argument that organizing creates establishment, which is constructed from the interaction of emotion and politics, and gives rise to characteristic organizational dynamics that limit learning. I also begin to explore the concept of strategic learning. Strategic learning is orientated towards the questioning of assumptions as an organizational imperative (set in the context of the tension between a desire to learn and a desire to avoid learning). The emphasis is on learning through collective experience, on the conscious and unconscious structures that are inevitably created through attempts to learn, and on organizational dynamics that both construct and constrain learning.

In Chapter 3, I construct a framework for understanding strategic learning at an organizational level of analysis, highlighting the theoretical difference between individual learning in an organization and organizational learning. A combination of psychodynamic theory and politics provides an additional perspective to current thinking about the relationship between learning and organizing. The suggested starting point of learning initiatives is collective inquiry aimed at understanding the nature and impact of establishment and its consequences for learning. Critical reflection and action on what has become established (and how) provides the basis of attempts to recognize and transform self-limiting organizational dynamics. Attempts at strategic learning can be understood to involve a desire to transform establishment that organizing has created, both in terms of ways of working as well as what 'the organization' is in the minds of its members. This requires an examination of the politics and emotions that are enacted and reinforced through organizational roles. It also entails speculation on the unconscious dynamics that guide the internalization of the organization in the minds of its members. The insights afforded by reframing organization as establishment may not immediately help members of organizations to imagine how to act, but this idea can help to clarify the current boundaries within which action is possible, and through such clarification raise the possibility of strategic learning.

In Chapter 4, I assert that individuals and groups continually manage and organize themselves on the basis of their emotional responses to organizational issues as well as on the basis of avoiding emotion, and that both of these have strategic implications. Two examples are used to explore this argument further. In Hyder, strategy was created as much by the fears and anxieties (the uncomfortable knowledge) of members of organizations as it was by their knowledge and skills. I suggest that HRD has an organizational role in identifying how strategic learning is made possible and blocked in organizations. This involves understanding the politics that arise from attempts to organize learning, as well as how organizational politics are created from and reinforced by emotions expressed both individually and collectively. A study within a local authority revealed not just the characteristics of a self-limiting approach to strategic learning in an organization, but also the political processes that informed and perpetuated it.

In Chapter 5 the theme of emotion and learning continues with a focus on the interplay between emotion and rationality at the time of the takeover of Hyder. The takeover of Hyder provided further insights concerning the relationship between emotion and politics. Managers created and carried a tension between emotions (pain and shame) and their rationalizations of or detachment from these emotions (self-interest and disinterest). Such tension was necessary to maintain a state and State from which their managerial role could continue to be enacted within difficult and emotionally charged circumstances. The value in studying the interplay between emotion and rationality (in the context of organizational politics) is in order to appreciate how emotions might transform rational processes from a coherent decision, plan or strategy into contested relations and disputed understanding. The example in this chapter shows how fears undermined the ability of managers to put their authority into practice and to act collectively within the organization. Managers attempted to rationalize emotions, rather than to look for the ways in which emotions associated with actions might reveal opportunities for critique and development. Emotions have the capacity to undermine the apparent simplicity of management or decision-making because they can point to and reveal the contradictions that are inherent in any attempts to manage. Therefore, the common idea that strategic thinking is and should be coherent and consistent does little to assist managers in relating to the contradictions that strategies mobilize, or to the differences of experience, expectation and understanding that they create in practice.

In Chapter 6, I argue that organizations are often thought of and experienced as if they are the stable containers of rational decision-making and problem-solving, a coherent entity that can be described in terms of mission, assumptions and underlying values. Organizational members relate and respond to the idea of an organization as fixed and coherent. To a certain extent, therefore, all members of organizations are subject to a fantasy of control and coherence, supported and reinforced by both conscious and unconscious personal, group and organizational processes for creating and resisting change. Strategic learning involves the identification of the *politics of imagined stability* that characterize and inform the limitations and possibilities of learning and change in a specific organizational context. 'The politics of imagined stability' is a phrase that describes the role that social and strategic politics play in the perpetuation of emotions and fantasies that have an impact on the various actions and inactions associated with organizing. In Hyder, for example, the politics of imagined stability involved a corporate fantasy constructed through three linked ideas: that Hyder was a confident organization, one coherent organization, and an organization that could change.

In Chapter 7, I provide an organizational view of reflection by addressing the question: what type of reflective practices might stimulate strategic learning? My emphasis is on reflection as an organizing process rather than on the individual, reflective practitioner. One common understanding of reflection for members of organizations is to do with 'looking back', 'thinking back' and/or 'examining personal performance'. Reflection tends to be on the individual and on the past, rather than from the collective and in the present. To illustrate the importance of this shift I describe one approach to organizing reflection in order to create and sustain opportunities for strategic learning. I suggest that specific practices that can contribute to reflection as an organizing process will be informed by three characteristics. First, such practices should contribute to the collective questioning of assumptions that underpin organizing in order to make power relations visible. Second, reflective practices necessarily provide a 'container' for the management of the anxieties raised by making power relations visible. Third, reflective practices should contribute towards participation and democracy in the organization. I continue by describing four reflective practices. These are: peer consultancy groups, Role Analysis and Role Analysis groups, action learning sets, and Group Relations conferences. I explain and explore each of these and define their impact at different levels of organizing.

In Chapter 8, I present a view of leadership as the product of human community: the collective capacity to create something of value, and suggest that management education and HRD can and should support the development of a perspective that goes beyond emphasising leadership as the authority or effectiveness of an individual. I provide two examples to illustrate the practical reasons why this is important. Mainstream definitions of leadership have tended to emphasize the individual's role as having an influence on others. There may be specific traits and styles that make this possible as well as situations where specific styles are likely to be successful. The leader may have a 'new' or more general task, the creation of corporate vision or culture, which is still achieved by influential and charismatic individuals who have discerned what puts others into motion. Such individuals may have engineered consensus or initiated dispersed leadership, both of which are political techniques for achieving greater employee output through making hierarchies seem less overt. Looking at this emotionally as well as politically, the leader spins dreams, and is subject to fantasies, which might stimulate defensive as much as charismatic behaviour. The leader's desire may also be to share authority, to collaborate in a social context where 'none of us is as smart as all of us'. However, the reality of individual accountability for outcomes implies a broader politics, where 'occasional regression to hierarchy' may be a necessary compromise. I argue that leadership is a collective as much as an individual process, which can be based on opening decision-making and organization to the critique and imagination of others. This does not mean that leaders must 'facilitate' others, rather that they can be responsible for creating spaces and processes for democratic dialogue and action. The leaders' role is less about having responsibility for making decisions, and more about creating shared responsibility for decision-making. Such a shift in the practice of leadership is part of the process for creating an organizational environment for strategic learning.

In Chapter 9, I reflect on the future practice of HRD, linking this to a discussion of intervention. HRD is a pivotal process in organizing for the future since its primary concern is learning and change. The future practice of HRD is the point of HRD; it can be characterized as evolving practice, as activity that inspires critique in order to create possibilities for learning, as the stimulus for attempts at organizing that seek to create the ways we will be thinking and acting. I explore what intervention means and involves, as well as the individual and collective role that internal practitioners and external change agents have in relation to learning. I am therefore exploring *the point of intervention*, both in terms of *reasons* for intervention and the *roles* that are taken and given by individuals and collectives with responsibility for intervention. My focus on role does not mean that I am primarily interested in, for example, the skills and knowledge of the individual. I am more interested in the roles of HRD practitioners or external consultants as one of the focal points for intervention in a system, as well as the institutional dynamics that are likely to be mobilized, experienced and created by the HRD practitioner or consultant as he or she engages with or disengages from the system within which intervention is made. I advocate a particular shift of understanding that is implied by the study of emotion, politics and learning. This involves balancing a tendency towards rationalizing the problem with an equal task of problematizing the rational.

In this final chapter I also reflect on my future thinking about 'rethinking strategic learning' as I start to move beyond the actual writing of this book. I use some of the comments from the people I invited to review the first draft of this book, as well as examples from organizational intervention and from management education. The various points I make in this section of the chapter are not intended as guidelines for thought and action. The idea is to open up further questions and reflections, certainly for me as the author, and I hope for you as the reader of this book.

2 Strategic learning and HRD

One of the aims of this book is to begin to outline a critical perspective on human resource development (HRD). HRD is used here as a general term that implies attempts at organizing learning and change. HRD is linked to other areas of scholarship including management and organizational learning, management education, organization development, intervention and consulting. These interconnected areas of theory and practice are brought together under the theme of *strategic learning*, which indicates that the emphasis of the book is more on the relationship between learning and organizing than it is on the development of individuals. The book highlights the role that HRD can play in the organization of learning and change. A central part of my argument is that there has been an over-emphasis on individuals' learning in organizations. In practice, this has meant that staff responsible for learning and change in organizations have put too much effort into the development of individuals (for example through individual performance appraisal linked to programmes of skill and knowledge development) and not enough into understanding and engaging with the organizational dynamics that limit and shape individuals' opportunities and abilities to learn and change. These dynamics are created as a result of the interaction between emotion and politics in organizations and they have an impact on both learning and organizing.

Consider the following example. Most people in organizations have at some point experienced the weight of 'expectations from above'. Where these are powerfully felt they can produce cautious and self-protective behaviour. Caution and self-protection stimulate a tendency to blame others for problems that arise. As blame becomes a habitual individual response it starts to have an impact on organizational processes, for example, how reflection is both undertaken and avoided. Reflection is undertaken in isolation from others (if at all) and becomes focused on 'looking back' at actions. Ambivalence about engaging in collective, public and strategic reflection reinforces difficulties of communication across organizational sub-systems. From a relatively simple emotional reaction (caution in the face of expectations) has emerged an organizational process or 'structure' that limits learning and change (see Chapter 4 for a fuller description of this process). Therefore, in addition to looking at, for example, the meaning of reflection or leadership in the minds of members of organizations, I explore the organizational dynamics that impact on concepts like reflection and leadership, and that help to construct them in practice.

The above is just one example from a very large set of possibilities mobilized by 'expectations', since caution is not the only possible response in this situation. Expectations from above might produce anxiety; they might encourage and support action, create confusion or indeed produce a mixture of all of these. This suggests the importance of studying the relationship between emotions and politics (power relations) in organizations, and through such study, to identify the dynamics that give rise to implicit organizational designs and structures. Therefore, I argue that an organizational perspective on learning is an important aspect of future thinking about human resource development because current HRD practices place considerable emphasis and energy on developing the knowledge and learning of individual members of organizations.

I will be exploring current themes in human resource development. McGoldrick, Stewart and Watson (2002: 396) have identified what these are. First, 'HRD has a central focus on and concern with learning'. Second, HRD is likely to have a wider constituency and purpose than organizational success, which suggests that HRD practice has a broader accountability than performance. Third, 'HRD is clearly a political activity' – it is central to power and control processes. With these themes in mind, I have constructed an exploration of HRD that attempts to be critical, collectively focused and situated in the emotional and political context of learning and organizing. Human resource development (despite the problems and criticisms associated with this phrase) is seen as an integral and necessary aspect of organizing; it may be the function of all members of organizations to some degree, but it is often undertaken by people who are in the middle of an organization in the complicated position of trying to provide intelligence to senior managers to inform strategy and organization as well as supporting the expression of the voices of their subordinates (Pedler, 2002). HRD is concerned with 'issues of individual, group and organizational learning and performance' (Woodall, 2003), it encompasses actions that vary from the everyday tasks of supporting learning and development through training, to the complex and at times impossible task of making change happen.

In the first section of this chapter I explore four interconnected themes that emerged from a small conference that brought together HRD and OD (organization development) practitioners with academics within the fields of Management Learning and HRD. The conference was organized as a way of discussing and developing some of the issues in this book. The title of the conference was 'The Future Practice of HRD' and a group of ten academics and practitioners were involved in the discussions and debate. It was organized over two days and involved both small group discussions and plenary sessions. All of the plenary sessions were recorded and transcribed. The following ideas and opinions about HRD come from a temporary community (a short-lived project team) of academics and practitioners, and the interpretations and choices I have made from the transcripts of our discussions. The outcomes from this conference particularly inform this chapter and the final chapter of the book. In this chapter, I cover four sub-headings: definitions and assumptions in HRD, why HRD needs to change, foundation knowledge for future practice and the role of the HRD practitioner. All of the quotations I have used in these sections come from the transcripts of the plenary sessions; they have not been attributed to individual conference members.

Definitions and assumptions in HRD

Definitions of HRD emerge from different areas of interests, both practitioner and academic. Practitioner or 'working' definitions offer a practice-based view of HRD. The idea of a working definition is useful because it implies that definitions can and will change in line with current perceptions and perspectives on how to do human resource development. A working definition reflects the current understanding of what it is HRD practitioners aim to do. This might include changing the organization, creating a collaborative work environment, making a difference to performance, developing core capabilities, making interventions, putting systems into place, and organization design and development. The question of why HRD practitioners aim to do this is linked to the function of HRD within organizations, which involves shaping and responding to the business agenda, informing and providing added value. Change is the underlying theme and strategy:

> My HRD strategy is to make sure that every member of staff is able to transfer knowledge from the classroom into the work environment, to bring about change in working practices. It is about making a difference and it is about change.

The desire for change inevitably interweaves with the complexity of attempting to make change happen:

> I want to be successful, I want to satisfy the needs of the people I serve and if I challenge their notions then I risk not being successful any more. Maybe that is my job . . . We enact our power and authority in a very focused and planned way because we are strategic, aren't we – but the reality is that we are not – we react and those reactions have an impact on others. This is the reality, of being, doing, responding, engaging in the organization in which we operate and in a way that assists the interests of the people we serve.

Leaders, managers and HRD practitioners often find themselves searching for certainty in a world of contradictions. However, in order to thrive, HRD may have to get more complicated, to be less well defined, to engage more directly with the unlimited supply of contradictions that organizing seems to create. On its own, a focus on training and individual development, however well connected into practice it may be, is not likely to be a sufficient justification for the use of resources, nor can it fully represent a business case for HRD. This is only likely where the idea that 'what is good for the individual is good for the organization' is transformed to include both the search for that most sought after goal, added value, as well as inquiry into the emotions and politics that are mobilized around attempts to add value.

Therefore, for academics studying HRD it is not only the practice-based view that is interesting. *Inquiry into definition* (in addition to *working definition*) is equally important because it is the basis on which speculation and critique can be mobilized in the service of changing the ways in which we think about what is HRD. Such critique is likely to involve asking: what does 'added value' actually mean, what function does HRD have within the political systems of organizing, how does HRD provide mechanisms for the control and manipulation of members of organizations, what role does fear (or other such powerful emotions) play in defining how HRD is and is not done? The academic role in relation to HRD is to inquire further into such questions and relate them back to HRD practice, to inform and support the emergence of additional working definitions.

Of course, the speculations and critiques of academics are a mixed blessing to practitioners – something that is simultaneously wanted and unwanted. As academics we provide ideas and suggestions from our inquiries much more readily than we do processes that translate smoothly into practice. For those who are working within the highly politicized context of HRD in organizations, critique can prove to be risky. Whereas academics might believe that improvements in practice (and performance) come from the integration of critique (theorizing practice), practitioners perceive the risk in critique, the danger of mobilizing resistance to change that undermines their role and sets back attempts to add value or make change happen. The interplay of theory and practice is therefore always a complex and important component of defining and redefining HRD for both academics and practitioners.

Part of the role that academics can sustain in relation to HRD is to express a critical agenda, arguing therefore for continuous discussion of what is undiscussable, uncomfortable and uncontrollable in organizations: the role of emotion, politics, ethics and system psychodynamics in the context of espoused values. From an academic point of view, the study of HRD is important because its practice provides many examples concerning the impact of emotion and politics in strategic attempts at learning and change. Change is unlikely to be sustained without a consideration of the various emotional, relational and political dynamics that underpin the organization of learning and change within specific organizational contexts. It could well be argued that, as far as emotions, politics and psychodynamic insights are concerned, 'this is an area into which we might want to say that HRD doesn't go'. However, because HRD is focused so often on attempts to change and to shape attitudes, it may already have arrived there. The fears and anxieties that are inevitably mobilized by attempts to learn and to change underpin and inform the choices that are made in the name of HRD.

This is not to say that individuals have to be aware of their fears and anxieties so much as attempting to understand how fears and anxieties have contributed to the emergence of particular 'ways of doing things here'. One risk that HRD managers may be able to take is to create processes for reflection on how inaction or constraint is being produced. For example:

> I'd like to see the organization develop collaboratively and engage in activities that allow us to explore the defences that we exhibit – looking at what inhibits learning. In practice we do have a cosmetic or perception that we are constantly adhering to . . . but I also see many instances where such behaviour (related to learning) is not materialising. In little discussion groups someone says that they have got this agenda and I say I will support them and then I don't. Why don't we engage in lifting that up to a larger group level and ask why does this occur in the organization? It must be because we are afraid of engaging in that discussion. Maybe we fear loss of control or authority or loss of engagement with what we profess to engage in.

Politics (in addition to emotion) is integral to HRD. Having a responsibility for HRD means being aware of the various interests that are served from this position in the hierarchy. HRD practitioners are often the intermediaries between different power interests in organizations, in the middle of competing or contested expectations, interpretations of events and desired outcomes. Practitioners are often expected to create processes that reveal what people think, to empower collective voices, and to mobilize participation in change. In addition, of course, when senior managers have ignored or filed away all of this consultation, the role is also to deal with the disappointment of undermined and unfulfilled expectations. This is not a passive role. Instead of waiting for the outcome of established power relations to become apparent it is possible for HRD practitioners to be direct about the likely impact of power relations on organizational processes of learning and change. Making this clear from the outset is a powerful contribution to understanding the possibilities and limitations of change within specific organizational contexts, as well as contributing to increased reflection on the political element of what we do.

In addition to reflection on politics there is also the politics of reflection. Reflection may not always be an attractive idea to managers since it might undermine the strategic decisions that they have spent time making. The emphasis is on both academics and HRD practitioners arguing the business case for reflection. This involves, at the very least, a transformation from the idea that reflection is the province of the individual practitioner. Reflection is an under-developed organizing process, which could provide information about the *organization* of learning and change. For example, project-based initiatives are currently popular in organizations. Project-based work, driven by business imperatives, is aimed at using diverse combinations of existing individuals' knowledge to find creative solutions to key issues within the organization.

Despite the impact that such projects have on key issues, there has often been little reflection on the ways in which project intervention has changed or reinforced the system dynamics of the organization in which they were built and whether the knowledge they generated could be usefully transferred across boundaries within and outside the organization. Much of the collective knowledge that organizing generates is not being used.

Collective knowledge is often an output of interventions made by HRD practitioners, but the flip charts produced in one part of the organization rarely get shared with other parts of the organization (or network). HRD practitioners also generate useful knowledge for the organization through the enactment of their roles. Anyone who has occupied a development role in an organization is likely to know that attempts at learning, even driven by our best intentions, can produce effects that are unimagined, unwanted and unworkable. The fact that they do is a mirror of a generic problem with management, the difficulty of accepting that rational techniques, no matter how good they are, do not guarantee the planned outcome.

There is one other issue that has an impact on definition in HRD: the continuing debate about differences between training, management development and organization development. HRD currently carries an implicit hierarchy, from the work of 'chalk-and-talk trainers' and instrumental skills programmes at one level, to intervention, consultancy and organization development at the other. Increasingly, the focus of HRD is organization development, which involves being an integral part of the business, and organizing interventions to help the business move forward:

> We need to do the chalk and talk, but I see it as someone else's role. I'm there to facilitate, influence, consult and ensure that training happens – but other people do it.

Within some organizations HRD is seen as organization development:

> What we mean by HRD is defining what the OD agenda is in our organization. We are also caught up in the history of before this role, when management development [MD] was seen as part of what the divisional centre did, labels that are still associated with some of the people in my team. We have moved from the MD element to what we see as organizational design and focusing on some key areas that are aligned with the business, the drivers that we are facing, and then trying to replicate that in our operating businesses. This was something the people in my team wanted to do – to move away from being known as MD people and be doing more of a consultant role within the business, working with directors in terms of sharpening the actual business and helping to deliver interventions that help to improve performance. These are people who were fed up with the view – you do training courses or MD.

In other organizations, training, management development and organization development blur:

> We will provide whatever is appropriate: professional and clinical courses, manpower management, leadership development, psychometric testing, IT training and health and safety. We have a massive range of opportunities because we have a critical mass of people, not just a team of seventeen (training and development staff). The organization has some confidence that if they need an event facilitated someone within the team could do it for them. We also encourage 'workplace fixers' who are given tangible support to undertake a training role as a part of their jobs. This type of model is working well for us. In all the professional groups it is stated on their job descriptions that developing others is a key part of their role.

This raises questions about the HRD role, both for practitioners and academics. Who exactly has an HRD role in organizations, is HRD something to be done by trained professionals or does everyone need to integrate perspectives from HRD into their role? This also has implications for academic institutions running courses in HRD. Are these courses orientated towards people who are going to do development work for a large part of their career or are they developing people who are going to do HRD as a part-role? HRD practitioners know that it is often useful to 'take people from different environments and get them to engage within the organization in order to challenge some of the notions they and others have'. Part of the role of HRD professionals therefore has been to undermine HRD as a profession, to convince managers that HRD is an integral aspect of their role. One of the reasons why HRD practitioners want to share the role with other managers is because to do so reinforces the importance of HRD as well as the legitimacy of what practitioners are trying to do. If the role is spread throughout the organization then it is less likely that the HRD practitioner or the OD section will be the focal point for the powerful projections that are associated with attempts to learn and to change.

If, however, HRD is seen as part of a professional role, then how can a broader understanding of HRD be developed to provide capabilities that relate more to organizational development and change than to training? Most people come into HRD through administrative jobs, most trainers are actually technique trainers and only very few end up in the areas that relate to OD and change, which are seen as the most crucial for organizations. Whilst the rhetoric in organizations is that 'we don't do sheep dip programmes here', this view often exists alongside a very low incentive for management development to be linked to OD and strategy development. There is still primarily an emphasis on providing individuals with generic skills and relying on them to apply these skills for the benefit of the organization. At the other end of the spectrum, it has been noticed that senior HRD practitioners who get on to the boards of companies find that they have to become generalists in order to exhibit credibility and to input into the debate at 'the top table'.

Why does HRD need to change?

Currently, the practice of HRD in the United Kingdom is rooted in standardized products and services, driven by competencies, defined by professional bodies and focused on predictability and consistency. There are too many organizations whose approaches require staff members to learn mechanistically, and only a very small number of models of development that are used and that make any lasting impact (the top three are the training cycle, Kirkpatrick's evaluation ladder and Kolb's learning cycle). Current training standards are not sufficiently strategic and are weak in relation to organization development, particularly in terms of a failure to establish links between people management development and business performance. There aren't many senior levels in HRD, nor is there consistent commitment to HRD from senior levels. The focus of HRD is on the development of people in teams in organizations, and this is too often informed by a tired humanism that imagines such development separately from the social, political, emotional and economic pressures on business. HRD, which has a central concern with change, has demonstrated a persistent inability to change itself. Approaches to change management have been based on rational planning and people development, more often than not failing to make the desired impact on organizing processes, practices and strategies. This reinforces the already compelling evidence that change initiatives are more likely to fail than to succeed (Palmer and Hardy, 2000). Until such time that there is a much more sophisticated, high-level demand for what experts in HRD ought to do these problems will continue.

HRD is currently driven by a need to respond to a narrow set of market perceptions. If this is the way that HRD is to be conceived, then ultimately it is not going to be able to contribute to organizational learning. Training people as HR practitioners simply to respond to market perceptions is tempting but short-sighted. It is tempting because the development of individual skills and knowledge is important in that it can reinforce confidence, help to broaden action and improve capability. It is short-sighted because it places the emphasis on individuals to learn, and largely ignores the wider contexts of organizing in which HRD exists and can have an impact. We need, therefore, to start thinking about HRD less as people development and more as an approach that supports the impact people can have on organizing.

HRD practice can and should make a discriminating contribution to organizing. HRD is an intervention within a political system, a practice of management and leadership, with all the difficulties that attempts to manage and to lead are likely to contain and reveal. HRD needs to construct itself critically, and as an integral part of continuous change. At the same time, HRD has to provide approaches to knowledge generation, as well as highlight the issues that arise from attempts to share knowledge. HRD is no longer easily seen as a function within a single organization, rather it is responsible for supporting moves beyond 'the organization', not only into configurations like supply chains and networks but also into wider contexts involving stakeholders, communities and customers. Organizing is now as much about shifting form and transience as it is about stability and coherence (although shifting organizational forms do not necessarily imply shifting assumptions), and the actions of HRD practitioners should reflect this. HRD can take a lead in creating the designs and developments for future business – and this means a focus on how change is avoided as well as planned, on the different forms and approaches to leadership required, and on strategic learning. The focus of HRD is on action, on developing the capacity to act, on generating credibility through action, and on influencing and working with others. HRD practitioners, therefore, may have to make a significant contribution alongside other people who have a monopoly on resource use or power.

Foundation knowledge for future practice

To organize is also to institutionalize. Organization is a process driven by the twin desires for stability and coherence, which necessarily involves defining the boundaries of what can and cannot belong in the organization. There are emotional boundaries – organization is built from values and mission statements that give the impression that there is a coherent direction that all members subscribe to and adhere to. There are political boundaries – organization reflects the outcomes of differential power relations and also the legitimacy of certain opinions and behaviours as well as the illegitimacy of others. People try and create something solid and bounded when we organize – we seek that kind of certainty. It allows us to delineate relationships, to manage meaning and to make sense of the complexities generated through interaction. The difficulty and the challenge facing us is to break through the dependencies we have created on those particular designs and forms of organizing.

The institutionalizing or stabilizing forces that inform and construct organization necessarily make change more difficult. Change is usually justified by stability – 'I want to change this in order to make that more stable' (or, less overtly, 'I want you to change to allow me to stay the same'). Such forces are inherently about the organization of clarity, of knowing what is involved and included. This also means that, in a complex and incomprehensible world of globalization, discontinuity, policy change and intervention fatigue (to name but a few) some members of organizations need to try to intervene in order to make change happen. The role of the HRD practitioner is therefore both complicated and interesting. It implies discovering how an organization has managed to become set in its ways, to organize opportunities for change that can challenge a tendency to resist change, and to imagine and deliver processes that can underpin organizational learning and transformation. Given the emotions and politics that inevitably surround any attempts at change, this means that HRD practitioners have to think about *transforming leadership*, both as a defining characteristic of their own role and as an organizational imperative.

In general, senior managers want both a compliant and a willing-to-adapt workforce. However, trying to make change happen inevitably means saying things about managing and organizing that others, above and below, will not want to hear or acknowledge. This is anxiety-provoking, but also intriguing and stimulating: it reflects the idea that underlying the roles of (e.g.) leader and manager is the ability to take risks, to challenge existing ways of working and to find new practices, approaches and solutions. The HRD practitioner therefore, from their position in the middle of organizing (between strategic and operational staff, between competing interests and functions, between different agendas and interpretations of change), has to take political risks. Given the difficulty of holding this most important aspect of organizing it is not surprising that HRD has tended to institutionalize itself into the smaller space of training and personal development. Because of the politics, the HRD practitioner has to be aware that there is a time and a place to say what you think:

> If the power base is trying to influence a director in terms of practice to do something and you have that power base with you then you use it to your advantage to get what you want. Sometimes if I said what I think, I wouldn't get what I want.

The role of HRD practitioner involves placing oneself in the middle of an enduring and ever-present dynamic between experiences at different hierarchical levels of an organization. The role involves both generating intelligence for above and helping to make voices audible from below. Attempting to generate both intelligence and voice means being in the middle of something political.

This also raises the issue of the tools and technique that might be needed to thrive in this role. In HRD, techniques are necessarily unclear, despite the extent to which they are sought. It is not necessarily useful to ask the question 'How do you do it?', when the success or failure of development interventions depends more on why you do it, who you are doing it with, how they feel about you and what you represent, and how you feel about them – none of which is actually to do with technique. It may be better therefore to approach learning from the position of not knowing how to act. Techniques can impose themselves on complex situations in order to simplify them, thereby undermining emotions, relations and knowledge that might lead towards learning and change. The leap of faith that is integral to the role of HRD practitioner is that learning and development are less about what is known or even knowable and more about what is *mutually discoverable*. One danger in doing HRD is that we might have to engage with each other collectively in order to change things around here. The HRD role is to make this happen; however, it is also to be aware that giving voice to people who don't normally have it and providing the intelligence to people who don't normally get it (and actually may not want it) is not something that can be engineered or planned.

The role of the HRD practitioner

Intervention is paradoxical because it implies both some kind of purposive activity to make something happen, at the same time as creating and/or entering situations with no clear idea or agenda about what is to happen. It is the importance of this paradox that makes HRD a necessary and integral aspect of organizing. In their role, HRD practitioners carry the insight that the knowledge we lack is as important as the knowledge we have. Not knowing is an HRD strategy, it is an acknowledgement that the things we have done in the past, and the previous knowledge and experience emerging from it, may get in the way as much as they may help. We may also defend against what we know because it is sometimes dangerous in organizations to have what we know up-front. People know a bit more about the emotions and power relations that characterize the organization than they are prepared to let on. Commonly avoided knowledge is as potent an organizational force as common knowledge. In their role, the HRD practitioner carries a developmental dilemma at the heart of organizing – the continuous and competing dynamics between trying to promote both stability *and* change.

On a day-to-day basis the HRD practitioner has to hold back from implementing what they know, and occasionally has to profess not knowing as a strategy for getting things to happen. This skill – not knowing – is particularly troublesome both for the practitioner and the people they may be working with. The point of doing it is to undermine the role of (expert) facilitator, and consequently all the anti-developmental expectations, dependencies and restrictions that accompany this role. It is to encourage a 'critical mass' of shared experience and knowledge in the hope and expectation that this will produce what is needed to support and encourage learning and change.

> If you go to the first meeting of a group and you are there as the facilitator, then everybody looks to you to start things off and to say what the right way to doing this is. If you think you know what you are doing you've had it. If I am coming to teach the HRD class on six theories of group behaviour then it might be reasonable to assume I know what I am doing and I will do it. If I am coming to help people in a unit to sort out a problem they have got, then there might be things I know – like problem-solving sequences, but actually if I go in there thinking that I know how to do this it's not going to work. The skill is in how you do this without seeming incompetent and useless.

The role of HRD practitioner also attracts the idea that 'in HRD they have the solution' – a fallacy that may originally have been initiated by an anxious HRD practitioner. As a result of not wanting to appear incompetent or useless, practitioners can be dogged by a sense that they have to *protect* themselves in some way against feeling a fool, seeming to know nothing, not doing what is wanted, not providing value for money. This means that HRD practitioners are in a unique position to understand a particularly powerful and useful form of authority in organizations. This is often the authority that senior managers need but don't have (or avoid), as well as being the authority that less senior managers might want but are afraid to take up. It is the authority that comes from experiencing and understanding the complexity and circularity of a development role within organizations.

The HRD practitioner as an individual in a role may well be aware of tools and analytic techniques that support learning and change. However, it is not the tools and techniques that make the most difference to members of organizations. This is made as a result of experience, the type of experience that tells you that the silence in the room is OK, that it doesn't intimidate you into saying something, into taking over. The importance is not in the solution, but in the sensemaking – being able to reflect on experience in a way that transforms it. The organizational role of the HRD practitioner has similar characteristics. It is not the role of the HRD practitioner to attempt to mechanistically recreate organizing processes that occur naturally, for example, communities of practice, mentoring relationships and informal patterns of coaching. It rarely works that organizing that occurs naturally, by chance, because of the specific situation or variables, can be recreated as a technique.

The first level of entry in HRD is to be invited, which implies an interest in a relationship aimed at development.

> I'm not going to be invited in because they think I'm a guru from the university, I'm going to be invited in because I show some interest in the people, because I really want to do something and because they perceive me as genuine in some way. It is about having the right conditions under which you are able to make use of your expertise, or your expertise can be made use of. That's why you have to be invited in, why the relationship has to come first. Then, when the relationship is there you find there is a surprising amount of knowledge and expertise around. When you get trapped in that position of being the expert you are isolated, aren't you?

The difference between change programmes that do and don't work can be about the quality of relations, but such relations are also inevitably part of the emotions and politics that are mobilized through intervention:

> I find that people invite me in and give me the legitimacy to work with them as a team. They do this willingly and openly and for good reasons, but then when the difficult work starts feelings change because other things emerge that aren't as positive as they had hoped for, and that have to be worked through.

The HRD practitioner is trying to make a contribution to processes of learning within organizations where learning is both sought and feared. There is much that is not out on the table, there is much that would not be recognized or accepted easily by other people if it was, and in some cases is most certainly best left where it is. It is part of the HRD role to bring difficult things to the forefront so that they become part of the debate. This is not always about difficulties – it is also about the value of 'the feeling that you have been part of something that opened some doors and windows'. The role of HRD practitioner implies 'heedful action'. Heedful action suggests that development involves the desire to move in a certain direction (an HRD agenda, which fits with an organizational world of operation), that people are aware of their responsibilities, and that through enacting these responsibilities they contribute to the necessarily fluid nature of organization.

The emphasis of HRD is development, not prescription. HRD is reductive when it seeks to identify practices that work in one context and apply them in a different context. Being an HRD practitioner is likely to involve critical acts of inquiry into current practice in order to change and develop it. The HRD role, therefore, is to try and make sense of and to transform the various processes and the practices that are used or that emerge within the specific development context within which we are working. Answers have to be lived, imagined and developed. As soon as they have been found they begin to be limiting as well as useful, so they have to be dispensed with or transformed. Perhaps a statement such as this can only be made in an academic voice. However, I think that there is currently a desire from many practitioners working in and with HRD to recognize the role HRD can have in understanding organizational characteristics and complexities, as well as the impact of these on the creation and enactment of new approaches and insights concerning – for example – reflection, leadership and learning. HRD has a role that goes well beyond the implementation of skills and techniques, the facilitation of models and approaches, and even beyond the development of performance and competitive advantage. Strategic learning forms the basis of this role, as well as underpinning continuous inquiry into organizational processes for reflecting, acting, leading, following, changing, managing and organizing. The question of *how* suggests that future practice always needs to be reinvented – that what emerges from the process of inquiry is of primary importance in understanding the relationship between learning and organizing. In the following section, therefore, I begin to discuss and develop some of the key components of an organizational perspective on strategic learning.

An organizational perspective on strategic learning

The ideas in this book are usually discussed and extended through examples that come from various organizations, in particular Hyder plc, which until its takeover in September 2000, was a multi-national, multi-utility and infrastructure management company that had grown and changed considerably from its original organization, Welsh Water. The emphasis of this change was in two directions. The company created Hyder Utilities, a multi-utility business within Wales. It also established Hyder Infrastructure Development, which undertook large engineering, consulting and infrastructure projects throughout the world. One general issue that these changes created for the workforce was how they might be able to transform from ways of reflecting and acting that were rooted in their public-sector, locally focused past towards clearer imperatives for commercial growth and global development. An analysis of approaches to learning and organizing in Hyder showed how difficult it was for the company to engage with the impact of entrenched organizational dynamics on individuals and collectives. Managers believed Hyder to be a learning organization – however, research in the company revealed that extensive learning and change initiatives made little impact on established power relations, which limited the influence that HR staff could have on learning and change.

As I have already said, the approaches that are commonly used to implement learning in organizations have over-emphasized the development of individuals. The effect of an emphasis on individuals' development has been to limit the ability of individuals and collectives to understand the many social, emotional and political issues that impact on learning and organizing. To put this more directly, the individual orientation of much current HRD practice limits strategic learning. In the rest of this chapter, I outline the thinking and action that might inform initiatives designed to explore the relationship between emotions, politics and learning. I ask what learning methods might best promote an understanding of this relationship as well as suggesting some of the implications of this approach for rethinking the implementation of HRD. An assumption that informs my discussion is that exploration of the different emphases between individual and organizational learning is a key issue in developing both the theory and application of strategic learning and in beginning to map out an emerging, critical direction in HRD.

There is a difference between 'individual learning in an organization' and 'organizational learning'. The sum of individuals' learning in an organization is frequently assumed to equate with organizational learning. Such an interpretation is based on the idea that the combined impact of individuals' applied learning in an organization probably means that organizational learning (or change) will take place. Organizational learning does not mean that an organization is learning, but it does imply that learning and organizing are related. This connection has been captured to good effect by Gherardi and Nicolini (2001) when they talk about organizational learning as 'learning-in-organizing', recognising that learning and organizing 'are not distinct activities within a practice' (2001: 35). Efforts to understand organizational learning have been assisted in recent years by the general shift of interest away from organizations and towards organization and organizing (Clegg, Hardy and Nord, 1996). An increasing focus on collective learning, situated learning, communities of practice, and on politics, power relations and learning have helped to shift the academic study of organizational learning away from individual learning, towards social, political and relational interpretations of learning and organizing (see Gherardi, Nicolini and Odella, 1998; Easterby-Smith, Araujo and Burgoyne, 1999).

So far, however, there has not been a concurrent shift in practice. In-use HRD strategies and organization-based approaches to management education and development remain focused on the knowledge and learning of individual members of organizations (Vince and Broussine, 2000). Programmes of individual appraisal, self-managed learning, personal qualification development and skill-based training have done little to assist an understanding of the subtle interplay between learning and organizing and the role of individuals and collectives in creating the power relations that characterize and limit organizational behaviour and design. Similarly, approaches to mentoring and role shadowing and/or exchange have focused on individuals' gaining new insights from or with other individuals rather than on the power relations that characterize and surround organizational roles, or the emotions generated within or by them. There has been relatively little reflection on the implementation of an approach to learning that enables members of organizations, both individually and collectively, to better understand what organizational designs are being constructed through simultaneous attempts both to learn and to organize. In this chapter, therefore, I begin to explore a question that this book attempts to answer – what are the underlying ideas and approaches to HRD that can assist in developing an understanding of both organizational and strategic learning?

The theoretical position I create emerges from the interplay between emotion, politics learning and organizing. I do not focus on the various rationalizations of emotion that are currently popular, like 'emotional intelligence', or on individuals' feelings. My interest is in the way that emotions and politics combine: to create organizational structures or processes that then limit (e.g.) knowing, feeling, sensemaking; to reinforce existing organizational designs or power relations; and to inhibit the organization of learning and change. One way to express this would be to say that I am interested in the ways in which emotional responses become political, which is to say how they help to maintain or challenge existing assumptions, values and/or power relations that characterize ways of working. The exploration of organizational dynamics inevitably involves engagement with emotions that are generated through organizing. Emotion is knowledge, often 'uncomfortable knowledge' (Fineman, 1993) about learning and organizing in both manageable and unmanageable forms. The individual and collective reaction to emotions mobilized through organizing (i.e. what is done to try to prevent things from feeling uncomfortable) is political. Defending against emotion takes up a lot of time and effort and, over time, is integrated into enactments of role, authority and responsibility. The relationship between emotion and politics is an everyday aspect of organizing (see my example earlier concerning 'expectations from above'). My interest is in the various ways that individual and collective emotional responses become organizational politics and designs, and this interest is linked to an acknowledgement of knowledge, learning and development as *emergent* concepts (Lee, 2001).

Knowledge that informs HRD as practice is also linked to and constructed from the emotional and political dynamics of organizing. This may be one reason why many interventions aimed at development reinforce the control processes of the current organization more than they help to imagine and underpin processes of change. There have been few attempts to include appreciations of underlying emotional and political dynamics in understanding HRD (something that this book tries to address). To do this involves recognition of the interaction between emotions and politics as well as the unconscious processes and strategies that are generated through this relationship:

> Many of the processes that contribute to organizational difficulties are unconscious in nature. By this I mean that the leadership, the management and the members are not aware of what the underlying factors are that motivate their behaviour, nor are they in touch with the fact that their behaviour has a destructive effect on the organization. In fact, they often believe the opposite.
>
> (Obholzer, 1999: 87)

The focus of HRD has been on the monitoring and development of individual knowledge in order to inform action. This strategy can be successful in the development of individuals' rational and intellectual capabilities – however, it is unlikely to assist in the development of knowledge about the emotional, political and relational nature of learning and organizing. 'The human individual is a political animal and cannot find fulfilment outside a group and cannot satisfy any emotional drive without expression of its social component' (Bion, 1962: 118). Bion's famous quotation is a reminder that emotional experience is located in a social as much as an individual context. This idea has important consequences for understanding HRD. It implies a continuing shift from the development of cognitive processes and concepts towards a better understanding of the type of social engagements that provide a context for learning. For example, this will involve a shift away from the idea that learning can be planned and implemented through the development and understanding of various models of application or coherent 'steps in a change process'. Understanding the emotional as well as the social and political context of learning involves an awareness that any attempts to make change happen are sought at the same time as efforts to contain or control it. An approach to HRD that goes beyond the current focus on the development of individuals will serve an important purpose. It will help individuals and collectives to understand the organizational dynamics within which strategic learning is both perpetuated and resisted.

The current understanding of strategic learning is that it is a form of organizational learning whereby assumptions that underpin corporate-level knowledge are reframed (Kuwada, 1998) and/or where the sensemaking and knowledge management structures of an organization are altered in potentially radical ways (Thomas, Watts-Sussman and Henderson, 2001). Strategic learning is seen to involve both the enactment of meaning from new, ambiguous experiences and the development of shared understandings of both current and future events. Kuwada (1998: 719) identifies four aspects to knowledge that underpin strategic processes, making a distinction between corporate-level knowledge and business-level knowledge. At the corporate level, the organization creates 'a universe of discourse or an enacted environment, the basic assumptions are used to define the framework of facts, perceptions and meanings by which the firm operates'. The organization defines the problem space or situation; it has rules, procedures and heuristics to specify environmental factors and the causal relationship among those factors (this is an 'ecological' process, not a planned change of assumptions). At the business level, the organization generates a rational planning process within the problem space and implements strategic behaviour within the environment. It 'observes performance and interprets the results'. As I have already mentioned, my own view of strategic learning is built on related but different ideas: that organizing creates establishment, which is constructed from the interaction of emotions and politics, giving rise to characteristic organizational dynamics that often limit the potential interaction between learning and organizing. Organizing generates an idea of stability, within which it seems possible to make and to manage strategic decisions. The emphasis of my understanding of strategic learning, therefore, is less concerned with rational planning and the observation of performance, and more with the impact of conscious and unconscious emotions on organizing, as well as the expression and enactment of these emotions as politics or power relations.

Organizational obstacles to strategic learning

Human behaviour and relations frequently contribute to the construction of organizational processes that become obstacles to learning. These include the fears and anxieties that the possibility of learning generates, habits of mind that put frenzy above reflection, managerial strategies to avoid conflict and difference, the protection of personal empires, or perceptions of work pressure and expectations. As the (conscious and unconscious) emotions and relations behind these processes intermingle with decisions, strategies and political developments, the need to try to control and contain learning and change are reinforced. There is a continuous tension within organizations between the need to have coherent and communicable values and structures that inform organizing as well as having the means to reflect on and revise the organization that is being created. In other words, organizing involves a continuous tension between attempts to control and to change. Strategic learning is necessarily orientated towards changes in the very processes of organizing; it involves making an impact on the assumptions that both guide and are created from organizational behaviour and that inform organizational structures and designs. The assumptions that underpin and inform organizing are shaped from and shape individual and collective behaviour in organizations. To learn, therefore, may involve letting go of habits that have formed about how to do things, attachments to knowledge that relates to the past, or ideas that have previously informed actions. Such habits and attachments can inhibit the development and utilization of new knowledge. Learning provokes anxiety, defensiveness, fear and retrenchment as much as it excites, stimulates, motivates and empowers members of organizations. The tensions inherent in organizing reflect the continuous pull between the desire to learn and the need to avoid learning, and the ways in which such tensions are played out in organizational processes and designs.

In Hyder plc there were various organizational obstacles to strategic learning that provided clues to the ways establishment was created and sustained within the company. These can be summarized as follows:

- the individual orientation of Hyder's HRD strategy and the expectations on individuals to put learning into practice;
- limited and self-limiting notions of reflection;
- fears about engaging with the interplay between politics and emotion in the organization, particularly conflicts between sub-systems, and the effects of this on authority and leadership in practice.

One assumption that informed Hyder's HRD strategy was that an emphasis on individual learning would improve personal performance and contribute to the development of new ideas and forms of practice as well as their implementation. Hyder had a highly competent and developed range of learning processes available to individuals, collected under the general idea of a 'learning journey' (see Hurlow, James and Lenz, 1998). These included personal opportunities for formal and informal training and development linked to individual appraisal and supported through mentoring. New skills, knowledge and perceptions were developed through this process and individuals were enthusiastic as a result of their learning.

However, individuals' learning had little impact on processes of organizing, strategic decision-making, existing power relations or entrenched political positions. In fact, despite the enthusiasm surrounding personal learning there was a general feeling from staff that learning initiatives have little effect on the organization as a whole, that they tended to 'sink into the sand'. The individual orientation of Hyder's approach to learning remained uncritical of the ways in which power was experienced and enacted within the organization. This inevitably had an impact on the emotions experienced by staff. One department in Hyder organized a consultation process aimed at stimulating change within the department. (This example is explored in depth in Chapter 3.) Considerable energy and resources were given to the project and it succeeded in generating much enthusiasm from the front-line and middle-management staff involved because it seemed that they were being asked to shape the strategic direction of the department. Over time it became clear that the initiative was going to have little or no impact on the senior managers who had supported it, and gradually staff enthusiasm was replaced by staff cynicism about the ability of the senior managers (and therefore of the organization) to change. This emotional journey from enthusiasm to disappointment, then to cynicism in the face of established organizational power relations seems to me to be a common aspect of individual and collective experience of participation in organizational change initiatives.

Difficulties of reflection and development in Hyder were experienced individually as well as in relation to collective attempts at participation and involvement. Managers experienced continuous pressure to deliver and develop performance and, because of the pressure of work, were 'happy to accept the first logical explanation that comes into your mind'. Reflection was understood as an individual responsibility, something that the individual does, when they have the time. The limited practice of reflection in Hyder meant that reflection served a limited purpose, contributing little to an understanding of how establishment was being created and sustained. Underlying both an individualized perspective on learning and a restrictive practice of reflection there were powerful emotions connected to organizational politics. Organization members felt fear and anxiety about engaging with conflicts or differences either across hierarchical lines of accountability or across the political intricacies mobilized by competition, envy or ambivalence between various organizational sub-systems. They would rather ignore or avoid such conflicts. The effects of this (largely unconscious) decision had considerable impact on the practice of leadership and authority in Hyder. Competition between different sub-systems minimized partnership and understanding across organizational boundaries, as well as discouraging risk. In an environment that lacks risk there is a greater tendency towards control. Anxieties over either losing or retaining control contributed to reticent managers who feared change, failure and conflict. Through these organizing processes a culture of leadership was created in Hyder that, despite being consensual or collegial in intention, was in practice cautious, controlling and reactive.

What I am attempting to illustrate with these comments about the relationship between learning and organizing in Hyder is that, despite considerable investment of time and money in learning and development for individual managers, efforts towards learning made little impact on established ways of organizing. When the organizational processes or dynamics I have described are added together, Hyder can be understood as a company with very little orientation towards strategic learning (despite the creative and developmental learning processes present for individuals). This therefore raises the question of what can be done in organizations like Hyder to assist the development of strategic links between learning and organizing. It also raises a more general issue in terms of organizational learning:

> The fact is – we don't know a lot about organizational learning. Sure we know how to improve the learning of an individual or a small team, but we don't know how to systematically intervene in the culture to create transformational learning across the organization . . . One of the greatest business challenges is to find some models for how a whole organization can learn.
>
> (Schein, in Coutu, 2002: 103–4)

Rethinking strategic learning

The individual orientation in HRD practice has been perpetuated both through approaches to university based management education and approaches to HRD that privilege individual learning and development. In the past few years there has been a growing recognition of the need for critical perspectives that inform both management education and HRD (French and Grey, 1996; Willmott, 1997; Reynolds, 1999a, b). My general argument for an organizational orientation in HRD is developed through discussions that cover both management education and in-company HRD, since these connected areas of scholarship and action both seem to be subject to the same individual orientation. Both management educators and company managers can find it difficult to engage directly with the organizational dynamics that define their roles, for example, the power relations that are inherent in the student–teacher or manager–subordinate relationship, or those politics that impact on educational or organizational designs. A focus on the (real and imagined) relations of power that are mobilized and enacted from a role are a key starting point for the transformation of the organizing processes within which that role is embedded. This is not a new issue for educators or for managers. The work of Paulo Freire (1972, 1974), critical thinking in adult education (Kemmis, 1985), and critical approaches to action learning and management learning (Willmott, 1994, 1997) have, for example, provided many clues about forms of education and approaches to management that work with and through power relations. In practice, however, it continues to be an issue that is more avoided than addressed.

In management education, the emphasis on 'learning from experience' (Revans, 1983; Kolb, 1984) is an acknowledgement that managers' own experience is central to their education and development. However, approaches to learning from experience have again placed the individual at the centre and obscured the politics and emotions that are constructed in any collective or group-based effort to learn (Vince and Martin, 1993; Vince, 1998). There is therefore an increasing need for an organizational form of learning from experience (or learning from organizing), which I have referred to as 'strategic learning'. Strategic learning places the emphasis on learning through collective experience; on the conscious and unconscious structures that are inevitably created through attempts to learn; and on the reflexive relationship between collective experience and on organizational dynamics that both construct and constrain learning. The practical focus of strategic learning is the development of different ways of undertaking processes and approaches to reflection, a different interpretation of the notions of leadership, and the need to rethink ways in which HRD is framed and implemented.

Transforming the practices within which organizational roles are embedded involves the development of approaches that encourage the questioning of the assumptions that organizing has created. Assumptions emerge, take shape and institutionalize for important reasons, giving security and coherence to the uncertainties of organizing, and defining the parameters of how to belong and develop. That assumptions promote constraint as well as coherence is an integral and inevitable part of organizing. The questioning of assumptions is a challenge to the rationality and stability that underpins organizing. Strategic learning involves re-framing the questioning of assumptions as an organizational imperative rather than a responsibility for individuals or of groups (for example, the HRD division). This implies that, individually and collectively, managers will be continually involved in reflection into the organizational dynamics that inform (e.g.) leadership or decision-making.

From this position, the various meanings, understandings, resentments, opportunities, and so on, created through established organizational dynamics become the starting point of attempts to learn and change rather than the consequence of them. Individuals' approaches to learning and change can be based on how the organization is reflected and enacted within their own practices, and what this means in terms of transforming the particular organizational context that surrounds them. The value of this perspective is that individuals will learn how the dynamics that characterize an organization (and the emotions and politics that create and sustain these dynamics) are an integral part of their own thinking and ways of working. Strategic learning is not therefore a prescription for 'better' or 'effective' learning. In fact, the results of engaging with uncomfortable knowledge, with power relations and established assumptions are often difficult and unpredictable. However, managers may be able to learn how they contribute to the creation of patterns of organizing that limit their and others' ability to learn and to change, even as they imagine that they are making it happen.

An example

The following example is from my experience as the director of a programme of management education, for doctoral-level students who are mainly senior managers undertaking their studies part-time and utilizing their own work contexts as a setting for action research. I do not claim this programme as radical or particularly new. Indeed the importance of 'backyard research' is already well established (Jacobs, 1997; Swanson, 1997). There are many such programmes (the Centre for Action Research in Professional Practice at the University of Bath, School of Management is an example), and sometimes the same or similar ground is covered in the various Doctorate of Business Administration (DBA) and individual programmes of research study.

The Guided Doctorate in Organizational Leadership and Change (GD) at the University of Glamorgan is a group-based doctoral programme with a focus on organizational leadership and change. It started in 1996, recruiting up to 12 managers into each intake (not necessarily annually, depending on the availability of senior research staff). The programme lasts at least four years and (as with all PhD's) students are required to produce a doctoral dissertation that constitutes a unique contribution to knowledge. The GD attempts to provide a context for an in-depth process of knowledge creation, recognizing that knowledge changes as we live it. The aim, in terms of both understanding the temporary learning group and the organizational context within which individual research takes place, is to study the organization in action. Inquiry inevitably raises the question of power, as well as conscious and unconscious relations to others and to a social context. In the GD, reflection on emotions and power relations – both internal to the group and within the organizational context of the research – provides the impetus for understanding strategic learning.

As a temporary organization for learning, the GD programme itself reflects the possibility of strategic learning, questioning the politics of PhD study as a process of supervision between a professor and their student. The GD programme does not intend to create and sustain an institution driven by dependency on staff experience and expertise. For example, it is not seen as the role of the professors to dispense knowledge, nor is it the role of students to project their anxieties in such a way as to turn professors into experts (even if they are expert). Both students and staff are required to acknowledge their different roles in the GD, expressing different responsibilities and expectations. It is easy for staff and students to fall back on traditional positions in relation to each other. A strong emphasis on peer supervision and group engagement in learning sets is important, as is providing opportunities to focus on whole-group dynamics through the integration of Institutional Transformation or Group Relations methods into the course workshops (see French and Vince, 1999).

A key aspect of the staff role is in sustaining and developing the relationship between learning and organizing. There are various aspects to this. First, the different emotions and power relations that are inherent in the roles of staff and students are raised at the beginning of the programme. This involves exploring the different types of authority that are an aspect of each role. For example, staff and students may be anxious at the start of the programme in different ways. Rather than ignoring or banishing the anxiety and tensions generated by beginning the programme, they are raised in the group. This is not to claim that such dynamics (e.g. apprehension, envy, rivalry, etc.) are necessarily understood or managed by staff or students. The importance in raising such issues *out loud* at the start is that they become an aspect of organizational memory and afford opportunities for future reflection. Second, a particular perspective on leadership informs the programme. The notion of a leader as a flexible individual with the sole authority to creatively direct operations is seen as a fantasy that minimizes the potential for collective knowledge and that steers the group towards controlling and compliant organizational designs. In the GD the underlying assumption that informs learning about leadership (for both staff and students) is that it is a process orientated towards others, something that emerges from within a group or between groups of learners. In terms of strategic learning, therefore, it is seen as helpful to explore the difference between the expression of authority (in a role) and leadership. Third, work-based research at a doctoral level is a powerful intervention into the organizational systems and sub-systems within which the leadership role is enacted. In our experience at Glamorgan, an action-research project leading to a PhD inevitably becomes more than the inquiry of one individual. In the GD, through the inquiry brought about by being in the role of researcher as well as a senior manager, individuals are provided with an opportunity to question and to transform the patterns of organizing within which their leadership role is contained and constrained.

Such research has a collective orientation: it is necessarily with others rather than on them (Reason, 1988). To construct inquiry in the way I have described is to mobilize possibility with and through others in a distinctive emotional and political context. This is a process that can connect learning and organizing, going beyond what individuals may learn from their experience. The approach to knowledge implied here allows for the idea that 'knowledge is not something people possess in their heads, it is something people do together' (Weick, 2002). The GD is just one example of a shift of emphasis in the delivery of management education and HRD away from the individual learner and towards educational processes that recognize and work with the complex relationship between individual and collective learning and organizing.

In summary, strategic learning generally implies:

- an approach to learning that raises the complexities of political relatedness;
- reflection on organizational dynamics – how the organization is created and recreated through the interaction of behaviour and structure, and the importance of *social* reflection-in-action;
- open engagement with the emotions and power relations that are created in collectives as they evolve.

Specifically, within the Guided Doctorate programme at the University of Glamorgan, this was expressed through a focus on:

- *The organization in action*. Programme members study the relationships between organizing and learning that are being created within the GD at the same time as undertaking inquiry into these dynamics within their own organizations. Since programme members bring with them conscious and unconscious ways of working that reflect the various organizations they come from, the organizational dynamics from both settings often inform and challenge each other.
- *The political relatedness of different roles*. Programme members and staff reflect on the nature and enactment of authority, leadership, learning and change in the GD. The emphasis is on opportunities for collective and critical reflection, attempts to develop a collective enactment of leadership, understanding the potency of inquiry as intervention in the social and political context of an organization.

The emphasis here is on an organizational perspective. This is not so focused on what an individual knows, can learn, may change, and so on – rather it concerns the transformation of the system that creates and constrains roles and that marginalizes collective capacity and action. To have a meaningful impact, HRD (whether undertaken in the academy or in-company) has to engage with the contextual politics, power relations and emotions that shape the possibilities and limitations of learning. I do not believe this to be a difficult shift of understanding, even if it represents something complex in practice. At present the emphasis is on the relationship between a person and his or her role in an organization (e.g. learning to be a more effective manager, leader or follower). A revised emphasis will be on the relationship between role and organization (on organizational dynamics and their impact on the enactment of a managerial or leadership role). For example, the Chief Executive of a company is not just a person: he or she is in a (possibly, the most) powerful role within the organization – one that attracts many relations, perceptions and fantasies. Whatever the behaviour of the person, it is often the collective interpretations of his or her behaviour over time which come to define the person *within their role*. The Chief Executive might be seen as: aloof from most staff, charismatic, a political animal, a fearsome ogre, and ineffectual . . . the list is endless. However, as collective perceptions of the individual are reinforced, escaping them becomes more difficult, and these perceptions can have a profound impact on collective behaviour in the organization. Examining the relationship between role and organization involves inquiry into the ways in which organizational designs, assumptions, values and expected behaviours create and constrain the ways in which a role is enacted, and vice versa.

In this book I argue that a revised notion of strategic learning can provide a starting point for exploring key organizing practices like reflection and leadership. The focus is on transforming organizational roles, not on developing the individual's ability to act from within a role. If university-based management education is to support such a shift then this means placing less emphasis on approaches to learning that are didactic, or even on experiential approaches that are designed primarily for self awareness. An understanding of strategic learning comes from opportunities to explore the organizational dynamics that are being created as individuals and collectives participate in organizing. In practical terms this involves questioning and exploring the emotions and power relations present in the roles of (e.g.) tutor and student, and the impact of these on the design, content and outcomes of learning. The focus of in-company HRD will be to support the relationship between learning and organizing. This will not happen primarily through the delivery of training, through appraisal or mentoring, but through collective attempts to transform the ways in which organizing is imagined and implemented in order to minimize constraints on learning in an organizational role. I provide a more detailed explanation and examples of what this means for organizing reflection and leadership in Chapters 7 and 8.

There is a need for HRD scholars and practitioners to better understand that development initiatives are not simply about improving individual performance or organizational effectiveness. Future developments in critical perspectives on human resource development can support the advancement of knowledge about emotional, relational and political processes affecting management and organization, as well as the implementation of this knowledge in practice. At this time, further knowledge about individual development is not imperative. More important now is a better understanding of the complex relations between people in an organizational context – what people collectively create and can imagine. For this to happen there will have to be increased interest in the emotional responses that are integral to organizing, as well as how these create, reflect and represent power relations that underpin emerging organizational experience and designs. In the next chapter I construct a conceptual framework that provides a theoretical basis for such development.

3   Power, emotion and organizational learning

In this chapter I develop and illustrate a conceptual framework for understanding organizational learning. Recent advances in the study of organizational learning, particularly a social and political perspective on organizational learning, provide a theoretical base for strategic learning. To emphasize this: in this book, the term 'organizational learning' particularly represents the academic side of strategic learning. 'Strategic learning' is a broader term, which links the academic study of organizational learning to the thoughts, reflections and actions of managers and other practitioners (concerned with learning and development). As I mentioned in Chapter 1, I use the term 'strategic learning' as a bridge between academic and practitioner voices, views and interests.

I explore in depth the difference between individual learning in an organization and organizational learning. As I explained in Chapter 2, this is an important distinction because, if the emphasis of strategic learning is on changes in 'the sensemaking and knowledge management structures of an organization' (Thomas, Watts-Sussman and Henderson, 2001), then it is the development of an organizational level of analysis of learning that is most likely to assist in imagining what such changes are, as well as how they might be attempted. I argue that an emphasis on individuals' learning within an organization and its possible eventual impact on the organization as a system is unlikely to lead to the transformation of organizing structures. Instead, I refer to organizational dynamics, constructed from the interaction between emotion and power, that create the social and political context within which both learning and organizing take place. Using a combination of psychodynamic theory and reflections on the politics of organizing I develop the idea that organizations are learning when the *establishment* that is being created through the very process of organizing can be identified and critically reflected on. I argue that this combination of psychodynamic theory and politics is an important addition to current thinking about the relationship between learning and organizing. I use an example of a change initiative within Hyder plc to illustrate and develop my thinking.

To remind the reader of the context, Hyder had two distinctive but interlinked business directions: Hyder Utilities, a multi-utility business mainly located in Wales, and Hyder Infrastructure Development, which undertook large engineering, consulting and infrastructure projects throughout the world. The emphasis of the change initiative I talk about in this chapter concerns Hyder's attempts to make clearer imperatives for commercial growth and global development. The prevailing understanding of learning in Hyder at that time was that individual staff would benefit from highly practical and applied on-the-job learning and training. The 'learning journey' that was available to staff had been built on links between various processes of appraisal and a wide variety of approaches to training and development. The Hyder perspective on learning was created and implemented by highly committed and hard-working corporate HR staff members, who were particularly concerned to ensure that all learning was transferred into action within the company, and that this learning had an impact on working groups. For them, the resulting changes and developments in working practices and attitudes would mean that the organization was learning. Organizational learning therefore was seen in terms of the results of the impact that individuals had on the organization. This way of thinking, despite being very common is not without its problems: "individual learning can be a dangerous thing when the organization's value system and culture don't have enough freedom to allow individuals to do what they need to do" (Schein, in Coutu, 2002: 105).

In my critique of the Hyder approach to learning I describe and illustrate the problems that resulted from entrenched or established organizational dynamics, as well as their impact on individuals and collectives. HR managers and staff genuinely believed Hyder to be a 'learning organization'; however, the evidence showed that even a well-thought-through, well-developed HR strategy for learning made little impression on established organizational structures and knowledge.

Approach, data collection and interpretation

The case example is drawn from an action-research project within Hyder that was designed to help the company think about the development of the learning journey at strategic levels of the organization (in addition to the existing emphasis on operational and business levels). I am using 'action research' as a broad term that covers various qualitative methods linking inquiry with learning and change (see Raelin, 1999). In general, the study was interpretative and impressionistic, capturing examples of the issues, meanings, relations and politics that were characteristic of the organization. It was an attempt to reveal what was hidden, stuck, obscured or undiscussable. The research was not undertaken in order to provide evidence to justify action, rather as one possible starting point of action that implied strategic learning.

There were a variety of aspects to the method that gave it particular relevance to the study of strategic learning in Hyder. Action research recognizes that language is not an individual act, assuming complex, interpersonally negotiated processes of interpretation (Winter, 1989). An important aspect of Hyder's struggle with learning was to move beyond the notion that individuals are the primary focus for learning, to understand the emotional, relational and political dynamics that were central to both learning and organizing. Action research is collaborative; it does not seek a consensus, but engages with dialogue and difference. Managers in Hyder tended to avoid and underplay differences, undermining dialogue and communication. Action research is a method that explicitly recognizes the interplay between reflection and action. In Hyder, managers placed more emphasis on action than they did on reflection on action. For whatever reasons, they often ignored, avoided or abandoned meaningful processes of reflection and inquiry.

Seven directors from different parts of Hyder were interviewed up to five times over a period of two months. The interviews lasted ninety minutes each and were largely unstructured. They were guided by an emphasis on the directors' understanding of their role in the company. Through discussion of their role, and the relatedness between person, role and organization, the research sought to reveal and explore the 'organization-in-the-mind' (Armstrong, 1991; Bazelgette, Hutton and Reed, 1997) of these senior managers, to provide one possible map of the experiences, impressions, understandings and interpretations of Hyder as an organization. The data collected were emotional, relational and political in nature, as well as reflecting the thinking of the directors individually and collectively.

Analysis of the interview transcripts sought to identify two areas of understanding, the *current themes and issues* present for this group of directors, as well as their *mental representations* of Hyder. For the themes and issues, I identified emergent categories within the transcripts, refined these categories and then grouped the data from each director around these categories in order to highlight a set of broadly collective concerns. For the mental representations of Hyder I highlighted the various images, metaphors and expressions within the transcripts and then grouped these into different images of the organization. The focus of the next stage of analysis was both checking back and extending the number of interpretations of the data. The participating managers were sent copies of the initial categorization and analysis. They were asked to comment and to reflect on the themes and issues that had emerged.

In this chapter my focus is on the 'Create Our New Company' initiative (CONC), developed and implemented in Hyder Utilities. This initiative constituted one of twenty-four categories emerging from the overall data on themes and issues. Discussion of the CONC initiative arose because the senior manager responsible for it wanted to explore his role in developing and attempting to sustain it in the company. The seven directors reflected a wide cross-section across the company, and each had views about the impact and relevance of CONC within their part of Hyder. All the interviews were tape recorded and transcribed. All the quotations that I have integrated into my descriptions about CONC in this chapter are taken from these transcripts. Before I talk about the CONC initiative in Hyder I take a step back, to explore some key issues in learning and organizing, which helps to set the context for my conceptual framework.

Power and emotion in organizational learning

The academic interest in organizational learning is very lively and creative at the present time, despite opinions I have encountered within some organizational settings, where the feeling is that 'we've done organizational learning'. The academic (and scholarly practitioner) community that is interested in organizational learning has produced a wealth of thought and reflection in recent years. Some classic texts have been updated (Argyris and Schön, 1996); there have been several edited books, some which have collected older material (Cohen and Sproull, 1996) and others that have collected new material (Easterby-Smith, Araujo and Burgoyne, 1999; Dierkes et al., 2001). In addition, there are edited collections of papers in notable journals that have been published every two years as a result of the scholarship from well-attended international conferences (Easterby-Smith, Snell and Gherardi, 1998; Easterby-Smith, Crossan and Nicolini, 2000; Vince, Sutcliffe and Olivera, 2002). The connected themes in this area of study are very varied, and interest in organizational learning has crossed (and continues to cross) a wide variety of academic disciplines (Easterby-Smith, 1997). The field continues to carry a dual emphasis: on practical interventions to create learning organizations (Senge, 1990; Pedler, Burgoyne and Boydell, 1991; Pedler and Aspinwall, 1998), and on scholarly observation and analysis of the processes involved in individual and collective learning inside and between organizations (Easterby-Smith, Araujo and Burgoyne, 1999). In addition, there is interaction between research and scholarship in the connected areas of organizational learning and knowledge management. In recent years the academic and scholarly work in the field of organizational learning has moved away from an emphasis on organizational learning as a technical process (i.e. learning through the effective processing of information) towards a 'social perspective' (Easterby-Smith and Araujo, 1999). A key theme in organizational learning as a social process is a shift away from the idea that politics is a problem in the way of learning (Argyris, 1990), or that political activity is a constraint on learning (Senge, 1990). Politics is seen as a natural feature of organizing and learning, and it is recognized that power relations directly mediate interpretative processes within organizations (Coopey, 1995; Coopey and Burgoyne, 1999; Vince, 2001).

Many approaches to organizational learning have been rational and pragmatic, focusing, for example, on the measurement of outcomes (Garvin, 1993), on specific behaviour sets (Ellinger, Watkins and Bostrom, 1999), on commercially significant prescriptions for organizational design and change (Lei, Slocum and Pitts, 1999), or in terms of gaining explicit capabilities (Ulrich, von Glinow and Jick, 1993). However, both learning and organizing are seen as much more than rational processes. Learning in organizations and organizational learning also happen by accident, from the unintended consequences of action and through paradoxical tensions that are integral to organizing (Vince and Broussine, 1996). The challenge of learning can be expressed in attempts to engage with the paradox, uncertainty and complexity of management and organization, with 'learning in the face of mystery' (Gherardi, 1999). Such engagement requires an examination of the complex web of social relations through which learning occurs as well as the impact of the emotions that are generated by attempts to learn and to prevent learning in organizations. Although there is widespread acknowledgement that emotions are integral to organizing, this is in itself uncomfortable knowledge that prompts members of organizations to try to 'de-emotionalise emotions [and] make them seem rational' (Fineman, 1993). Increasingly it is recognized that learning primarily occurs in the context of social relations and as a result of complex interactions which are profoundly influenced by both individual and collective emotions and relations.

In addition to the importance of politics and emotion to the theory and practice of organizational learning, it is useful to understand how the words 'organizational' and 'learning' connect, or indeed contradict each other (Weick and Westley, 1996). Is there any way in which learning can be considered *organizational*? 'Perhaps the idea of organizational learning is an anthropomorphic fallacy, that leads to an inappropriate reification of the concept of organization' (Prange, 1999: 27). However, there is also the view that 'complex organizations are more than ad hoc communities or collections of individuals. Relationships become structured, and some of the individual learning and shared understanding developed by groups become institutionalized as organization artefacts' (Crossan, Lane and White, 1999: 524). In other words, organizations can be seen as more than the sum of their individual or collective parts. Organization level learning has been seen as important because it 'captures the elements of strategic alignment' (Bontis, Crossan and Hulland, 2002: 444).

It is this second interpretation, on the importance of dynamics created through group interaction (both internal and external), which provides a key underlying assumption informing the conceptual framework I outline in this chapter. Strategic learning involves the acceptance of a dynamic relating to the organization-as-a-whole. Recently, Lipshitz and Popper (2000) have attempted to 'solve the problematic link' between individual learning in an organization and organizational learning. They have proposed a conceptual framework whereby 'organizational learning mechanisms' can be identified, emerging from the experience of members of organizations, but ultimately becoming the 'property of the entire organization, either through distribution of lessons learned to relevant units or through changes in standard operating procedures' (p. 347). They make the distinction between 'learning-in organizations' and 'learning-by organizations'. The first implies learning that is directed at improving the proficiency of members of organizations, the second has organizational-level outputs, which implies changes in informal norms and procedures. The research by Lipshitz and Popper (2000) is useful because it describes aspects of the difference between the development of individual cognitive processes and the social processes that underpin organizing. However, their research was not concerned with describing key components of these social processes, the emotional or unconscious dynamics and the politics that shape organizational behaviour and design. It is this particular task that I develop within the rest of this chapter.

Conceptual framework

The conceptual framework I discuss and develop in this chapter is based on the interrelation between politics, emotion and organizational dynamics. The framework is designed to promote reflection on what is organizational learning, thereby helping to clarify what the word 'organizational' means in the phrase 'organizational learning'. Such reflection is useful to academics and scholarly practitioners because it attempts to provide greater clarity as to what constitutes an organizational level of analysis. It is also useful to other practitioners in considering how organizational dynamics are created and expressed through individual and collective behaviour and engagement, and therefore in assessing the possibilities and limitations of learning within a specific organizational context.

There are three premises that underpin my notion of organizational learning:

Premise 1: Learning processes are directly mediated by power relations.
Premise 2: Emotion determines the possibilities and limitations of both learning and organizing.
Premise 3: There exist organizational 'dynamics', which are more than the sum of individual or collective learning.

There are two particular aspects to the thinking behind the premise that learning processes are directly mediated by power relations. One of these concerns theory, the other is to do with practice. As theory, 'a political perspective widens our understanding of the processes that constitute learning in organizations' (Coopey and Burgoyne, 1999: 292). It achieves this by addressing how employees relate to organizational practices and constructions of reality, to the structural features that locate them in positions of inequality or impotence. It addresses the interface between structure and action, and shows how such interactions create and establish characteristic power relations and regimes. From this viewpoint, politics is neither a problem to be avoided, nor a set of conflicts of interest. Rather, it affords a critical stance on the complexities of power relations through which organizing takes place. When I use the word 'politics' therefore, I am talking about the power relations that moderate how learning (and change) does or does not happen in organizations.

As practice, a political perspective invites critical reflection on what managers think they know and how they come to know it within an organizational context. Managers can find ways to doubt taken-for-granted assumptions, and learn through their capacity to question and to engage with the particular regime that both they and the organization have jointly created. The political struggle in organizations in terms of practice is often represented in the reluctance managers have towards expressing leadership openly and in public (a theme I develop in Chapter 8). The ways in which managers are able to open out processes of leadership and decision-making to others and to reveal rather than avoid power relations will be crucial for strategic learning. Managers defend against the impact of socially constructed power relations because of the anxieties that struggles with issues of power, authority and responsibility provoke. However, engaging with such issues can provide considerable opportunities for learning about the emotional, relational and political processes involved in managing and organizing. The revelation of how power is expressed and enacted in organizations offers opportunities to move beyond interactions that are created from managers' defensiveness and towards new forms and processes of communication and interaction.

My second premise, that emotion determines the possibilities and limitations of both learning and organizing, is influenced by psychodynamic theory. The subject of emotion in organizations has an established literature, reflecting both a social-constructionist standpoint (Hochschild, 1979, 1983; Fineman, 1993, 1996) and the psychodynamic exploration of emotion at work (Kets de Vries and Miller, 1985; Hirschhorn, 1988; Trist and Murray, 1990; Hoggett, 1992; Obholzer and Roberts, 1994; French and Vince, 1999). Both approaches challenge the ways in which emotion in organizations have been 'narrowly perceived' (Hosking and Fineman, 1990), as well as a tendency to ignore the impact that emotions have on organizational development and design.

There are two aspects to psychodynamic theory that are particularly important to my understanding of emotion and organization. First, there is the idea that learning and change are inevitably associated with anxiety. At both a conscious and an unconscious level, the management of learning is the management of anxiety and of resistance arising from the anxiety (Obholzer, 1999; Coutu, 2002). In addition, this implies something about the role of a manager or leader: that such a role involves an emotional connection to the anxiety arising from the nature of work. As several authors have pointed out, anxiety is an important ingredient in managers' understanding of learning in organizations, in terms of both how learning occurs and how it is prevented (Kofman and Senge, 1993; Schein, 1993; Vince and Martin, 1993). Also, Bain (1998: 414) has identified the 'absence of attention to unconscious processes influencing individual, group and organizational functioning' in the writing on organizational learning.

The second contribution that psychodynamic theory makes to this chapter is with the theory of 'relatedness' – the 'conscious and unconscious emotional levels of connection that exist between and shape selves and others, people and systems' (French and Vince, 1999: 7). People in organizations are inevitably 'creatures of each other' (Hinshelwood, 1998) involved in a mutual process of becoming that obscures as much as it highlights the notion of a separate self. Relatedness implies a range of emotional levels of connection across the boundaries of person, role and organization, which emphasize the relational nature of organizing. In using the word 'emotion', therefore, I am talking about emotions (e.g. envy, guilt, joy and fear) that are ignored or avoided and how these consciously and unconsciously impact on organizing. To put this briefly, I am saying that emotion *is* political.

My third premise is that there exists something that can be referred to as 'organizational dynamics' (see Miller and Rice, 1967). These are more than the sum of individuals learning and more than learning in a collective context. Organizational dynamics refer to the system or more precisely the establishment that is unconsciously or unknowingly created from organizing. In using the term 'establishment' in addition to 'system', I am trying to find a way of expressing the importance of politics to an understanding of organizational learning. Establishment (as opposed to family, community, or all working together) is expressive of the connection between emotion, power, learning and organizing.

The idea that organizing gives rise to establishment is useful in two ways: first, it connects to insights about the ways in which an 'internal establishment' is created and perpetuated within individuals' inner worlds (Hoggett, 1992). In other words, how individual psychology and organizational power relations combine to create the temporary truths or realities that underpin individuals' enactments of their roles, as well as perceptions about their roles. Second, it implies a controlling force, which is inevitably brought to bear on ideas and experiences in order to contain them (Bion, 1985; Bain, 1998). Establishment is recognition of a strategic relationship between learning and organizing. Organizing, in part and mostly unintentionally, involves the containment of learning so that it can be assimilated into existing organizational power relations, so that learning can be 'exploited' as much as 'explored' (March, 1996). This implies that the juxtaposition of organization and learning is desirable, as long as it is learning that can in some way be managed, limited or controlled.

Organizational dynamics are created from the interplay between (often unconscious) emotion and (existing and emerging) power relations generated through organizing. I am using the term 'organizational dynamics' to describe the organizational characteristics that are unconsciously or unknowingly created from individual and collective experience and action in the organization-as-a-whole. The term exists as a device to focus on an organizational level of analysis. To refer to such dynamics both avoids the problem of personifying or reifying an organization, and acknowledges that as emotions and politics interact they produce processes that have an impact and influence beyond the individuals that imagined them, and beyond the specific group contexts that produced them.

The 'Create Our New Company' (CONC) initiative

The specific case example from Hyder that I am using here to illustrate the concepts and ideas I have presented concerns the development and implementation of a significant initiative (in terms of both staff time and financial resources) aimed at increasing staff participation and involvement in organizational change. On the surface the motives for the initiative were about the empowerment of staff; however, the politics and emotions surrounding the initiative were more a representation of competition between different parts of the business, fears about conflict, and control.

Senior managers and HRD staff in Hyder Utilities devised CONC. Their strategic focus was on doing something to marry the very different management styles and organizational cultures that were represented in the previously separate organizations, Welsh Water and SWALEC (South Wales Electricity Company). The initial enthusiasm and desire that built the CONC initiative was a genuine feeling that 'with time, this process will definitely improve the shape of our business', that it was a 'nurturing process' of change. The design of the change programme was to take a cross-section of the company staff (500 from the 5,000 in Hyder Utilities) away for a two-and-a-half-day residential workshop facilitated by external consultants. The company ran twenty-six of these seminars over three months. The brief for the participants was 'to look at visions and values for the future and to develop a change model that will take us from where we are, to the company we want to create'. The workshops were developmental in the sense that the first twelve were used to bring out ideas; the next ten reviewed, reflected on and developed the ideas from the first stage of workshops; and the final four workshops asked staff to pull all the ideas and actions together into the vision and values of the new company. A small steering group of participants was created to sustain and develop the initiative.

CONC was initiated in the Utilities business a few months after the launch of the company-wide re-branding that created Hyder as one organization. Corporate Human Resource staff in the Group Development section of the company led the re-branding. The idea of 'One Hyder' was 'to identify a market position and to represent a promise to customers and other stakeholders'. The underlying value seen to be driving the re-branded organization was the earning of 'confidence' (hence the name Hyder, the Welsh word meaning 'confidence'). Internally, this would happen 'because managers had the self-confidence to go forward and to create a confident business, one that generates external business confidence, both from the client and the Stock Market'. Managers in Group Development saw CONC as a waste of time and money. It seemed to them to cut across the re-branding exercise and to have very different organizational aims and purposes. The dynamics between the staff leading the CONC initiative and those promoting the corporate re-branding exercise were to an extent expressive of tensions between managers who wanted the company to remain focused on its 'core' (utilities) business in South Wales and those who wanted 'growth' in the company towards becoming a key global enterprise. The organizational dynamics being played out over CONC were constructed from the tensions between the desire to assert Welsh Water's public-sector values in the face of an evolving and demanding commercial imperative within the new company (Hyder). The CONC initiative can be understood as a process designed to promote change within the Utilities division. It can also be understood as a reaction against changes taking place within the company as a whole.

Organizational dynamics

A key point in my argument is that an understanding of organizational learn-ing involves comprehending the organizational dynamics created from the interaction of politics and emotion. I suggest that organizing generates an identifiable establishment, created from the interaction between politics and emotion, within which both behaviour and structure are contained and con-strained. The following quotation offers an insight into the contextual dynamics characterising Hyder at this particular point in the history of the organization.

> That Create Our New Company initiative is very, very similar to a considerable other number of initiatives during recent years which have been undertaken with the best possible motives in mind, they really are, they are quite laudable, it is about empowerment, it is highly participative, with the right objectives in mind, but we do seem to struggle if we revisit only a handful of the ones that I have been on myself, as to what on earth happened afterwards.

The interviews provided the impression of an organization where change initiatives were enthusiastically created yet could not be sustained and fully implemented. As another senior manager put it, 'they sort of sink into the sand'. One reason why CONC sank into the sand was because it was designed to represent a political position within Hyder Utilities, as well as an emotional and strategic response to attempts at organizational change emerging from Group Development.

The dynamics created from politics and emotions that were visible in the CONC initiative reflected the wider establishment in Hyder. Managers were working in the context of a continuous pull between two directions or dual identities. For some Hyder was a (Welsh) utilities company, for others it was a global, commercial company. Communication between the people with these two perceptions was not good: 'it is almost like the old iron curtain'. The tension between managers wanting to develop the utility business and the commercial business became a powerful underlying aspect of the organizational design of Hyder. As one senior manager remarked: 'if you structure a business to be split down the middle that's what you are going to get'.

The politics of this split did not only concern the difference between discrete divisions of the organization but also different perceptions of the organization. As these perceptions were reinforced through everyday decisions, interactions and the avoidance of interaction, they created an organizational dynamic. The emotions connected to this split were primarily fears about the conflict that might arise between the two sides, and such emotions promoted a lack of communication in the company as a whole.

> I think the big problem with the organization is that everybody knows what needs to be done, but everybody is dead scared of doing it because of the consequences and the fallout and the issues that come with it.

Discussions with senior managers on the CONC initiative revealed that the emotions and politics mobilized around two competing organizational change initiatives were ignored and avoided. There was little or no communication about the ways in which the CONC initiative and the re-branding exercise might conflict or complement with each other. Managers in Utilities and Group Development ignored, avoided and undermined the change initiative that least represented their view of the company, thereby sustaining the competition between them. The unresolved competition and the inability of the CONC initiative to make the desired impact created defensiveness and consequently a desire to protect and justify the initiative. The CONC initiative was set up (in part) to compete with the re-branding exercise. It was a process designed to promote change, but at the same time it was a reaction against Group Development's view of change.

Politics and learning

I have argued, along with other commentators on organizational learning (Coopey, 1995), that inquiry into the politics of organizing widens our understanding of the processes that constitute learning, and the internal and external structures that locate people in positions of inequality or impotence. My thinking emphasizes that the politics or power relations that organizing has generated moderate how learning happens (or not) in organizations. The way in which the CONC workshops were set up meant that promises about involvement, participation and empowerment were made to staff. They were sold the idea they were being involved in the creation of a new company. The senior manager responsible for CONC reported that the staff members involved in the workshops were pleased and excited by this idea. However, these staff members were not involved in the creation of a new company – to a certain extent they were pawns in a power struggle between two versions of the organization. The eventual impotence of staff involved in CONC was an inevitable aspect of the process. The initiative certainly gave rise to considerable enthusiasm from a group of staff that believed that they were being empowered to be involved in organizational change. Despite the overt response from Group Development (which was, broadly speaking, 'go ahead and do it if you think it will work'), there was a lack of interest and commitment from the part of the organization most responsible for organizing corporate change.

The power relations mobilized by the CONC initiative were cautious and controlling, motivated by fear of failure and reinforced by a fear of conflict. Conflicts tended to be covered over rather than dealt with. Managers feared that 'things will get personal', and as a consequence interactions were motivated by the question 'how do I avoid this row?'. Managers' difficulties with conflict undermined the extent of their authority.

> We don't explore the differences long enough to actually expose the differences and therefore to deal with those differences and actually understand them.

That sort of intelligent inquiry without fear is something that is absent from our behaviours. Of course you end up having a conversation where one thing is being said but something else is being thought.

The politics of trying to initiate change in a climate of mistrust between two competing perceptions of the organization made the Director of Group Development's espoused view of collegiality in the organization look (at best) optimistic. The politics that were created in Hyder, visible in the CONC initiative, were not about collegiality. Managers did not enact their authority and leadership openly through dialogue, and they were unable to open leadership and decision-making to others in ways that might address rather than avoid the various power relations that arose. This meant that opportunities to move beyond defensive interactions were lost, excluding the possibility of effective communication across organizational sub-systems.

Emotion and learning

Individual and collective emotions, generated through organizing, come to define characteristic organizational politics or power relations. These then have an impact on what are possible (or legitimate) emotional responses. I summarize this idea by saying that emotion is political. An understanding of organizational learning involves asking how emotions are ignored or avoided in an organization, and how what is ignored or avoided impacts on organizing. Corporate HRD managers in Group Development felt that CONC was unnecessary and divisive, since it cut across their corporate re-branding exercise. In addition they did not rate the initiative highly. For them, the conclusions that emerged from the workshops 'were values that we have probably been espousing since about 1986, there wasn't anything new about it'. Managers within Group Development felt that 'the outcome was built into the process, you got the impression that there was a certain leading going on', and that the steering group arrangement was an artificial expression of authority.

> So it seemed to me that it reinforced the divisions . . . it seemed to vest in a group of people quasi decision making authority which is artificial, and I think it told of a prospectus of change which was not as vigorous as it needs to be.

In turn, the HRD managers in Hyder Utilities didn't rate the re-branding exercise. For them, it was seen to come from a 'corporate communism mentality'. Their imperative for undertaking CONC was 'an urgency to get on and do something' because Group Development 'weren't attempting to shape anything'. It was felt that the re-branding exercise did not represent the needs of staff in Hyder Utilities, and that the Director of Group Development (who led the re-branding exercise) was to blame:

Now there is someone who should actually be representing the interests of the people and this is a very positive, people based initiative, there is someone who should be on board helping to lead it and yet feels threatened by it.

Managers both in Hyder Utilities and in Group Development acted as if the competition, envy, mistrust and lack of communication between them did not exist or have an impact on the organization. However, it did, and the avoidance of the powerful emotions surrounding the CONC initiative both represented and reinforced existing organizational power relations.

There was considerable anxiety surrounding the expectations both on individual managers' commercial success as well as the commercial success of the organization as a whole. In all organizations, expectations are handed up and down, consciously and unconsciously through relations between individuals, and between sub-systems, as well as through political processes of action and avoidance. Expectations have a powerful impact on the ways in which members of organizations feel about and do their jobs. This, in turn, shapes organizational habits and characteristics, creating established ways of organizing.

One emotional pressure on managers in Hyder was the high expectations of people to deliver. Such expectations were both managed from above and self-imposed. The imperative from above was for commercial success, and the internal experience of this was the pressure to be successful, always right and to stay in control. Hyder managers lived with considerable anxiety about 'not achieving what one imagines one ought to achieve'. In terms of the CONC initiative, 'what one ought to achieve' was the change that staff had been promised. The managers and staff responsible for CONC became protective, defensive and ultimately controlling of the initiative as they saw it sinking. Their defensiveness meant that the CONC initiative 'had to be kept alive in people's minds' which, given the organizational politics, involved much frustration and anxiety. In an effort to keep things alive, the CONC steering group members devised statistical measures and processes to monitor the behaviour of managers. Controlling the behaviour of managers would be achieved through monitoring their improvements in relation to a prescribed list of acceptable behaviours.

We put that pamphlet out to all of our people and it shows the . . . behaviours and what some of those behaviours look like in practice. We are going to build that into development reviews with people and also use the same values in appraisals for managers . . . We will do that in a way in which we can actually get a fix on what people's perceptions are, of how they are operationalizing those values. So, if we get an overall score, which is a very crude score admittedly, that says our managers have been scored at sixty-six out of a hundred so to speak, the next time we get the fix on it is a score of seventy. I want to measure how well managers are developing against those values, not to stifle them but to say to people, look, last year we looked like this, do you think we look like this now? There is more sort of empowerment if you like in this process, you feel more relaxed about yourself and we try and build positives to encourage people to do more and not less.

The steering group's policing strategy generated even more direct criticism, and this in turn produced more defensiveness and self-justification.

Some people have said that this thing is very manipulative and it is not consciously designed to be manipulative but we have been very definite to put a framework around it.

As it gradually but inevitably sank into the sand, those managers and staff involved in the steering group were the ones who felt the frustrations over the apparent failure of CONC most powerfully. They saw themselves as the guardians of all the enthusiasms and expectations that had been generated in the workshops, as well as being responsible for the impossible task of sustaining and developing the initiative. They were angry about the consequences of the failure to implement the vision and strategy that they had been responsible for creating. The manager in charge of the steering group felt that failure would be 'an ongoing black mark against the organization for ever and a day'.

Discussion of the framework and the example

I have described some of the organizational issues associated with the CONC initiative, highlighting various aspects of the politics and emotions that gave rise to CONC and contributed to its demise. My impression, based on experience within various organizations, is that this example from Hyder is a reasonably common occurrence. In fact, Hyder is a good example of an organization that was doing much to support learning within the organization. One problem was that managers had not done what they could to understand the strategic impact of learning, by reflecting and acting on organizational dynamics, on the establishment that organizing had created and that limited learning and change. In this part of the chapter, therefore, my focus is on some of the conclusions that arose from the example I have just provided, as well as further reflections on the theoretical implications of these conclusions for organizational and strategic learning.

Establishment was created and reinforced through the underlying emotions and power relations in Hyder. Power is not something external to members of organizations or relationships – it 'penetrates the very essence of our being' (Knights and McCabe, 1999). Power cannot be separated from the emotions and relations that reinforce it. There are three interlinked organizing processes that helped to construct the distinctive politics I have described in Hyder. First, all organizing for change took place in the context of strong emotions and political manoeuvring between members of organizations who supported what they saw as the core work of the company (Hyder Utilities) and members within other parts of Hyder (particularly Group Development) where the desire was to promote commercial growth. Second, such different political perceptions of the business and the emotions attached to them led to an 'iron curtain' between the core and growth lobbies within the organization. Relations between Utilities and Group Development were based on attempts at control rather than dialogue. Third, as the emotions and politics surrounding this difference became more entrenched, their separateness needed to be protected and justified. The power relations shifted from being concerned with organizational change to being concerned with protecting the rights of these two parts of Hyder to create organizational change in the ways that they wanted, as well as defending their part of the organization from the other's perceptions of change.

In an organizational context it makes little sense to talk about emotions in organizations separately from organizational politics. Emotions were politically expressed and enacted in Hyder in the following ways:

- Competition, driven by emotions like envy, mistrust, or personal dislike, was ignored or avoided.
- The CONC initiative invested in its participants an unrealistic feeling of involvement or empowerment in organizational change. The initiative did not have the wider political legitimacy it needed and therefore it could not create the necessary authority and ownership for the implementation of change.
- In whole organizational terms the initiative generated conflicting emotions. The enthusiasm of Utilities staff was concurrent with a lack of enthusiasm from managers within Group Development responsible for re-branding.
- The motives driving some of the managers in Utilities were aimed at protecting their own turf. They were trying to build a groundswell of values unique to Hyder Utilities that would counteract the commercial values at the base of the re-branding exercise.
- The initial enthusiasms for CONC could not be sustained because it did not have the wider organizational legitimacy it needed. There was disappointment that it was not progressing as planned, defensiveness towards the criticism that it engendered, and anger at the failure of impact of a large and expensive initiative.
- The emotions generated around the CONC initiative both connected to and mirrored company-wide emotions generated from expectations about delivery. Managers in Hyder were generally anxious about failure and the potential destructiveness of conflict. The avoidance of conflict reinforced communication difficulties between the different sub-systems of the company.

Differences of thinking within sub-systems of the organization, and the emotions and politics mobilized around them, were organized into an inability to communicate across organizational boundaries. Such differences exerted increasing influence on the behaviours behind managing and organizing. The resulting sensitivity to criticism and reluctance to debate promoted further attempts to control, protect or justify what was communicated between different organizational groupings, thereby reinforcing difficulties of communication. The dynamic was circular and self-limiting, unlikely to assist in the promotion of learning. Managers espoused a desire for dialogue within the company, to involve staff and take the organization forward. However, in practice they felt threatened and acted defensively. They focused on the development of their own part of the company to the extent that considerable competition, mistrust and envy was generated between sub-systems, undermining communication across organizational boundaries and reinforcing a lack of confidence in the whole. To express this a different way, the company formally became one organization and changed its name to mean 'confidence' at the time when there was very little confidence inside the company about its ability to communicate and develop as one organization. At this time in its development, Hyder was not concerned with organizational learning but with creating an image that contradicted the actual organizational politics.

The case example in Hyder reveals how particular organizational dynamics were being constructed and maintained (see Figure 3.1). Organizational dynamics were constructed from strong emotions and political manoeuvring between members of organizations in different sub-systems, which led to distinctive ways of avoiding communication, which led to their separateness being protected and justified. This circular, organizing process provided further opportunities for reinforcement of the emotions and politics originally involved. Differences of understanding between competing perspectives of Hyder as an organization, and the emotions and politics that sustained them, became organized into an inability to communicate across boundaries, were further limited by protection and control, and by attempts to cover up the importance of these differences. Given these organizational dynamics, an initiative constructed on the basis of empowering staff to make change happen came to

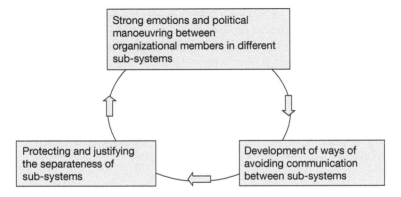

Figure 3.1 Organizational dynamics in Hyder plc (from Vince, 2001).

represent and mirror ways of working that meant change did not happen. To put this simply, the example illustrates how a collective desire for empowerment was transformed into a collective representation of establishment.

The organizational dynamics I have identified in Hyder are helpful in beginning to pinpoint key aspects of a theoretical approach that seeks to map the connections between learning and organizing. The example in Hyder provides a vivid picture of the difference between the idea of learning as a strategy in the minds of managers and the implementation of learning in the context of emotions and power relations that underpin organizing. Strategic learning, therefore, is not only represented in the ability of individuals in an organization to have an impact on the ideas and practices that characterize the organization. Strategic learning is demonstrated through the ability of an organization to transform the self-limiting establishment that it has developed (unconsciously, deliberately, through its history, through habit, by default, through the very action of organizing). Both in theory and in practice, this implies some collective effort to understand the nature and impact of the establishment that organizing creates, as well as its consequences for learning.

Politics, emotion and the ways in which politics and emotion interact, are an integral aspect of understanding strategic learning. This interplay between politics and emotion provides scope for an understanding of learning that represents the complexity of social and political interaction in organizations. Therefore, learning and organizing are not limited by a perspective focusing on individuals' power to achieve personal advantage or preferred outcomes (Pfeffer, 1981). Neither is the relationship between learning and organizing distorted by those writers who are to an extent ambivalent about politics (Argyris and Schön, 1996; Senge, 1990). My discussion of the interplay between politics and emotion in Hyder offers an additional development to the perspective that political activity 'frees people up to voice their opinions [and] generates a creative dialectic of opposites' (Coopey and Burgoyne, 1999: 286). I would say that political activity might also mute people's voices and distort their opinions, generating a defensive practice that reiterates differences and promotes scepticism about the point of dialogue. It is an understanding of the interplay between the politics and emotions involved in organizing that make it possible to identify how such different feelings are being enacted and expressed within an organization, and how they contribute to defining the boundaries of inequality or impotence. Whatever the individual or collective feelings expressed by members of organizations it is likely that there will be both desire and ambivalence concerning learning. The example shows Hyder as an organization that organizes through conscious and unconscious behaviour and action, both for and against learning and change. Any analysis or implementation of strategic learning will therefore need to take account of this dynamic, that learning is simultaneously likely to be both desired and avoided.

Organizing tensions in Hyder

The organizational dynamics highlighted in the example reflect particular tensions at work in processes of managing and organizing. I will summarize what these tensions are, as well as linking them to organizational learning:

The tension between the idea of learning and the implementation of learning

Managers in Hyder believed that learning and change were possible. Hyder had a clearly identified 'learning journey' for individuals, and many initiatives, like CONC, were designed to make change happen. However, it was difficult to sustain and implement the initial enthusiasm generated by the idea of learning. Whatever the individual and collective enthusiasms may have been for learning in the organization, the organizational dynamics identified in the research revealed emotions and politics that restricted learning. An analysis of the interplay between emotion and politics provides one possible starting point from which to make sense of organizational barriers in relation to learning.

The tension between empowerment and establishment

Organizing in Hyder was undertaken in the context of a characteristic dynamic, the confusing interplay between involvement and control, between attempting to change and trying to remain the same. The espoused desire for collegiality sat alongside politics driven by fear of failure and a perceived need for control. Cynicism about learning and change occurred when 'empowered' individuals were confronted with organizational power relations that blocked learning and change. The discovery of the limitations of involvement after the event reinforced managers' cynicism and confusion. Strategic learning involves attempts at such discovery both before and during the event, through more developed and organizationally situated processes of reflection and action.

The tension between individual learning and organizational learning

The Hyder experience of learning was built on the company's commitment to individual development and the collective difference that this might make in practice. Whatever the managers involved in the CONC initiative learned as individuals their learning actually had little impact on established organizational power relations or on organizing processes. However, the analysis of the emotions and power relations involved in learning and change provided scope to interpret why Hyder's strategic emphasis was on the individual 'learning journey'. An emphasis on the learning of individuals within the organization placed the responsibility for learning with individuals. In this sense, learning was linked to individual and collective experience but not explicitly to key organizing processes like reflection and leadership.

The tension between creating a 'new' organization and recreating the 'old' one

It was easier for many of the individual managers and staff involved in the company when Hyder was a public utility serving South Wales, rather than a global enterprise. There was considerable resistance in parts of the company towards the type of learning and change that would give rise to a shared, commercial future. As the CONC initiative showed, an initiative designed explicitly for creating something new can represent the desire to recapture the past as well as a desire to design the future. In practice, Hyder was an organization containing a complex mixture of emotions and politics that combined in ways that prompted members of organizations to both embrace and to avoid learning.

The CONC initiative was explicitly set up as a process for building learning and change. An analysis of the initiative showed that it was also created to represent a political position in the organization; it was an emotional response to others' attempts to change the company; and it was an attempt to recreate the organization as it used to be. The study in Hyder suggested that an understanding of the emotions and power relations that underpin initiatives designed to promote learning is a necessary aspect of any attempt to organize learning. The organizational tensions that I have identified in the example can be summarized in terms of their theoretical implications for organizational learning. Organizational learning involves:

- A collective inquiry aimed at understanding the nature and impact of the establishment that organizing creates and its consequences for learning. Critical reflection on what has become established can provide a way out of self-limiting organizational dynamics.
- An inquiry that identifies organizational politics or power relations and the potential impact that these might have on initiatives designed to promote or to avoid learning. Such inquiry would be the starting point of learning initiatives.
- A focus on the organizational dynamics that underpin and impact on both learning and organizing. Such a focus implies attempts to understand and develop more than an individualized notion of learning.
- An analysis of the interplay between emotions and politics, and how this links to the paradoxical desire within organizations both to promote learning and to avoid learning. This recognizes emotion as politics, adding something more to the analysis than the idea that emotion is the public expression of individual feelings.

Conclusion

Learning implies some discomfort with the state we are currently in – some desire to change. Organizational learning can be understood in terms of actions that emerge from a desire to transform the establishment that has been constructed through the very processes of organizing. This involves the transformation of politics and emotions that characterize the organization as an establishment and that are enacted and reinforced through organizational roles. It involves the identification of conscious dynamics as well as speculation on unconscious dynamics that guide the internalization of the organization in the minds of its members. In practice, making politics, emotions and organizational dynamics visible in order to create new mental and structural models for organizing is not an easy task, either for individuals to comprehend or for organizations to achieve. Learning is not a comfortable state precisely because to learn is to challenge the current State. However, an emphasis on organizational learning (rather than individuals' learning in an organization) provides an opportunity to frame an organization not only as a system of 'complex patterns and structures' (Senge, 1990) but also as an establishment of emotional and political processes that restrict the relationship between learning and organizing. This insight does not necessarily help managers and other practitioners to act, but it does clarify the boundaries of potential action, and through such clarification raises the possibility of *strategic* learning.

In the next two chapters I explore and develop specific examples of emotional and political processes that restrict the relationship between learning and organizing. In Chapter 4, I give three short illustrations from Hyder in order to develop my thinking about the relationship between emotion and organization. I then discuss emotions that were generated from attempts to implement organizational learning in Fairness Borough Council (a pseudonym), in order to demonstrate how emotions underpin political processes of organizing. In Chapter 5, I return to Hyder and discuss the emotions and rationalizations generated during the takeover of the company. Not surprisingly, the takeover of Hyder produced strong emotions, providing an opportunity to examine managers' approaches to the management and organization of emotion. Both of these chapters build on what I have started here, further developing ideas about the ways in which emotion and politics are connected in organizations, as well as how this connection informs strategic learning.

4 Emotion and strategic learning

Hyder corporate HRD managers and staff were justifiably proud of their approach to learning in the organization. They had devised a comprehensive performance appraisal process for the entire staff, supported by programmes of training, both formal and informal, delivered by both internal and external providers. In fact, as a result of their experience within training events, several of the staff and junior managers acted in more authoritative and autonomous ways, much to the annoyance of some of their own line managers who, while being supportive of their individual learning, resented having their views or decisions directly questioned or challenged. For some of the senior managers, further reflection on decisions took up valuable time. Some of the front-line workers and junior managers felt as though they were either 'banging their heads against a wall', or worse, jeopardizing their career progression, and that for all the good ideas and intentions behind the company's learning strategy, nothing was really going to change. Managers' experience of individual learning within the company was constructive, but there was much cynicism generally about the company's claim to be a learning organization.

In order to progress beyond the point that they had reached, Hyder would have needed explicitly to acknowledge (at least) one aspect of the emotional life of the organization: how threatened managers can feel when challenged, especially by subordinates, and their consequent defensive and attacking responses to this. In terms of strategic learning, the key to its development in Hyder was to find ways of legitimizing challenge as an integral aspect of management practice within the company. This does not arise as a result of training individuals in the skills of challenge, but from prolonged and continuous daily support for a critical approach to how management is experienced and expressed within the organization. To support strategic learning, Hyder would have needed to design and implement ways of legitimising learning processes that question the assumptions informing existing power relations and practices, in addition to their provision for individuals.

In Hyder, the emphasis on individuals learning, while it genuinely encouraged individuals to learn, was limited by fears about learning and change. The discourse behind individual learning was informed by managers' fears concerning the consequences of action, reluctance to reflect on weaknesses, disinclination to speak out, and ambivalence about differences between sub-systems in the company. Enthusiasm for individual learning within the organization was not matched by an open and legitimized organizational context within which individuals were meant to apply their learning.

There is an unwritten rule in many organizations that it is inappropriate to bring emotions to work. This idea, that emotion is 'not a part of the job' and can 'get in the way' of effectiveness is pervasive. Also, in one sense it is true, our emotional responses – particularly fears and anxieties – can and do get in the way, but they can also provide the basis for learning, both individually and collectively. Several authors have noted that learning and change are unlikely to occur without anxiety (Kofman and Senge, 1993; Schein, 1993) and the impact of anxiety on management learning has been illustrated by Vince and Martin (1993) who show how it both promotes and discourages learning (see Figure 4.1). For the individual, anxiety may be provoked by having to say something difficult or challenging, by the effects of unwanted decisions, by the pressures of an unfamiliar task. For groups in organizations, anxiety may be provoked by external deadlines or demands, shifts of decision-making that occur in other parts of the organization, or through interactions across inter-group boundaries. In all of these examples the individual or the group is faced with a 'strategic moment', where the anxiety can either be held and worked through, towards some form of insight, or it can be ignored and avoided, creating a 'willing ignorance'.

Figure 4.1 shows the two directions that it is possible to travel from the starting point of anxiety. In the top cycle, the one that promotes learning, the uncertainty created by anxiety can be held long enough for risks to be taken.

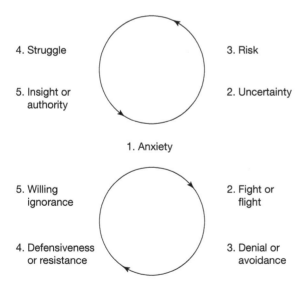

Figure 4.1 Anxiety and learning (from Vince and Martin, 1993).

Risk, and the struggles that it makes possible, often lead towards new knowledge or insight. In the bottom cycle, the one that discourages learning, uncertainty cannot be held and anxiety promotes the denial or avoidance of emotions that seem too difficult to deal with. In this cycle, the resistance emerging from anxiety leads towards a willing ignorance of the potential for learning and change. For individuals and groups, in that moment driven by anxiety, it is possible to move in either direction, towards learning or away from it. Anxiety therefore can be seen to have a strategic dimension, to be an emotion that may equally promote or discourage learning and change. Emotions, such as anxiety, that underscore the experience of organizing create both the possibilities for making the most of these strategic moments and the capacity for ignoring them. Individuals and groups both face strategic moments created from emotional responses to experience. This emotional aspect of organizing is frequently difficult for individuals and groups to acknowledge and work with.

The first part of my argument in this chapter, therefore, is that individuals and groups continually manage and organize themselves both on the basis of their emotional responses to organizational issues and on the basis of avoiding emotion, and that both of these have strategic implications. The second part of my argument is that organizing creates and sustains this dynamic. For example: Stephen was one of the most successful managers in Hyder in terms of developing business income, and his success created expectations of further success, especially at a time when other parts of the business were being grown and supported by the profits his part of the business generated. These expectations started to be reflected in Stephen's behaviour. He seemed never to have enough time to do his job. He rushed from one issue, one meeting, and one decision to the next. His communication with his staff was authoritative, yet it increasingly reflected this pressure. The staff around him 'caught' his way of working, and they too started to feel pressured in their roles. This pressure resulted in the loss of an important contract. Stephen was criticized as a result of this incident, and at a subsequent assessment centre appraisal it was suggested that 'his effectiveness in any role remains contingent upon his ability to address his personal development needs, specifically those relating to the management of stress'. All this made Stephen even more determined to push towards winning new contracts, as well as maintaining and developing his status in the company.

There are several possible interpretations emerging from this example. At first sight, it could refer to the common pressures on individual senior managers. Stephen's work became stressful and his performance suffered. All Stephen needed to do was 'address his personal development needs', to learn how to cope. My interpretation of the example, however, is that the problem belonged as much (if not more) to *established* ways of being and working within the organization as to Stephen, and that, through his reactions and behaviour he was expressing organizational as well as individual anxieties. Feelings of urgency concerning the generation of increased profit were certainly an issue for Stephen, but they are also a reflection of leadership anxieties and issues within the organization as a whole.

Such dynamics are an integral aspect of everyday organizational life. Emotional experience is not only something that occurs within an organization, it is also a central part of what creates and sustains that system within its current organizational forms. In this sense it is a crucial component in the possibilities and limitations that organizations may create towards learning. Hyder had few mechanisms (other than financial ones) for reflection on the current state of the organization. In such situations, the individual managers easily became the focus for systemic issues, and their behaviour represented and reflected broader problems. Despite many days of discussion on statements of values, or on the corporate identity that they wanted to create, Hyder managers had few ways of understanding the organizational dynamics that they had already collectively created. In the above example, company-wide strains and tensions about profitability and competitive advantage were mirrored in the behaviour of an individual and his team. They had done well in the company and were seen as one linchpin of profitability. Their failure in relation to an important contract reflected a more general fear of failure concerning the continued growth of the organization.

In my first example, the focus on individual learning in Hyder had unintentionally created limitations for the development of strategic learning. In my second example, the lack of organizational processes for reflection (which might involve recognizing the existence of powerful emotions where, for example, bidding for contracts is concerned) meant that key individuals represented and acted out wider organizational issues and problems. In both examples, yet in different ways, organizational politics were mobilized against strategic learning. In the CONC example in Chapter 3, two separate change processes designed explicitly for the promotion of learning, came to reflect organizational conflict that blocked learning.

Managers in Hyder Utilities and within Group Development were not openly hostile to each other's development initiatives, but acted in ways that were critical or ambivalent towards them. They did not completely avoid working together, but they were slow to comment, or they claimed lack of knowledge about what was being done in the other sub-system. Both sides thought that their initiative was of benefit to the company as a whole, and both sides found ways of criticizing either the other initiative or the people responsible for it. Such politics seemed to reflect a desire to keep the initiatives separate from each other so that conflicts did not arise. They feared the consequences of not being able to control development within their part of the organization. Faced with the possibility of having to work together to resolve differences, they found ways to ensure that this did not happen. Inevitably, conflicts did arise, not directly, and they were not faced 'head-on' so that they could be dealt with quickly, as an integral part of the daily business. Rather, they lingered (for example) in the ways in which decisions were made, in terms of who was involved and who was not, in relation to what was and was not spoken out-loud, and in informal gatherings rather than formal meetings. These political processes of avoidance had strong emotions connected to them, especially where they had become habitual or reflected long-term interpersonal histories. They also helped to create and reinforce characteristic ways of organizing, and consequently helped to shape the behaviour that was and was not seen as legitimate within the organization.

Uncomfortable knowledge

The three examples I have identified from Hyder show how 'uncomfortable knowledge' was produced and reinforced. They demonstrate some of the ways in which emotions were constructed as uncomfortable, as well as the consequent effects of this on learning – both individual and organizational. They illustrate various points.

First, limits to the impact of (and possibilities for) organizational learning were created through HRD strategy with an orientation towards individual managers' development. Managers' enthusiasm for generating new insights and their involvement in strategic learning was dampened when their hopes encountered a disappointing reality. Individuals who were enthused by the possibility of learning became disappointed with the experience of acting on and trying to implement their learning within the context of existing power relations. In such a context it is easy for managers to behave either cynically or mechanistically – indeed this type of behaviour was likely to be reinforced. Second, an organization-wide issue was seen only in terms of its impact on a particular individual (and their team), within only a part of the whole organization. The individual manager felt the weight of expectations and frustrations that were company-wide, but were not overtly acknowledged in this way. Criticism of individuals or sub-systems is a likely consequence of situations where mechanisms for reflecting on assumptions do not exist (because espoused 'values' tend to be 'written in stone', they inform behaviour but are not changed by it). An inability to reflect on the assumptions underlying everyday work processes reinforced feelings that strategic leadership was lacking and that decisions were made only in relation to crisis. Third, in the Create Our New Company initiative, two different parts of the organization worked independently to keep the emotional charge between them out of their interactions and communication. They did this ostensibly in the service of avoiding conflict, but they instead created more complex and difficult relations out of their competition and rivalry. They established competition and rivalry as a 'normal' aspect of their communication and interaction. In Hyder, such underlying, organizing dynamics, built from everyday emotions and relations, meant that strategies to progress learning were informed as much by the fears and anxieties of members of the organization as they were by their knowledge and skills.

Knowledge about appropriate and inappropriate emotional responses (for example, that conflicts should be avoided rather than directly addressed) quickly becomes an integral part of standard approaches and established ways of working. I now want to consider three ideas about how established ways of working that have been developed through fears and anxieties might be transformed.

First, attempts at understanding and developing individual learning within an organization will benefit from being allied to a more organizational analysis and understanding. Such understanding can be based upon increased attempts to engage with the impact of emotions (for example, fear and defensiveness) as well as the ways in which politics and structures arise that reflect, reinforce and institutionalize such emotions. Second, defensive reactions, both conscious and unconscious, serve the purpose of attempting to make the uncomfortable comfortable (for example, it is often in other parts of an organization where incompetence exists, not here). Strategic learning is more likely to be supported where individual or group projections, denials and avoidance strategies, the core of relations between self and other, are utilized as knowledge about the organization (for example, why has a part of the organization come to particularly represent 'incompetence' and what can be learned from this about the organization as a whole?). Finally, members of organizations can benefit where the prevalent idea of communication as a rational process is balanced with awareness of emotions that may drive it, especially emotions that reflect differences between groups in organizations. It is the extent to which an organization can create either processes or habits that 'contain' the complexities of emotion and relations that will make the difference to their ability to both acknowledge and utilize them in relation to learning and change.

My reflections on the organization of learning in Hyder have led me to think that a critical approach to HRD inevitably involves engagement with the impact of emotion on how strategic learning is made possible or is blocked in organizations. In order to develop this I will provide a further example, which demonstrates the organizational impact of emotions as well as the impact they have on strategic learning.

The politics of caution and blame

The following example comes from a study within a UK local authority. I refer to this local authority as Fairness Borough Council (BC). The background to the research is the continuing organizational imperative for learning and change within the UK public sector, both centrally and locally. Local authorities have been faced with nationally driven attempts to promote change with initiatives such as 'Best Value', and locally, the expectations of communities are increasing while the resources available to fulfil these expectations are remaining static or being reduced. For local authorities, such external and internal drivers of change have generated considerable pressures. Financial constraints and the need to address local issues have meant restructuring in an attempt to face present and future challenges. In Fairness BC, learning was seen as synonymous with change. Statements such as 'learning from our mistakes', 'learning from our customers', 'learning to change' and 'becoming a learning organization' were often quoted by senior managers.

The research involved inquiry into managerial perspectives on learning in the Council. It was concerned with identifying some of the emotions and politics generated through attempts to implement both individual and organizational learning. The study identified organizational issues and processes that characterized the Council's approach to strategic learning, in terms of how this was limited and was promoted. Understanding how learning was perceived and enacted within the organization provided clues both to the way learning was being undermined and to how the possibilities for learning could have been extended. The interviewees were managers who were all involved either in leading and/or developing strategic learning or having to lead and to manage its implementation directly within services. In addition, the emphasis on emotion and on 'political relatedness' (Sievers, 2001) provided material from which it would be possible to speculate on the organizational dynamics involved in or set in motion through the implementation of strategic ideas.

Fairness Borough Council is an organization of approximately 5,000 staff, organized within five Directorates and the central Chief Executive's Office. The total numbers of senior managers at each of the levels interviewed for this study were: the Chief Executive (1 of 1), Directors of Departments (2 of 5), Heads of Service (2 of 15), Operational Managers (4 of 32). At the time of this research, the organization had emerged from a period characterized by poor political and managerial leadership. A new Chief Executive had been in post for six months. The research was undertaken within a cross-section of the management structure (Operational Managers to Chief Executive) and was particularly located within the Directorate for Economic Development. Six of the nine managers interviewed were from this Directorate. The focus of the research was managerial perspectives on learning and their impact on organizing.

The sequence and process of data collection and interpretation in this study was as follows. The research interviews were conducted with nine managers. There were two rounds of interviews with each of the managers. The first interviews used a loosely structured set of questions, which were:

- Ideally, how do you see learning taking place in an organization?
- In your experience how is learning actually taking place in the Council? Can you give any examples?
- What are the barriers to learning in the Council? Can you give some examples?
- In the current environment of change what emotions are present? (Are these emotions different in your idealized learning environment?)
- How do you think the Council is managing learning and change?
- How has the recent restructuring had an impact on learning in the Council?
- How do you feel about the challenges that lie ahead?

The audiotapes were transcribed and the transcripts were seen by each of the interviewees. Various themes were interpreted from the data and turned into propositions (see Table 4.1). The second round of interviews was based around discussions of the propositions developed from stage one. Again, the audiotapes were transcribed, leading to a review of the differences in the sample (see Table

4.2). The original propositions were revised on the basis of these interviews (see Table 4.3). All of these data were interpreted in terms of managerial perspectives on learning and their impact on organizing (Figure 4.2).

Interpretations of the first set of interviews involved the identification of statements that related particularly to managerial perspectives on learning and organizing. These were then grouped under seven categories: learning (formal and informal), emotions, communication, reflection, blame culture, barriers to learning, and challenges (Best Value). The contents of each category were reviewed to check on and to further develop an understanding of what managers had said. A proposition was formulated for each category to take back to the participants for further discussion and development, and as the basis of the second stage of interviews. The initial propositions developed from stage one of the research are outlined in Table 4.1.

Table 4.1 List of propositions developed from first-stage interviews

Learning	In Fairness Borough Council learning is predominantly a formal process. This limits the development of individual and organizational learning.
Emotions	The characteristic emotions underlying the work of managers in Fairness Borough Council are fear, anxiety and cynicism.
Communication	Poor communication is producing an incoherent interpretation of the vision espoused by senior management.
Reflection	The limited opportunity to reflect individually and collectively at all levels is a barrier to the successful implementation of the desired changes.
Blame culture	The blame culture in Fairness Borough Council limits learning.
Barriers to learning	The four key barriers to learning are seen as lack of resources, lack of opportunities, fear and blame.
Challenges	Best Value is seen as the key challenge for the future. This will lead to a narrow development of organizational capability.

By reviewing the propositions collectively, it was possible to create a working definition to outline perceptions of organizational learning in Fairness Borough Council. This was:

Organizational learning is perceived as the aggregation of formal and informal learning undertaken by individuals. Learning is affected by emotion, reflection and communication. Collectively these processes interact to create a culture which both encourages and limits organizational learning.

To further explore and refine this working definition, participants were interviewed a second time and invited to comment on each of the propositions. The responses were again recorded and categorized. Table 4.2 provides general information about agreement and disagreement with the propositions. The opinions of each of the interviewees are included. "A" stands for agreement, "D" for disagreement with the proposition, and "U" stands for undecided. Further discussion of each proposition follows.

Learning

All but one of the managers interviewed believed that a formal approach was necessary to facilitate a basic level of learning across the Council. The general view was that learning is the responsibility of the individual and should be marshalled through personal development plans instigated by the Council. One senior manager thought that learning was perceived as a formal process but in fact was predominantly an informal process. In an environment of reduced resources, formal learning through the use of structured training and development programmes may not be possible, thus leaving individuals with the view that learning has little impact on their daily work. A perspective on how informal learning could be harnessed by the Council was not offered and therefore leaves unanswered the important question of what is the relationship between informal learning and formal organizational processes. The proposition was revised to include these views: in Fairness Borough Council learning is predominantly perceived as a formal process. This limits the development of individual and organizational learning.

Emotions

Seven of the managers interviewed disagreed with the proposition, two agreed. After further discussion, some of those who disagreed acknowledged the presence of such emotions (fear, anxiety, cynicism) in the workplace but questioned, externalized or denied their impact. Anxiety and cynicism were accepted as an aspect of managers' experience, but the idea of fear as an underlying emotion was disputed. One manager said that if fear existed, it was 'elsewhere' and not in the respondent's immediate environment. One manager distanced himself from the issue by placing it in the past. The level of defensiveness about emotions increased with hierarchy. Only one operational manager saw these emotions as an organizational issue. These were accepted as underlying the work of managers and legitimate symptoms of the recent corporate restructuring process. Based on the responses the proposition was modified to: the characteristic emotions underlying the work of managers in Fairness Borough Council are anxiety and cynicism.

Table 4.2 Agreement or disagreement with stage-one propositions

	Learning			Emotions			Communication			Reflection			Blame culture			Barriers			Best Value		
	A	D	U	A	D	U	A	D	U	A	D	U	A	D	U	A	D	U	A	D	U
Chief Executive	X			X				X		X			X				X				X
Director A		X		X				X		X			X			X					X
Director B	X			X			X			X				X		X			X		
Head of Service A	X			X			X			X			X				X			X	
Head of Service B	X			X			X			X			X				X			X	
Operational Manager A	X				X		X			X			X				X				X
Operational Manager B			X				X			X			X			X				X	
Operational Manager C	X				X		X			X				X			X				X
Operational Manager D	X			X					X	X			X			X					X

Communication

At the most senior management level (the Chief Executive and one of the directors), poor communication was not acknowledged as an organizational problem but as an issue for individuals to resolve. The corporate vision and its delivery were considered adequate and therefore not open to question. The emphasis was placed on the unwillingness of individuals to find out more about corporate issues. A view was expressed that an organizational culture had developed whereby some junior managers expected to be 'spoonfed' information. Operational managers believed that individuals were being 'communicated to' in an instructive and 'top-down' manner yet at the same time they were being asked to take equal responsibility, but were not being offered equal participation in the process. One operational manager thought that problems with communication were partly being reinforced by incoherence within the strategic management and decision-making processes. Not all strategic decisions had been closely aligned with the espoused corporate vision and this may have led to confusion. The original proposition was not amended.

Reflection

The importance of reflection was clearly acknowledged by managers at all levels. Most responses focused on reflection as a personal process, yet due to the pressures of work, individual reflection was seldom undertaken. One manager saw reflection as needing to be collective. His view was that it is reflection within groups that can 'really make things happen'. Another manager, whilst acknowledging the value of reflection, questioned its purpose. There seemed little point in reflecting if the insights that emerge meet organizational resistance because they challenge the objectives that have already been set. The original proposition was not amended.

Blame culture

This proposition produced some of the most extensive and emotive responses, which varied from acceptance to complete rejection. There was a belief that if a blame culture existed it was 'elsewhere' in other parts of the organization but 'not here'. Several managers found it difficult to accept the existence of blame, whilst others reluctantly accepted its existence but questioned its intensity. In an attempt to deal with this issue, blame was seen as having been in the past and that the new (i.e. the current) organization was somehow different. One manager related an explicit and recent example of how the blame culture operated. Blame was attributed to individuals when mistakes were made, even if it was the first time a particular action had been undertaken. Focusing blame on individuals 'causes hurt, jeopardizes career prospects and limits their learning'. However, this was not seen as limiting organizational learning because other individuals might learn at someone else's expense. This manager was convinced that a blame culture would continue to operate in the future. The original proposition was not amended.

Barriers to learning

Four managers (the two directors and two operational managers) supported the proposition that a lack of resources and opportunities limited organizational learning. The remainder were unsure. The tradition of 'doing things the way they have always been done' and the inability to appreciate the importance of learning were also cited as significant barriers. Fear and blame were not acknowledged as contributory factors. The proposition was amended to reflect these views: the key barriers to learning are seen as lacks: lack of resources, opportunities, appreciating the importance of learning and the will to change.

Best Value

There was an even distribution of opinion about 'Best Value'. One manager thought that Best Value was likely to evolve into a 'tick box' culture and that this would limit the development of organizational capability. Another believed that Best Value would provide the organization with a much broader outlook. One of the directors was concerned that Best Value was producing a negative sentiment amongst some staff. The existing proposition was not amended.

The revised propositions are outlined in Table 4.3.

Table 4.3 List of propositions with amendments after the second-stage interviews

Learning	In Fairness Borough Council learning is predominantly perceived as a formal process. This limits the development of individual and organizational learning.
Emotions	The characteristic emotions underlying the work of managers in Fairness Borough Council are anxiety and cynicism.
Communication	Poor communication is producing an incoherent interpretation of the vision espoused by senior management.
Reflection	The limited opportunity to reflect individually and collectively at all levels is a barrier to the successful implementation of the desired changes.
Blame culture	The blame culture in Fairness Borough Council limits learning.
Barriers to learning	The key barriers to learning are seen as lack of resources, opportunities, appreciating the importance of learning and the will to change.
Challenges	Best Value is seen as the key challenge for the future. This will lead to a narrow development of organizational capability.

The general view of learning in Fairness BC was the same as in Hyder: that it was the responsibility of the individual and should be marshalled through personal development plans instigated by the Council. There were complementary and conflicting views of individuals' responsibilities in terms of strategic learning. Some senior managers believed that subordinates were often unwilling to find out more about corporate issues. In their opinion, junior managers expected to be 'spoonfed' information. Junior managers, however, believed that they were often being 'communicated to' in an instructive (patronizing) and 'top-down' manner, yet at the same time they were being asked to take equal responsibility, but were not being offered equal participation in the process.

Political processes linked to learning

The context of strategic learning in Fairness BC could be understood (using the managers' own words) as follows:

- 'We are an organization terrified of getting it wrong' (emotion)
- 'I know who is going to get the blame!' (blame)
- 'I would describe it as reflection in a hurry' (reflection)
- 'People . . . want to be spoonfed' (communication)

The study highlighted how emotion, blame, reflection and communication were interrelated, in the sense that they follow in sequence, one after the other. I can summarize this as follows. Expectations from above and a focus on individual responsibility meant that individuals were afraid of getting things wrong. Fear of getting things wrong made individuals behave with caution and in the interests of self-protection. When things went wrong, the caution manifested itself as blame. Blame undermined the ability of managers to reflect (the individual is too anxious and therefore too 'busy', and the collective is

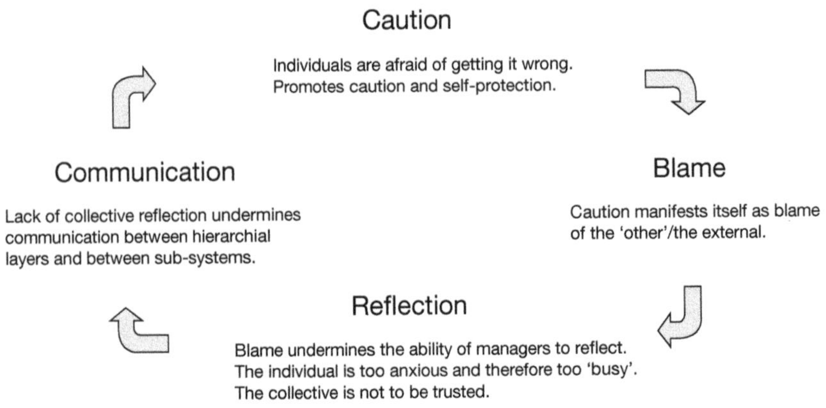

Caution

Individuals are afraid of getting it wrong.
Promotes caution and self-protection.

Communication

Lack of collective reflection undermines
communication between hierarchial
layers and between sub-systems.

Blame

Caution manifests itself as blame
of the 'other'/the external.

Reflection

Blame undermines the ability of managers to reflect.
The individual is too anxious and therefore too 'busy'.
The collective is not to be trusted.

Figure 4.2 The impact of caution and blame on organizational learning.

not to be trusted, because decisions are an individual responsibility). Lack of collective reflection undermined the practice of communication between hierarchical layers and across the boundaries of organizational sub-systems. In this sense, therefore, the study revealed not just the characteristics of the Council's approach to strategic learning, but also the *political process* that informed and constructed it (see Figure 4.2).

I can provide some more detail on the situated context of strategic learning in Fairness BC by using some of the quotations from the interviews.

'We are an organization terrified of getting it wrong'

The focus on individual responsibility and accountability for managing, organizing and learning contributed to the creation of a defensive and therefore cautious culture in the organization. The study showed two ways of looking at this. First, the impulse managers have a impulse to withdraw and defend:

> When things go wrong, basically people withdraw backwards. It is the Bart Simpson philosophy, it wasn't me, nobody saw me do it, you can't prove a thing.

Second, everything has to be checked and controlled to an excessive degree:

> I suppose one of the things you learn, particularly around a Performance Indicator, you check it twice, you check it three times, you check it four times and you get four other people to do it as well just to check what you've done it right!

The perception of the manager who thought that 'we are an organization terrified of getting things wrong' was an apt reflection of the organizational dynamics. In part this reflected a recent period in the history of the organization. The Council had developed a reputation for poor management and inefficient use of resources, promoting public outcry, the removal of the Chief Executive, and a number of significant changes in personnel. The political control of the Council also changed as a result of public dissatisfaction. The new management were concerned to put the past behind them and sensitive about being labelled by the problems of the past. Both politicians and senior officers were eager to maintain a positive image of a council that was now different, that had learned from the past, but was now leaving it behind. Getting things wrong was not really an option. If you are terrified of (or even cautious of) getting things wrong then one solution is to look around for others to blame.

'I know who is going to get the blame!'

There was a relationship in the organization between different views of management that contributed to the building of organizational defences. On one hand there were the views of the Chief Executive, that it is important for individuals to be accountable:

> I think there is an element of people not taking responsibility for what they do, being held accountable for their actions. I think that is important in any organization, particularly at a senior level. The staff below must see that, that individuals whether it is me, a director, a head of service or an operational manager take responsibility for their actions.

On the other hand, more junior managers felt genuinely apprehensive:

> I think the organization suffers a bit from a blame culture and many people are reluctant to advance themselves further than their job description might require, for fear of making mistakes.

One difficulty was that there were no organizational processes or mechanisms for meeting somewhere near the middle between these two views. This was further reinforced by managerial rhetoric based on a sense of how things should be in the organization:

> Part of the learning process is that people must be allowed to progress slightly beyond their current capabilities to gain experience by extending themselves and this is the best mechanism for learning there is. This has to be tied in with the acceptance by the organization that any error or failure from this process does not result in blame being directed at the individual. The organization needs to change to encourage people to extend themselves. The idea of empowerment and allowing individuals to progress to their natural level of ability must recognize that mistakes will happen.

Managers were rarely insensitive to the differences between the rhetoric and the reality, even when it was difficult to admit that there was a gap:

> The culture in the Council results in most people working in an environment where they are not praised for achievement and where there is a tendency to take low risk and decisions in order to avoid blame.

'I would describe it as reflection in a hurry'

Processes for collective reflection can be utilized to break through the impact of caution and blame. However, managers in Fairness BC recognized that reflection was rarely undertaken and seldom encouraged as a group activity. Some of the reasons are explained in the following extracts:

> There is limited opportunity to reflect; occasionally it is non-existent. At best I would describe it as reflection in a hurry. You grab a few minutes here and there to reflect on what you do but not necessarily as you are doing it.

Our capacity to learn from what goes well and what doesn't go well is limited because we don't take the time to do it properly. It is a real effort when you've finished one task to call people together to ask, what can we do better next time? When we do this, it is very powerful. I don't think it is happening often enough.

Managers in Fairness BC were sometimes caught in a trap of their own making. The cautious need to exert tight controls (on what is said, done, decided, implemented) meant that the results of reflection could be problematic as well as useful. On one hand 'it may be time badly spent because it's diverting you from what you have been told to do', on the other 'we don't take time to do it properly'. The idea of reflection was popular, but the impetus to do it was avoided. This was particularly true of collective reflection, which might generate ways of bringing established strategies, values and/or power relations into question.

'People . . . want to be spoonfed'

When established strategies are challenged or criticized one managerial response can be to reassert existing power relations. This can involve making statements guided by a more general notion of blame:

> A lot of people, and I don't really regret saying this, want to be spoonfed. It is a bit of a culture of this organization.

> The fact that there is a Big Picture and the fact that there are corporate documents that point out the main themes and development as far as the Council is concerned . . . people have presumably read these? I think these statements are quite clear and they are there to be read as a fair and coherent vision, as far as the Council is concerned. I go back to the individual in the end. If you want to be aware of corporate issues it is down to the individual.

Such statements tend to annoy and to provoke a similar or mirror response:

> I've been fed the Big Picture, I've been told about Best Value and the Community Plan and so on . . . I don't feel I have signed up to something which is very cogent.

> I think if you asked Council employees, they wouldn't know exactly where we are going, who is leading us, they wouldn't know the thinking of the Management Team.

Communication between different hierarchical levels of an organization, or across sub-system boundaries, becomes even more difficult when such generalizations get established. Senior managers can feel that junior managerial staff members need to be spoonfed information (that this is how senior managers can best communicate what they want). Junior staff members feel that senior managers cannot or will not communicate with them directly (which may actually be a desire on their part). However, organizational activity depends on effective communication, and implicit in good communication is the idea of a shared responsibility, that the other person can make sense of what is being said (Isaacs, 1999).

General reflections

Fairness Borough Council is not an unusual organization in the sense that the espoused idea of learning is rather different from its manifestation in practice. Nor is it exceptional in appearing to have a grasp on learning while perpetuating emotional and political processes that limit learning. In this organization these limitations were built from the workings of caution and blame, they were enacted in an organizational ambivalence about reflection, and reinforced through resulting difficulties of communication between different hierarchical layers of the organization. Many organizations, both public and private, face the type of issues and organizing processes that were identified in Fairness BC. Many organizations have a high motivation to engage with learning; the rhetoric surrounding learning is coherent; however, implementation is undermined by collective anxieties as well as an inability to question established power relations and political processes of organizing. This provides a challenge for organizations in the development of strategic learning that implies attention to collective learning, and that is sustainable in the context of everyday organizational emotions and politics.

The question then follows, how might Fairness Borough Council or organizations with similar organizing issues and characteristics go about changing the self-limiting processes that have been created? As the study suggested, the prevalent organizational discourse on reflection is insufficient for the task, and reinforces difficulties of communication rather than promoting opportunities for more collective thinking. There is a need therefore to test and develop different forms of individual and collective reflection in order to break through the structures of organizing that have been created from caution and blame (as well as other emotions that underpin attempts to learn). Organizational members will have to understand reflection as something more than the creation of the 'reflective practitioner', suggesting the need for the development of broader insights that go beyond the individual capacity or responsibility to reflect, and that can underpin the further development of an organizational perspective on strategic learning.

A different understanding and experience of reflection – one that is not based on the individual trying to find time to look back – also implies a different approach to leadership. The impact of processes for collective reflection will be to shift the responsibility for making decisions away from individual managers, giving them a broader responsibility to enable group decision-making. A new understanding of the (collective) practice of leadership can be related to the need to improve communication within organizations as a whole (acknowledged as crucial by many of the managers involved). These issues – reflection, leadership, practice and change – are further developed in the final three chapters of this book, as illustrations of the practical implications of rethinking strategic learning and a critical approach to HRD.

I have discussed examples from Hyder plc that illustrate how emotions and politics informed and reinforced organizational dynamics. I have shown how emotions had an impact on political processes of organizing in Fairness Borough Council, which limited the potential for strategic learning. In Chapter 5, I continue to explore emotion and politics, examining how a specific event, the takeover of Hyder, and the rationalizations that accompanied it, assisted members of organizations in creating responses to the emotions that were mobilized by the takeover.

5   Being taken over

Every organization . . . is an emotional place. It is an emotional place because it is a human invention, serving human purposes and dependent on human beings to function. And human beings are emotional animals: subject to anger, fear, surprise, disgust, happiness or joy, ease and unease.

(Armstrong, 2000: 1)

In two previous chapters I have discussed how emotions and politics combine to create organizational dynamics that limit or define emotional responses and perpetuate existing political relations. Also, emotions can be seen to underpin and influence strategic initiatives in organizations in ways that create distinctive political dynamics and organizing processes. I have been trying to bring to the surface various questions and answers about *how* organizations are emotional places – for example, how strategies are subverted by unacknowledged emotions, how individuals internalize and enact organizational dynamics, how links between individuals' behaviour and organizational structures are created and recreated and how initiatives designed for change come to represent or replicate existing anxieties or stuck relations. The journey into a better understanding of emotion in organizations is not about understanding emotions so much 'as their *meaning*, what they have to say about the organization as a system in context' (Armstrong, 2000: 3; emphasis in original).

Emotions are linked to knowing and learning, knowing and learning are linked to politics. Emotions are therefore essential to control processes and need to be understood in terms of the social and political structures of which they are a part (Fineman and Sturdy, 1999). Organizational power structures evolve in ways that can undermine the legitimacy of emotions that are not attached to an organization's vision. They can therefore prompt the denial or reorganization of individual experience (Turnbull, 2002). In this chapter I discuss managers' experience of the takeover of Hyder in order to provide more information on the various ways in which emotion and politics impact on individuals and organization. My inquiry explicitly focused on managers' experience of an emotive issue (takeover) in order to reveal how emotions and associated rationalizations of emotions interacted to shape the experience and practice of managerial roles and relations. The emotions and experiences mobilized during the takeover of Hyder provided further insights about emotions in organizations and their connection to organizational politics. My research on the takeover adds to the knowledge I have already highlighted about how organizations are emotional places. In this chapter, I show how managers use their role to reduce or rationalize emotion, and at the same time to create an emotional state from which a managerial role can continue to be enacted under emotionally charged circumstances. Emotions are likely to be balanced by rationalizations aimed at making difficult emotions manageable. I ask, therefore, how emotions are transformed by rationalizations and vice versa. There are also strategic implications that arise, because emotions invariably turn coherent plans and strategies into *contested relations*. How managers respond to contested relations is an important consideration for strategic learning.

Before I describe the research on the takeover of Hyder, I want to explain briefly my thinking about emotion and rationalization, and the link to broader dynamics and relations. Perhaps the most direct way to start is to repeat the words of Stephen Fineman (1996: 550), who says that in organizations, 'much of what we describe as rational is in fact emotional'. Emotion is a continuous and integral aspect of organizing, but this does not mean that emotions should be studied separately from the various rationalizations that relate to them. The everyday activities of members of organizations tend to be defined and justified rationally, therefore there would be little value, for example, in privileging emotion in the study of organizations if doing so meant ignoring how rationality is used in organizations to block emotions (Domagalski, 1999).

In all organizations, members of organizations need to acquire a degree of emotional literacy in order to survive or thrive in the job (Fineman, 1997). The difficulty is in understanding, for example, what can or cannot be expressed in particular settings and whether and how emotions might be utilized strategically to gain desired ends. Blocking, suppressing, containing and neutralizing are all political activities in the sense that they are strategies that attempt to advance or to avoid interests, and they imply actions related to desired outcomes. The value of studying the interplay between emotion and rationality, as well as how these are linked to organizational politics, is in order to appreciate how emotions might transform rational processes from a coherent decision, plan or strategy into contested relations and disputed understanding. In Chapter 6, I develop this further by exploring how organizing creates a fantasy of coherence and clarity that underpins rational decision-making, but also reduces the scope of knowledge available from which to reflect and change. Such knowledge includes emotional, relational and political dynamics as well as rational capacities. Emotions contribute to the impetus for and outcomes of strategic initiatives, and can provide many clues for ongoing reflection and development. Approaching the relationship between emotion and rationality in this way is also, potentially, a shift in managers' understanding of the strategic component of their role. It implies a shift from looking at how rationality is used to try to manage emotion, to looking at how emotion provides an additional critique of rational responses.

In studying managers' experiences of the takeover of Hyder I was concerned to identify the feelings and emotions that arose within a specific organizational context. Fineman (2001) has explained the difference between feelings and emotions. He suggests that feelings are fundamentally private experiences and that emotions are the public performance of feelings. Emotional display depends on an audience on which the performance of feelings is designed (consciously or unconsciously) to have a strategic effect. The nature of individuals' emotional display is regulated by the actor's internal state as well as by a web of social rules. Therefore, 'emotion can be understood as the culturally based interpretation of a physiological state that enables an individual to act' (Callahan and McCollum, 2002: 6).

While it is clear that emotions are always located within a web of social rules or power relations, the construction of feelings as private experiences may promote a misleading distinction. Psychodynamic theory offers the insight that feelings are not only private experiences, but are shaped by and linked to the internalization or denial of self–other relations. In this sense, therefore, both feelings and emotions are always social. In addition, one has to ask who is being represented in the public performance of feelings: is it the individual, or might it also include those persons and collectives whose influence on the individual encourages the 'acting out' of relational and/or collective conflicts and defences? The experience of being the 'scapegoat', for example, expresses one way in which individuals become the conscious and unconscious victims and mouthpieces of interpersonal or group dynamics, or the politics that relate to specific group and organizational contexts.

The differences and similarities between the social constructionist and psychodynamic perspectives on emotion in organizations have been outlined in detail elsewhere (see Gabriel, 1999; Antonacopoulou and Gabriel, 2001). To summarize these in very brief terms, from a social-constructionist perspective emotion guides the individual in appraising social situations and responding to them, therefore emotional display is part of an interpersonal, meaning-creating process. From a psychodynamic perspective, understanding both emotional dynamics and unconscious processes is seen as essential to transforming self-limiting organizational behaviour as well as the organizational structures and designs that are associated with and emerge from it.

To repeat what I quoted earlier, the importance of studying emotion in organizations is not only about understanding more about specific emotions, it also concerns what specific emotions say about the organization as a system in context (Armstrong, 2000). Both feelings and emotions are defined by, and are part of defining, the social and political context within which they are experienced. The experiences of an individual within an organizational role are constructed in part through internal and external expectations, which is to say through the interplay between emotion and politics. Experience is what characterizes and contains individual emotions, as well as individuals' everyday thought and action. It is an expression of the individual within a social world, never detached, even when alone, from the impact of the relations between self and others. Political relatedness generates feelings and emotions both directly through interpersonal processes and indirectly through a web-like connection to social and strategic politics.

One aspect of the interplay between emotion and rationality concerns how rational processes apparently transform emotions to make them (seem) manageable. Rationality helps to reinforce and emphasize a plan or strategy. So far, there has been little or no management research that has examined this equation from the opposite way around. One of the aspects of studying the takeover of Hyder was the opportunity it afforded to investigate how emotion might provide knowledge in addition to the rational processes that inform strategies. My argument is that reflection on emotion helps to reveal assumptions and expectations, as well as the political processes that have mobilized and reinforced them. Second, both feelings and emotions need to be understood in terms of the social and political dynamics of which they are a part. Given this perception, focus on the individual or on individuals' emotions would not provide sufficient connection to the social and political context within which emotions are located. This can be achieved by recognising the political relatedness between the person and the organizational role she or he occupies, as well as how an organizational role shapes and is shaped by organizing. Emotions that are felt and communicated from an organizational role are inevitably part of broader power relations and politics within an organization.

The takeover of Hyder plc

I will briefly remind the reader of the situation in Hyder. The company, which existed between 1996 and 2000, was the largest private company in Wales, with a global workforce of approximately 10,000. It was a multi-utility and infrastructure management company that grew quickly after privatization from the original public-sector organization, Welsh Water. The emphasis of corporate change was the creation of a multi-utility business with a firm base in Wales and a global infrastructure development company. The company vision and strategy was to become 'worldwide infrastructure specialists . . . to create the UK's first truly integrated utility'. In order to achieve this the company created the Hyder brand (meaning 'confidence') to express the coming together of former public sector utilities with the newer, entrepreneurial parts of the organization.

> The public sector organizations and private companies which form our customer base have a specific need. They need help to finance, design and operate infrastructure. And that means more than just construction companies. They need one company, with many specialist skills, able to deliver a complete service.
>
> ('Creating Our Brand', company publication, September 1996: 7)

The slogan to accompany the brand was 'One Hyder: Altogether Stronger' (this slogan was made into a screensaver and spoke out from all company computers).

As one senior manager reflected at the time, 'the idea of "One Hyder" is a very strong desire, but a very bad representation of what it is actually like'. As I have illustrated with an earlier example, 'One Hyder' was an attempt to create a clear corporate identity within a company characterized by established conflicts across organizational divides.

There were two particular issues that seemed to undermine Hyder's business stability. First, the company was required (by the Labour government that came into power in 1997) to repay £300 million in 'windfall tax' to the UK Treasury. Second, Hyder's purchase of SWALEC, the former South Wales electricity company was seen as being overpriced and likely to place too big a burden on the company, undermining its ability to invest and grow. Hyder's share price gradually collapsed from a high of £10.49 in mid-1998 to £1.79 in March 2000, and the company amassed debts of £1.9 million. In the summer of 2000, Western Power Distribution (WPD), a US-owned company, paid $840 million for Hyder, beating a rival bid by Nomura, the Japanese investment bank. The British Takeover Panel was involved in the final decision, after ordering the bidders to submit sealed bids. This saw the end of a complex and acrimonious, four-month battle for the company, with 'more twists and turns than a Frederick Forsyth novel' (*Western Mail*, 19 August 2000), and it finally sealed the fate of Hyder. Although the windfall tax and buying SWALEC were seen as a crucial aspect of the financial difficulties, others saw the causes of Hyder's problems as: 'too much expansion, too much debt, too many irons in too many fires, and not enough management experience or skill' (Fanning, 2000: 32).

The few thoughts and quotations above allude to the fact that there were many and varied ideas and opinions about the demise of Hyder. It was a protracted and politically charged process, connected to both external and internal issues. As the largest private company within the Principality, Hyder was seen to represent the successful business and economic development of Wales (the company was informally known as 'Wales plc'). Internally, the takeover of Hyder prompted the expression of strong emotions as well as rationalizations of thought, feeling and action. Insights emerged because the managers interviewed were willing to express their feelings about the demise of the company, and there were a number of possible explanations of the event. The impending loss of the company may have promoted the idea that managers now had less to lose in saying what they felt. The emotional tensions created by actual or imagined loyalties to the organization decreased as the company's demise became inevitable. In addition, the competition, envy and the need to avoid conflicts that had underpinned managers' silences and avoidance strategies were relaxed. As constraints and expectations were lifted, they became less powerfully felt, enacted and adhered to. The study of emotion in Hyder provided an opportunity to question the interaction of emotions and politics and their impact on the organization.

Research approach and results

Five managers were interviewed (between April and June 2000); all the interviewees were men, three of whom were directors and were part of the senior management group, two were senior/middle managers. All managers interviewed had been centrally involved in the organizational thinking and strategy that gave rise to the company re-branding initiative that created Hyder. The interviews lasted about sixty minutes each and were recorded. Interviews were loosely structured around the theme of 'your emotions, thoughts about and experiences of the takeover of Hyder'. Interview transcripts were loaded into a qualitative data storage, retrieval and management system (MAXQDA). My interpretations of the interviews can be explained in the following way. First, I reduced the data on the basis of identifying feelings that were expressed about the takeover and brought these together into a synopsis of five key points. These were:

- *Anger towards oneself, pain, impotence and self-blame*: individuals are angry with and blame themselves for not being able to influence events. They feel impotent and agonized by not being able to find a solution. Individuals feel hurt by the experience.
- *Disinterest and self-interest*: individuals are detached from the motivation to act. Enacting their role in the organization seems pointless. Individuals are looking outside of the organization and/or looking out for personal interests, or what they feel is due to them.
- *Shame, disloyalty, questioning of self in relation to others*: individuals feel ashamed and regretful, disloyal to the staff involved, conspiratorial, sad and unconfident, nervous and frustrated.
- *Frustration and anger towards the organization*: individuals are angry and frustrated with the organization, for their (individual and organizational) failure to make the strategy work.
- *Confusion and uncertainty mixed with some excitement*: individuals don't know what to feel and how to go forward. There are mixed emotions, which point to both the possibilities and the pitfalls in the experience.

This synopsis provides a basis for further discussion and interpretation of the emotions mobilized by the takeover, as well as the rationalizations that accompany them. I elaborate and develop these five points under two general headings – reflections on self and role, and reflections on organizational politics.

Reflections on self and role

The managers interviewed felt angry with themselves, for letting what they had built be dismantled and 'for allowing it to actually happen to me'. The takeover was something that confident, experienced senior managers had not expected or planned. It was a 'very unpleasant, not to be repeated, kind of experience' that pained the individuals involved.

That was frustrating and that was horrible because you just had these countervailing personal pressures, I mean it was like sleepless nights time.

Frustration is not a strong enough term really, it was agonizing, just couldn't bloody make anything move either way.

When that kind of dream is locked from you I mean it's worse than not having a dream at all.

In part, the anger that they felt was with their inability to enact their expectations of themselves as managers of other people's expectations:

The feeling of impotence, vulnerability, impotence and people asking you things you can't answer.

No sense of purpose, no power, no control, no influence on events at all, trying to manage lots of people who thought they were being taken for a ride.

Feelings of pain and impotence were balanced by expressions of self-interest, the need now to put personal needs before 'worrying about this bloody firm': 'the quicker I can get out the better', making sure of 'a decent pension' and the importance of not walking away before what 'I'm entitled to' has been negotiated.

I recognized some time ago that my priorities were really myself, secondly those who work for me and around me, and thirdly the organization.

The enactment of a management role was increasingly difficult as the financial demise of Hyder and the takeover battle gathered momentum. Managerial roles are constructed and perpetuated more in relation to others (the managed) than they are towards making decisions or devising strategies in isolation. Although the individual occupies a role, it takes a collective to give that role meaning and impetus in an organization. Individuals' feelings of shame and disloyalty were related to letting others down, to decisions made that had impacted negatively on the lives of staff, to the times when they 'felt shabbily conspiratorial', 'unconfident' or 'incompetent' in their role:

And then you're stuck now with all this kind of gut-wrenching feeling of disloyalty and should the loyalty be to the wider company and all the people or to personal things?

I suppose ashamed of it really. I'm ashamed for what's happened to the organization and I feel a lot of regret about not being able to influence it to a greater extent than I did and not having the confidence, if you like, to do that.

Managers eventually became detached from enacting their role because to do so seemed pointless, 'a lot of us have really been just wandering around doing almost nothing'.

> As far as the organization is concerned I mean there's a cutoff point where people just say, well, you know, work is a four-letter word.

> I've found it rather difficult to bother coming to work, you know, I'm sort of helping, I'm still working with that business but everything else that I was involved with has ceased basically.

Through my interpretations of the interviews I identified two particular pairings of emotion that characterized managers' experience of the takeover, and the relationship between self and role. First, pain was balanced with self-interest and, second, shame was balanced with disinterest. Expressions of self-interest and disinterest were a defence against the pain and shame generated for individuals by their experience in the role of manager (at such a time).

Reflections on organizational politics

Organizing produces mixed emotions in managers. All of the managers interviewed were enthusiastic supporters of 'One Hyder' – they were the members of the organization who had devised the strategy, led it or were responsible for its implementation in practice. The change from Welsh Water to Hyder was 'exciting', 'expansive', and rooted in a 'passionate' vision of the organization as a successful global business and 'a great place to work'.

> I think it started with the fact that you had a relatively small team of enthusiastic people who were looking for a new future, were looking for something that stimulated the thinking of the whole senior management team, not knowing exactly where it was going to go but actually trying to get people to think in an expansive way to move the business on, you know, in leaps and bounds.

It was difficult for managers both to rationally defend and develop the 'One Hyder' strategy and to express the emotions involved in living its failure as members of the organization. Their emotions about the failure of their strategy can be set in the context of a broader and more habitual or established organizing process in Hyder.

One characterization of the emotions involved in the management of change in Hyder was that most attempts at the implementation of change involved a gradual but seemingly inevitable move from excitement to disappointment. This was as true of the 'One Hyder' strategy as it was of other change initiatives that had gone before. In terms of 'One Hyder', the 'huge optimism' at the start of the strategy was eventually underpinned by the realization that several key people in the organization 'at the end of the day really didn't want it'. From here the managers experienced a growing awareness that the strategy wasn't going to work. Finally, from a position of hindsight, there was a feeling that the strategy was naïve.

> You start to think this is not going to happen in a million years and that was really the evidence of the start of the wakening, if you like, of what the difference between the potential of the business and what the reality was going to be, although it's easy for me to see that more starkly in hindsight than I would have seen it at the time.

> I think it was an ideal, which was about leveraging off each other's capability in different businesses within the group, which sounded nice but was quite a naïve thought process in terms of how things really work. I do think there was a naïvety about what it was we were trying to achieve.

Despite the inevitable and impending destruction of the organization as they knew it, and their own plans to move on or get out, the managers interviewed had a continuing sense of belonging to Hyder. They still remained 'a part of the organization'. The rational expression of this was focused on the conviction that their 'One Hyder' strategy was 'such a good set of ideas'. Their emotions reflected the considerable effort they had put into developing a sense of corporate oneness, and when this was destroyed it inevitably had an emotional impact on their expectations about the organization, not just their experience within it.

> I think the irritations, frustrations, anger – you name the emotion – you get a bit of it, are driven by the fact that the body corporate and its ambitions and everything else are so clearly intertwined with one's personal ambitions and objectives in life and stuff, that if you separate one from you it's like cutting a limb off.

Their disappointment involved some self-criticism about the failure of the strategic development of the company, but also motivated broader criticisms about the lack of 'organizational momentum for that vision', the 'disunited' and 'bloody awful' organization of which they were members.

> There was a huge gulf between what was said and what was done and I don't know what the root of that was, one could be just sheer lack of energy and not knowing how to do it, the other one is it's probably equally true if not truer that actually the organization, however you describe the organization, didn't believe it.

The disappointment at the failure of a 'wonderful dream' made managers question their own skills and abilities, not knowing how to make things work out the way they wanted them to, not feeling confident in the legitimacy of their wants, or in whether or not they could transcend the frustration inherent in existing power relations, the question of 'what do you do to get them shifted?'

> I'm sitting there thinking I don't know how to do it you know, I'll not pretend to know how to do any of this, I can do my bit and somebody else can do their bit but quite frankly I don't know how to do it, but unless you bring that collective capability to actually address that, then you will never get there, that's a certainty.

> We were not confident enough in ourselves to actually feel that we had the right to take it on further than we did.

The difficulty of breaking through established power relations (even it seems for some of the most senior managers in the company) encouraged fears about the consequences of trying to challenge them. 'The more you lift your skirt the more leg you show', said one director, to illustrate the fears involved in 'stepping out of line, stepping off that edge'. 'We could have ended up with us sacked, which I would have found very difficult.' The less senior managers had another interpretation. It seemed to them that the directors were unable or unwilling to act. They were indecisive, they were afraid of 'the personal risk about stepping out of line', they lacked 'ambition', 'drive', 'they lacked the bottle'. Established expectations about power relations and patterns of change created the conditions for managers' inability to sustain their confidence in 'One Hyder'. The lack of belief in 'One Hyder' reinforced and perpetuated existing organizational politics and established power relations.

I have identified and illustrated emotions mobilized by the takeover of Hyder in relation to managers' experience of self in role, and their enactment of their role in the context of organizational politics. In summary, these are:

- *Reflections on self and role*: feelings of pain balanced by a drive towards self-interest, and feelings of shame balanced by disinterest.
- *Reflections on organizational politics*: fears about power undermined managers' willingness and ability to act; feelings of enthusiasm about the organization's strategy and direction gradually transformed into disappointment and inaction.

Conclusions

In my interpretations of the takeover of Hyder I am trying to raise three issues. These concern, first, insights into the relationship between emotion and politics in organizations; second, contributing to the further understanding of emotion and the rationalization of emotion in organizations; finally, implications for strategic leadership in the role of manager.

Understanding the relationship between emotion and politics in Hyder

The study revealed a tension between the emotions managers expressed in the interviews and their descriptions of how they understood and enacted their managerial roles. Despite emphasizing how 'pointless' it seemed to manage, they continued to do so in a way that was consciously or unconsciously designed to reduce the emotional burden of blame and shame mobilized by the takeover. Individual experience was focused on self-interest and/or disinterest. Managers, however, continued to utilize the authority of their roles to try to reduce the impact of feelings of impotence, shame, regret, disloyalty or anger. It was not that managers felt that self-interest was a better strategy in this situation, rather they seemed to be finding ways to compensate for difficult and unwanted feelings with other emotions that they were happier to experience during these troubled times. In addition, self-interest and disinterest provided a means for reinterpreting organizational politics, minimizing felt or imagined expectations within and on their roles.

All of the managers interviewed felt the impending loss of the organization; all the managers found ways of distancing themselves from these emotions. The emotional process of managing the takeover (both internally and externally) depended on being able to sustain the link between self and role, between individual experience and (revised) expectations. Individuals felt anguished by the impending loss of their jobs and the demise of the organization. This was expressed, for example, through sleepless nights, or an inability to act, as well as in feelings of impotence, purposelessness and vulnerability. The self-interest that eased personal anguish was mirrored in an imagined disinterest, or detachment from 'work', making feelings of shame and disloyalty towards staff easier to manage. Managers made work a 'four-letter word', a place where it was 'difficult to bother coming'. However, they also continued to defend the idea that they had been trying to create 'a great place to work', as well as living with the experience of failure and separation, which felt 'like cutting a limb off'. The interplay between pain and self-interest, shame and disinterest is not contradictory; rather it succinctly describes tensions necessary to create an emotional state from which a managerial role can continue to be enacted within difficult and emotionally charged circumstances.

Rationalizations in relation to their role made it more manageable for the individual, but this was transformed within the broader political context. In looking back at the 'One Hyder' strategy, it was clear that all the managers interviewed (in theory) had the authority within their roles to realize the strategy. They had invested considerable emotional effort into using their own managerial authority to create and defend the strategy. Their frustration came from a feeling that people with more power 'didn't really want it'. For them, this meant that the organization became 'disunited', lacking in 'organizational momentum', a 'bloody awful organization'. These were some of the most senior managers in Hyder and yet they were afraid that (sic) 'the more you lift your skirt, the more leg you show'. The takeover of the company was experienced primarily as the failure of their 'One Hyder' strategy, the end of the idea of an 'altogether stronger' organization. The tension that had characterized the strategy, between the exercise of their own authority in a managerial role and the willingness to act in the face of the perceived power of others, continued. The interviews suggested that even the most senior managers had managed to make themselves uncertain about their power to act. Managers were unconfident in the legitimacy of their wants, frustrated that they did not have what they needed to make it 'work'. Whether it was feelings of impotence about the self or opinions about the lack of 'drive' or 'bottle' of others, the outcome was the same. The emotions associated with the failure of their strategy meant that managers both felt differently about their role and communicated differently from their role. This had happened well before the company's shares started to drop dramatically, but it contributed to the inevitability of the takeover.

Managers experienced a tension between emotions (pain and shame) and their detachment from these emotions (self-interest or disinterest). In terms of the difference between individual feelings and the emotions associated with a role, this was a way of containing, an attempt at controlling the emotions mobilized by the takeover. It was also a revised basis from which the authority of their managerial role could continue to be enacted under difficult and emotionally charged circumstances. However, managerial authority had been undermined as well as revised. Managers were juggling attempts to use their authority to minimize their own emotional burden, to carry on being (good) managers, but also to avoid existing and entrenched company politics. Managers' actions were driven, not by any rational relationship to organizational strategy, planning or decision-making, but by avoiding the political conflicts mobilized by the 'One Hyder' strategy. Given these emotions and their political consequences, a question arises about the context of this data. Was managers' detachment an emotional response to the takeover or was it something that to an extent had been there all along, an established aspect of the politics of management within the company? My view is that the emotional tensions I have described represent a continuation of the interplay between emotion and politics that characterized Hyder, but that the takeover allowed them to surface and find expression.

The contribution to the study of emotions in organizations

The results of this study have reinforced and further illustrated existing research suggesting that emotions are likely to be balanced by rationalizations aimed at making difficult emotions manageable (Hopfl and Linstead, 1997). In this study, managers' emotions – anguish, impotence and fear – were contained by a rational focus on self-interest or rationalizations aimed at disinterest. This was not simply about an individual's ability to balance the emotional and the rational, but part of a dynamic process representing managers' attempts to stay within their managerial role. In Hyder this specifically related to a desire managers had to maintain their (benevolent) role in relation to staff while at the same time find a good way of leaving a dying organization. There is potentially more research to be undertaken here, especially in identifying the ways in which individual and collective emotions and rational facilities combine to create and reinforce other distinctive organizational dynamics.

At a theoretical level the research points towards the advantages of a dual approach. What is borne out in this study about the social-constructionist theory of emotions in organizations is the idea that meanings emerge and are communicated through specific cultural events (for example, the takeover of a company). Surrounding political, social and cultural forces assist managers in finding emotional responses that reflect the organizational contexts within which feelings are mobilized. Psychodynamic theory provides insights about political relatedness, that we are social beings in a very profound and complex sense. In addition it helps to comprehend how unconscious behaviour, stimulated by either the avoidance of or adherence to emotions, contributes to organizational politics and therefore to emerging structures and designs. There is potential agreement within these two theoretical standpoints in terms of the mutual desire to understand the interplay between emotion and politics, and to study the impact of the relationship between emotion and politics as a fundamental aspect of organizational concepts like leadership and learning.

There are also implications for research into emotion in organizations that emerge from this study. If, as the study suggests, emotion is likely to be balanced by rationalization, then it is useful to include analysis both of the ways in which emotions have been transformed by rationalizations and how rationalizations may have been transformed by emotion. This implies a shift in the current perspective on researching emotion, from looking at how rationality may be used to try to manage emotion, to include a focus on ways in which emotion constitutes a critique of rational management within an organization. In Chapter 9, I describe this as a shift from rationalizing problems to problematizing the rational. The political context within which emotion is experienced and enacted is an integral part of the study of emotion in organization. One way to link inquiries into emotion and politics is through a focus on emotion that is associated with the person-in-a-role and with recurring political dynamics that seem to point to (conscious and unconscious) limitations on authority within a role. The insights that can be drawn from this study about the relationship between emotion and politics are situated: they describe aspects of the organizational dynamics of Hyder plc. A task for the future will be further research aimed at revealing and comparing the interplay between emotion and politics across a variety of other organizations and organizational domains.

Implications for strategic leadership in the role of manager

Earlier in this chapter I said that the additional value in studying the interplay between emotion and rationality (in the context of organizational politics) was in order to appreciate how emotions might transform rational processes from a coherent decision, plan or strategy into contested relations and disputed understanding. This may seem like a strange direction to want to go, and I hope to explain why it is important. Managers have attempted to rationalize emotions rather than look for the ways in which emotions associated with actions might reveal opportunities for critique and development. Emotions have the capacity to undermine the apparent simplicity of management or decision-making because they can point to and reveal the contradictions that are inherent in any attempts to manage. In Hyder, for example, the mixed emotions experienced by managers both supported and undermined managerial authority within a role. The idea that strategic thinking only represents decisions, plans and intentions that are rational (and thereby coherent and consistent) does not help managers to perceive the emotional and political tensions and contradictions that strategies mobilize, or differences of experience, expectation and understanding that emerge in practice.

An analysis of emotions associated with managerial roles can provide opportunities to understand the politics that attempts to manage and organize inevitably create. Speculations on emotions that are generated through organizing extend the data available and capacity for reflection. Emotions that are stimulated by the implementation of managerial roles can be an integral part of reflection on, review of and development of strategies as they progress and impact on organizing. This idea has a wider application in management studies, especially in relation to reflection and leadership (see Chapters 7 and 8). Understanding the impact of emotion is potentially part of a shift in managers' comprehension of the strategic component of their role. The identification of managers' emotions at the time of the takeover of Hyder provides an example of the contradictions that are a part of strategic initiatives. There was no solely rational explanation for the inability of senior managers to make the 'One Hyder' strategy work. These were some of the most powerful managers in the organization, who had led the development and internal marketing of the strategy within the organization. Their strategy failed primarily because they were collectively afraid that the conflicts that underpinned the strategy (and that the strategy had been designed to remove) were going to have a destructive impact on them – that they would lose their jobs – or a destructive impact on the organization – they would tear the organization apart. In this latter regard, they were right. Such fears undermined the ability of managers to put their authority into practice and to act collectively within the organization. The senior managers interviewed were afraid to put their heads above the parapet in order to face organizational politics that they had decided were best avoided.

The study into the takeover of Hyder has clear limitations. It is only one organizational study with a small sample of (only male) managers. However, it does show the potential for additional lines of inquiry based on the ways in which politics and emotion combine to create organizational dynamics, and the consequences of these dynamics for understanding strategic learning. In this chapter I have been exploring connections between emotions mobilized by the takeover of Hyder and various rationalizations attached to individuals' attempts to manage the takeover. This was especially related to the emotions and rationalizations of key individuals within management roles. In the next chapter my focus shifts from explorations of the ways in which emotion, politics and organizing are linked. I return to broader issues that concern how *establishment* is created and sustained. My particular focus is the politics of change in organizations.

6 The politics of imagined stability

This chapter explores the politics of change in organizations in order to clarify the broad organizational conditions and potential impact of strategic learning. The discussions are linked to the issues I have raised in previous chapters and are particularly related towards understanding processes that both contribute to and question the *establishment* that organizing creates. There is already a very considerable literature covering planned change, which conceptualizes change in relation to an event, as the solution of problems, or as the implementation of a strategic process. The focus of this chapter is in a different area. My starting point in thinking about change is a continuation and development of previous writing, where I have reflected that change 'happens in connection with others, through friendships and collaboration, it happens as a result of uncertainty and risk, through organizational politics, and it happens for reasons I cannot fathom' (Vince, 1996: 88). Change is seen as an ongoing process with unpredictable outcomes (Orlikowski and Hofman, 1997) and the management of change is bound up with the internal dynamics of organizing, with 'interests, values, power dependencies and capacity for action' (Greenwood and Hinings, 1996: 1023), as well as with the potency of the emotions and fantasies that shape organization.

My thinking in this chapter once again emphasizes the interrelation between individual and collective emotional experience and politics. I try to represent and explore some of the emotional and political complexities and connections involved in the management of change. The study of the interplay between politics and emotion plays an important part in understanding and organizing change because, as I have shown from previous examples in this book, political behaviour and action frequently emerge from fears and anxieties about the direction and consequences of change. In any attempt to manage change, the change process will be bound up with internal organizational dynamics, with unconscious processes and defences, with emotions, power relations and capacities for action and inaction.

I am also seeking to further develop an understanding of political perspectives on change, supporting the move beyond the fantasy that once politics have been understood they can be managed (Knights and McCabe, 1998). My use of the words 'management of change' is to an extent informed by doubt as to whether the emotions and politics mobilized through organizing can be managed. Although I am advocating a process that informs the management of change I am not suggesting change itself is always to be desired, or that it is necessary, always possible, or of itself a good thing. One aspect of the understanding of change presented in this chapter is that the management of change is never free from the political and emotional context that surrounds it. This might include, for example, attempts to control the nature or extent of change, what is and is not legitimate to change, or discourses concerning times when change may have gone too far.

The thinking behind the phrase 'a politics of imagined stability'

Organizations are often thought of and experienced *as if* they are the stable containers of rational decision-making and problem-solving. They are subject to a *politics of imagined stability*, a fantasy of control and coherence, supported and reinforced by both conscious and unconscious personal, group and organizational processes for creating and resisting change. The idea of a politics of imagined stability both built from conscious and unconscious processes and behaviour is fundamental to the thinking that frames this chapter and the book as a whole. Individually and collectively, members of organizations act as if an organization is a coherent entity that can be described in terms of mission, assumptions and underlying values (or even a primary task). In other words, people tend to relate more to organizations as fixed and coherent than they do to the idea that organizing generates diverse, contradictory and/or confused collective identities.

The idea of organization as an imagined stability resonates with Weick's (1995) notion of 'generic sensemaking', where people in organizations enact scripts, express roles and follow rules that both reflect and construct organizational behaviours and structures. Here, I am using psychodynamic thinking to capture something of the nature of political processes that constitute *imagined stability*, and I link these to implications for the management of change. In using the phrase 'imagined stability' I am acknowledging the extent to which organization involves acting on fantasy and imagination, that is, mental representations of things not actually present or concrete. In addition, this phrase is intended to capture some of the ways in which organizations might be 'taken in by their own fantasies' (Gabriel, 1999) and therefore how collective perceptions that limit behaviour and action are generated. Imagined stability is fantasy in the sense that it may well be the product of the interaction of collective imagination and organization over time. An organization is a product of collective imagination, built as much on the strength of its own illusions of stability as on procedures that underpin established ways of working.

I can further develop what I mean by the phrase 'a politics of imagined stability' by explaining how I am using the word 'politics' and identifying the links between politics, emotions and the psychodynamic study of organizations.

In general, when I use the word 'politics' I am referring to attempts at the management or control of relations and interests within an organization, as well as activities concerned with the acquisition or exercise of authority or power. I highlight three ways in which politics has an impact on the imagined stability of an organization. First, one characteristic of the politics involved in the ways organizations are imagined is that organizing is located in, and is a reflection of, broader social and societal contexts (Schneider and Dunbar, 1992). I refer to this as *social politics*. This may include the politics emerging from social power relations, of gender, race, class, disability or other socially constructed differences or inequalities. It may include social and economic forces that are linked to national opportunities and identities or stereotypes. It may include world events that have an impact on the social context within which organization takes place. From a psychodynamic viewpoint this recognizes that 'there is an implicit sociology within psychoanalytic theories of organizational life' (Cooper, 1998: 283).

Many psychodynamic studies of organization have looked at the relatedness between individuals and social or societal forms and dynamics. Early studies were concerned to examine the link between anxiety and the creation of institutionalizing processes (social defences) within social systems (Menzies-Lyth, 1990). Further development of this theme has been related to specific organizational domains (Obholzer, 1994; Bain, 1998). In addition, the wider politics relating to social issues has been shown to have unconscious effects on the behaviour of professional staff. For example, the organizational behaviour of a team concerned with young people and drugs came to mirror aspects of the (anti-social) behaviour of the clients (Cardona, 1999). In another study, the murder of four staff in a mental health project is linked to deeper questions of social change in Israeli society (Erlich-Ginor and Erlich, 1999). One of the examples in this chapter provides a description of how social politics are expressed and enacted in ways that can be related to or represent national feelings or expectations at a time of political change in Wales. The psychodynamic study of organizations therefore involves an interest in 'how the social becomes part of the psychological' (*Organizational and Social Dynamics*, 2001).

The second aspect to my definition of politics concerns *strategic politics* that are associated with language, history and actions within an organization. Strategic politics emerge from and express the nature of the political relatedness between individuals, groups and other collectives. For example, strategic politics include conflicts that get repeated; habitual behaviour that reflects usual or characteristic approaches to leadership or authority; and patterns of communication or organization that have become taken-for-granted. The usefulness of a psychodynamic approach here is its focus on system psychodynamics (Miller and Rice, 1967; Neumann, 1999) rather than with individual psychology. The individuals' role is part of a broader system, whatever personal histories and processes are being enacted. Although individual and interpersonal dynamics contribute to organizational behaviour and structure, emotional experience is rarely located within an individual space (Armstrong, 1991, 2000). Strategic politics therefore is concerned with the strategic consequences of behaviour in organizations and how this links to the emergence of organizational structures and designs that then have an impact on behaviour.

The final part of my explanation of how I am using the word 'politics' concerns the politics surrounding the management of change in organizations. Change is thought about, contested, imagined and implemented through both social and strategic politics. It is also managed alongside the avoidance of a variety of difficult individual or collective emotions mobilized by change. Psychodynamic studies show that a great deal about an organization, its structure as well as the limitations and possibilities of behaviour, is shaped through the conscious and unconscious avoidance of emotions. Defences against emotion tend to diminish the likelihood of organizational objectives being achieved (Stein, 1996). Attempts at organizational change necessarily involve recognizing and addressing the system of individual and collective defences that have been built up over time and that form the traditional way of doing things in the organization (Statt, 1994). All organizations are seen to have socially constructed defences against the anxiety of carrying out the primary task, which prevent learning and change (Bain, 1998). Social defences are shaped by shared assumptions concerning change and by the wish to avoid conflict and negative feelings (Diamond, 1990). They are also an integral part of maintaining and perpetuating organizational identity and design (Vince and Broussine, 1996).

Organizing involves attempts to make change happen at the same time as creating ways to contain or control it. Attempts at change inevitably lead to differences between intentions about organizing and the outcomes of organizing in action – what Argyris (1982) has famously termed the gap between the 'espoused' and the 'in-use'. A psychodynamic approach provides ways of thinking about and enquiring into this gap, especially the anxieties and defences that provoke it. A focus on the interplay in organizations between politics and emotion provides a way of recognizing that attempts to manage change are inevitably interventions into the fantasy of stability that organizing has created. A dual emphasis on both emotion and politics helps to locate emotional experience within an institutional (rather than individual) context, and to minimize a tendency to avoid addressing power relations as a part of change (Baum, 1993; Vince, 1996).

I am proposing an approach to the management of change that has a focus on the political and emotional dynamics that contribute to and maintain *imagined stability*. The framework is not designed to identify the culture of the organization, what the organization is like or how the organization needs to change. It does not seek to explain what is involved in the implementation of change, or follow through with the idea that the organization is like this (e.g. too hierarchical), and therefore it needs to become like that (e.g. flatter and more networked). The framework I propose can help to identify the imagined state that is being experienced, created and maintained; the dominant power relations, fantasies and emotions; and the general context within which these are represented. Actions that are developed after such an analysis have the benefit of being informed by an understanding of the politics and emotions that characterize an organizational context. Appreciation of the emotions and power relations that characterize an organization is more likely to give rise to strategies that are related to the specific situations that change initiatives are designed to address. In addition, an important assumption in this chapter is that the management of change is always contested, and always bounded by an imagined stability. I return to this in the concluding part of the chapter and discuss why this assumption is important and the contribution it can make to the theory and practice of strategic learning.

In summary, *the politics of imagined stability* is a phrase that describes the role that social and strategic politics play in the perpetuation of emotions and fantasies that have an impact on organizing.

- *Social politics.* An analysis of the social politics that contribute to imagined stability is attempting to discover the impact of, for example, gendered social relations, national expectations, global issues and events, on how organizations and institutions are internalized, imagined, experienced, maintained and developed.
- *Strategic politics.* An analysis of the strategic politics that contribute to imagined stability provides an understanding of 'the way we do things here'. Such understanding emerges from exploration of the link between individual and collective emotions and the creation and expression of procedures, practice and systems. Emotions and politics combine to create *establishment* – organizational values, ideas and boundaries within which it becomes increasingly difficult to challenge the various assumptions that have emerged through organizing.
- In general terms, organizing produces both the desire to make change happen and a need to avoid and resist change. Understanding organization as an imagined stability can help members of organizations to identify characteristic emotions and power relations that legitimize restrictions on how, what, where, when and why change can be implemented, as well as finding creative ways to perceive and undermine conscious and unconscious organizational limitations on change.

Attempts at the management of change, therefore, are likely to involve the identification of the politics that characterize and inform the limitations and possibilities of change within a specific organizational context. I illustrate this once again with examples from Hyder plc. The quotations I have used came either from interviews with Hyder managers or from company documents. My assumptions about the directors and senior managers I interviewed were as follows:

- The company's most senior managers are the key actors in the creation and perpetuation of the power relations that characterize Hyder.
- They are a powerful focal point for emotions, expectations and projections concerning organizational stability and change.

- The clearest way of expressing the role of managers at such a senior level of the company is that their role is to change the organization.

I am mindful that the generalizations I have identified come solely from an analysis of interviews involving senior managers whose job it is to make change happen, whether they are specifically aware of this role or not. I am also aware that change is not only something that is led by senior managers, but happens (and is resisted) throughout the whole organization both deliberately and by accident.

The impact of social politics on Hyder

At the height of its global development, Hyder represented something of 'the new Wales'. The national press in Wales saw the organization as 'a standard bearer for the new Wales' (*Western Mail*, 1999), a representation of Welsh development in the global economy at a time when the country had a new Welsh Assembly government with increased political autonomy from the British parliament. Hyder had grown dramatically and quickly from its original identity as Welsh Water. As I have already noted, the emphasis of this change, initiated formally in 1997, was the company's transformation from a Welsh public utility company to a global, commercial enterprise. In addition to its global aspirations, Hyder had a unique position in the Welsh economy. It was the biggest private company in Wales, and it carried a powerful national and social projection ('Wales plc'), which had considerable impact on the ways in which the enterprise was both seen from outside and imagined from within.

Organizational change and development in Hyder was emotionally and politically connected to a wider, social function of being Wales's largest private organization. Hyder was seen by many to represent the success of the new Welsh economy, especially in the political climate in Wales, which has its 'first home rule for 600 years'. There was considerable anxiety and desire to ensure that devolved authority was successful and that the new Welsh Assembly government 'must be seen to make a difference'. (Both of these quotations are taken from the national news programme *Wales Today* broadcast on 20 December 1999.) Threats to the organizational stability of Hyder (i.e. as a significant local employer) were by implication linked to the political and economic stability of Wales. The organizational imperative was to continue to develop as a global, commercial enterprise. However, the implementation of this was influenced by a powerful, national, social and economic responsibility within Wales.

The impact of strategic politics on Hyder

On 6 October 1997, to mark the re-branding of Welsh Water as Hyder, the Chief Executive gave a keynote speech to most of the senior staff in the company.

The speech was constructed around imaginary newspaper clippings from five years in the future. These were designed to communicate something of the vision in the development plan. For example:

> Infrastructure services experts Hyder yesterday celebrated a significant milestone – they doubled their market capitalization, to just over £2 billion, compared with five years ago.
>
> (Imaginary quotation from the *Financial Times*)

> Hyder, the worldwide infrastructure specialists, has announced a further round of price cuts as it reaps the benefits of its strategy to create the UK's first truly integrated utility.
>
> (Imaginary quotation from the *Daily Telegraph*)

The re-branding was designed to identify a market position and to represent a promise to customers and other stakeholders. It was also an attempt at change based on creating greater collegiality within a company characterized by conflicts across the divides of different organizational sub-systems, between the former electricity and water companies and between the (formerly public-sector) combined utilities company and the infrastructure management company. The idea of collegiality, that people were part of 'an association of equals', was the historical and philosophical underpinning of the re-branding exercise. 'We are, or we feel we are kind of egalitarian by nature.' However, it did not represent the divided and fragmented nature of Hyder. 'There isn't anywhere in the organization where you can see any commonality . . . there is no corporate method of working.'

The re-branding of Hyder was an organizational change that mobilized both the desire of managers for a new beginning and sharpened the conflicts and problems of the past. The re-branding highlighted the existence of various discrete empires and different views of company strategy (stay within the 'core' utility business or 'growth' as a global infrastructure company). After the re-branding, some senior managers were reluctant to address the conflicts within and between these views and empires. At the time, Hyder was a divided company and the branding exercise was certainly intended to address this divide. However, individually and collectively, senior managers were unwilling to work through the conflicts that were thrown into focus by re-branding. As a result the re-branding became more a way of wallpapering over the actual identity of Hyder than an attempt to change it.

The company name was changed to 'confidence' at a time when there was little internal confidence about being one organization. The company directors imagined that Hyder's high share price and continuing commercial success would be followed by an increasing ability within the organization to pull together as a whole. However, between September 1998 and January 2000 the share price dropped by more than 50%. The lack of internal confidence was therefore reinforced by a lack of external confidence. By the third anniversary of his speech, the Chief Executive had left and the company was being broken up. The imaginary newspaper clippings were a long way from the real ones:

> So will it be back to Welsh Water? The man who ignored all the silly suggestions that water and electricity do not mix is now considering whether to break up his Hyder-headed monster. He doesn't really have much choice. He still reckons that his 'multi-utility strategy' is a wonderful idea . . . It is time for the nice Welsh accountant to realise that he is out of his depth.
>
> (*Daily Telegraph*, 10 December 1999)

Organizing attempts to manage change

I have already mentioned that Hyder had created a well-thought-through human resource development process (the learning journey) available to all staff, built on a link between mandatory processes of appraisal and various different approaches to training and development. These included formal and informal training interventions, on-the-job learning strategies, mentoring, fast track programmes, cross-departmental secondments and links to management education run by providers both within and outside Wales. Considerable resources were put into the learning journey on the basis that it constituted a strategy for the gradual management of change. Several of the senior managers interviewed thought that, despite the energy that was often put into change, there was rarely any significant impact on organizational behaviour and design. 'We haven't managed the learning journey very well; there is no question about that. I think what we did in terms of setting it up was fine, conceptually, but its implementation in the business has been poor, to say the least.' In addition, the view from some senior managers was that they were too busy to get involved in a learning journey, and that the organization had other more important things to think about. 'I think that a lot of us are much too busy to think about things like that. The learning journey in that sense probably is a little counter productive to what we as a senior team are trying to do.'

The imagined stability of Hyder

An analysis of the politics and emotions communicated by senior managers reveals three general fantasies about the organization that collectively depict the imagined stability of the organization. Hyder was seen to be a global company, one company and a learning company. The politics of imagined stability in Hyder can be represented in the following emotional and political dynamics, which also describe the context within which change was both managed and contested. Table 6.1 presents a review of each of these and the associated politics that were involved in sustaining imagined stability.

Interviews with Hyder managers provided evidence that their perception of the company could not be divorced from the national dynamics mobilized by

Table 6.1 A summary of the politics of imagined stability in Hyder plc
(from Vince, 2002)

Hyder representing Wales	'One Hyder'	The learning journey
The fantasy of a global Welsh company: Hyder is a global company with a strong future in a new Wales.	*The fantasy of one company*: Hyder is one organization – stronger because all staff members are pulling together in a multi-utility, infrastructure management company.	*The fantasy of a learning company*: Hyder will implement a process of learning to complement the new organization – focusing on the skills and knowledge necessary for growth.
Social politics: The socio-political context for managing change – Hyder represents the business and economic growth of Wales.	*Strategic politics*: The organizational context for managing change – two businesses, a 'core' utility business or a 'growth' infrastructure business.	*The support and avoidance of change*: The individual/ collective context for managing change – senior management is not part of the learning journey.
A lack of confidence in being Hyder outside of Wales.	Collegiality is espoused but management is cautious, controlling and reactive in use.	Change initiatives can only go so far before they start to collapse.

the company's position in Wales. Managers in the company were well aware of the role Hyder occupied as 'Wales plc', and that the company represented the aspirations of Wales in the global economy. This was especially powerful because it coincided with the launch of the new Welsh Assembly government, bringing increased political and economic independence from England. As the social politics surrounding Hyder became clearer (Hyder is Wales's largest private company and represents the 'confidence' of Wales in the global business community), defences seemed to emerge within the company designed to help the company to resist this role. These defences were particularly associated with the name of the company. The Hyder 'branding booklet' stipulated that the pronunciation of the company's name is the Anglicized version (High–der) rather than the Welsh pronunciation (Her–der). It was as if, outside of Wales, the 'confidence' had to disappear. Anglicizing the word rendered it meaningless, removing both the emotional and political connection to Wales. For those who knew nothing of the meaning of the word in Welsh, it was assumed that Hyder had something to do with the word 'hydro', because it used to be a water company. One aspect of imagined stability in Hyder can be seen in the choice to call itself 'confidence'. Underlying this representation were contradictory emotions: a potent set of external expectations (which were embraced by senior company managers) mixed up with ambivalence about whether Welsh confidence could be meaningful out of Wales.

Another aspect of imagined stability in Hyder was the idea of being one coherent company. The imaginary newspaper quotations that formed the basis of the Chief Executive's speech allude to the importance of an institutionalized fantasy of oneness in terms of company success and development. Despite an imagined and espoused commitment to 'One Hyder', to a vision of collegiality across and between all departments and functions, there were at least two different organizations that rarely worked well together. A major change initiative, the re-branding of Welsh Water and the creation of Hyder, was based on an idea of organizational coherence that was a considerable denial by senior managers of the power of well-established conflicts between different organizational empires. The partnerships and alliances that would have been necessary to make 'One Hyder' were unlikely to emerge. The established ways of working in the organization were built more on caution and control than on collegiality. The strategic politics surrounding 'One Hyder' communicated a confusing message, on the surface the organization was meant to be collegial, involving and confident, whereas underneath it was controlling, cautious and risk-averse.

Despite their imagined participation in the equal value of the core and growth parts of the business, senior managers were emotionally occupied with the day-to-day task of defending themselves and/or their part of the organization from unwanted corporate agendas. The actual experience of collegiality was in a shared expectation on individual senior managers to be 'successful, always right and to stay in control'. Managers feared the consequences of failure and this was expressed in organizational terms as a fear of risk. The uncertainty that senior managers felt contributed to the creation of an idea that failure was unwise. They lived with a sense of 'not achieving what one imagines one ought to achieve' and therefore both risks and conflicts were avoided. The impact of this avoidance was primarily on managers' authority to act corporately. An underlying emotion in the company that undermined the fantasy of One Hyder was a lack of confidence in authority, both the uses of personal authority and in the effectiveness of the authority of others. The strategic politics at work in Hyder were primarily anti-collegial, based on the personal need to retain control and on collective fear of conflict, failure and loss of authority and influence.

The learning journey was not a poor HRD strategy; on the contrary it was a highly developed strategy for the learning of individual managers at the operational and middle-management levels of the company. As a corporate change initiative it was meant to underpin learning in the new company. However, senior managers in the company were not part of the learning journey themselves and saw it in the main as a training and development intervention for (other) staff rather than as a strategic initiative designed to put the re-branding into action. In the identification of a clear, corporate set of learning objectives orientated towards company growth, the learning journey potentially provided senior managers with a process for transcending fears of conflict and problems of communication between different empires. However, this would have meant changes in existing power relations. Senior managers imagined that Hyder was 'a learning company', without recognising learning as an aspect of their own role. Change processes were difficult to sustain because they did not have the support of senior managers and because they potentially might encourage shifts in the balance of power in the company.

Implications for understanding change

Identifying the politics of imagined stability in Hyder showed that any attempt to manage change in the company would necessarily be influenced (consciously and unconsciously) by three key factors. First, an analysis of the *social politics* of imagined stability in Hyder reveals external national, social and economic pressures on the company in the context of 'the new Wales'. The management of change was attached in the minds of managers to the development of Wales. However, this reinforced the difficulties of an already potent split between the core Utilities business in Wales and the growth of Hyder Infrastructure Management globally. One of the managers expressed this as follows:

> Are we a Welsh utilities business or are we a global infrastructure business? Is it really a utility business in Wales that has got other bits tagged onto it, which one can put a spin on, which actually says we are global? I have to pull in two directions. Part of me is trying to make global aspirations work, but I also feel the elastic pulling me the other way.

The management of change in Hyder was undermined because the organization and senior managers were being pulled in two directions at once.

An analysis of the *strategic politics* of imagined stability in Hyder reveals something of the difference between the fantasy Hyder created and the organizational dynamics that were driving management and organization. On one hand the fantasy was of an organization promoting oneness, collegiality, involvement and confidence – on the other hand, patterns of authority and leadership that were disconnected, controlling and cautious. The management of change in Hyder therefore was situated within a set of unacknowledged assumptions that implemented the opposite of what was felt to be desirable. This undermined the implementation of changes that might reveal the idea of One Hyder as fantasy, or shift the emphasis of what One Hyder actually meant in the organization, which was more to do with confusion than collegiality.

> To actually go the whole hog and call it the One Hyder is completely confusing, you can't show the outside world it is One Hyder, and I think it has been confusing them and to some extent it is divisive. Unless you understand the dynamics of the businesses and really buy into those, it won't work because it is going to look very different on each side of the business because the drivers are different and we haven't got anywhere near the maturity to do that.

Understanding imagined stability in Hyder can help members of organizations to identify characteristic power relations that legitimize restrictions on how, what, where, when and why change can be implemented. Change initiatives in Hyder were undermined because senior managers had, despite their apparent enthusiasm, become detached from the desire to contribute to change. As one manager said: 'the long-term strategy looks like indecision'. Indecision was preferable to change because change might involve the loss of individual power and control, as well as shifts in the balance of power relations within the organization. Despite the potential of the learning journey to produce organization development it represented one of many missed opportunities to reflect. Senior managers did not perceive or participate in the learning journey as a corporate opportunity and therefore did not legitimize it.

> If managers really believe in their people as really being the source of the energy that is going to create this business going forward then logically the same common element is that their ongoing development is fundamental to business development, then managers would be, you know, encouraging people in droves into the learning journey. The fact is that managers don't encourage people in droves into the learning journey, managers by and large, a very high proportion of them, don't even do performance and development reviews.

It is useful to summarize my discussion and analysis so far in order to clarify what I think were the politics of imagined stability in Hyder, and how the organization developed ways of working based on mental representations that were not that concrete. The corporate fantasy was constructed through the interaction of three linked ideas: in short, that Hyder was a confident organization, one coherent organization, and an organization that could change. Having discussed some of the individual and collective emotions involved, as well as identifying social and strategic politics and dynamics concerning change, the picture of Hyder that emerges is understandably of a more complex, fragmented and unstable organization. The examples illustrate the importance of the tensions that arise between the fantasy of stability and the internal and external politics involved in maintaining and challenging this stability. The fact that Hyder means 'confidence' in Welsh did not make Hyder a confident organization; the decision to rename the whole organization 'Hyder' did not provide the organization with wholeness or coherence; the decision to implement change did not mean that the desired changes were going to occur.

A key proposition in this chapter is that the management of change involves the identification of the politics of imagined stability that characterize and inform the limitations and possibilities of change in a specific organizational context. The purpose of my interpretations and analysis here is to demonstrate the usefulness of identifying the politics of imagined stability that characterize an organization in order to highlight the tensions that are an integral part of managing change. In Hyder, limitations on the ability to manage change were constructed from the tensions inherent in trying to make change happen in relation to a fantasy of the organization. Senior managers were obliged to carry into their roles contradictory experiences of and desires around change. On one hand they were motivated by the idea of Hyder as a global company, one company, a learning company, and on the other hand by the contradictory experience of the emotions and politics that sustained and undermined this imagined stability. In the concluding section of the chapter I review connections between politics, psychodynamics and change and then highlight the contribution that these interpretations make to knowledge about the management of change.

Concluding thoughts

An analysis of the politics of imagined stability in Hyder provides material for a different agenda for the management of change, one that focuses less on what to do in order to make change happen, and more on what has already been created that mitigates against managing change. To reflect on this (individually and collectively) as a part of organizing provides opportunities to review established politics and understand the emotions that might underpin them. From here, different approaches to change can begin to be imagined, as well as the forms of leadership and expressions of authority that might help with the management of change.

The general understanding of strategic learning I have outlined throughout the previous chapters of this book proposes the inseparability of politics and emotion in any process of organizing. Understanding this relationship involves reflecting on the imagined stability of the organization in the minds of its members. I have asserted that organizations are experienced as if they are stable containers of coherent visions and rational decision-making. I have used the term 'a politics of imagined stability' to describe more or less fixed representations of Hyder plc, which influenced how change was created and contested within that organization. A politics of imagined stability is constructed through the interaction of emotions and politics, creating an institutionalized fantasy or imagined stability that reinforces particular emotional and political responses, as well as associated actions and inaction. Over time this process becomes *establishment*, characterizing and informing the possibilities and limitations for managing change.

The study in Hyder showed that attention to the politics of imagined stability affords opportunities to engage with key organizational dynamics that underpin the management of change. Fear of change is an integral aspect of any attempt to make change happen. Such fear – and the defences created from it – decreases the likelihood of change, since conflicts, differences and power relations are avoided. The avoidance of power relations that inform and create attempts at managing change limits managers' ability to find ways of enacting their authority that are inclusive and open to view. Change is more likely to occur when opportunities are created to review and reflect on the real and imagined power relations that are a part of any attempt to manage change.

It has been estimated that as many as 70% of change initiatives fail (Palmer and Hardy, 2000: 192) and whatever the specific reasons for this, some general points are clear. Managing change is a highly unpredictable, speculative and resource-consuming activity. Successful outcomes are not necessarily planned, but can equally emerge by chance. The management of change is retrospectively justified as well as ignored and avoided. Change, whether it is being promoted or resisted, is often a process replete with emotions and politics. These points suggest that any model for 'managing' change whether it is rational and mechanistic or intuitive and developmental is likely to be as deficient as it is effective. The idea of a politics of imagined stability is not a model for the management of change. However, the idea is effective in identifying key elements in understanding the relationship between managing and change, particularly the various political and emotional dynamics mobilized by attempts to change.

In this chapter I have suggested and explored how aspects of psychodynamic theory may help to access the emotions and politics of managing and organizing that accompany attempts to change. For Hyder plc, in the end, the change that occurred was not the one set out in the Chief Executive's motivational speech. The company did not become a leading player in infrastructure management globally. What is left of Hyder has changed to become a not-for-profit organization, similar in many ways to its original form, Welsh Water. The failure to achieve the changes desired by some of the senior managers in Hyder cannot be explained simply and certainly not solely in terms of the examples and conclusions in this chapter. However, my discussions have provided examples of the political and emotional tensions that are present in and that undermine attempts at change. They have also described how psychodynamic thinking can contribute to an understanding of what the management of change might fully mean and involve.

So far in this book, I have outlined the components of an organizational understanding of strategic learning and HRD, providing examples of how emotions and politics combine to create organizational structures or processes that limit knowledge (both rational and emotional), that reinforce existing organizational politics and that inhibit the organization of learning and change. This reflects my specific interest in the ways in which emotional responses become political, how they help to maintain or challenge existing assumptions or power relations that characterize 'the way we do things here'. A concept that I introduced to help frame this view of strategic learning was the idea that organizing creates an *establishment* constructed from the interaction of emotion and politics, giving rise to characteristic organizational dynamics that limit the potential interaction between learning and organizing. Strategic learning involves the transformation of politics and emotions that are enacted and reinforced through organizational roles. It entails speculation on the unconscious dynamics that guide the internalization of the organization in the minds of its members. Individuals and groups continually manage and organize themselves on the basis of their emotional responses to organizational issues as well as on the basis of avoiding emotion, and both of these have strategic implications. Various examples have been used to explore and develop this argument. Strategic learning also involves the identification of the politics of imagined stability. This describes the role that social and strategic politics play in the perpetuation of emotions and fantasies that have an impact on various actions and inactions associated with organizing. The politics of imagined stability characterizes and informs the possibilities and limitations for organizing learning and change.

Strategic learning, therefore, is orientated towards informing changes in *establishment*, towards reframing the questioning of assumptions as an organizational imperative. Strategic learning places the emphasis on learning through collective experience, on the conscious and unconscious designs that are inevitably created through attempts to learn, and on organizational dynamics that both construct and constrain learning. The practical focus of strategic learning is the development of different ways of undertaking processes and approaches to reflection, a different interpretation of leadership, and the need to rethink ways in which HRD is framed and implemented in the future. These are all the subjects of the remaining chapters of this book.

7 Organizing reflection

I have suggested that an important shift in the study of learning moves it away from a focus on what individuals learn and how this is applied in an organization. I have explained and explored the thinking that underpins a strategic perspective on learning, particularly how politics and emotions interact to create organizing processes that may limit or undermine learning and change. In the final three chapters of the book I shift the focus away from the development of theory or ideas about strategic learning and towards practice, discussing what this means for three key organizing processes, reflection, leadership and intervention/future HRD practice.

In this chapter I discuss an approach to reflection that can assist in rethinking strategic learning. My emphasis is on reflection as an organizing process rather than on the individual, reflective practitioner (Schön, 1983). I am attempting to describe one way of organizing reflection in order to create and sustain opportunities for strategic learning. I suggest that the specific practices that contribute to reflection as an organizing process will be informed by three characteristics. First, such practices should contribute to the collective questioning of assumptions that underpin organizing in order to make power relations visible. Second, reflective practices necessarily provide a 'container' for the management of the anxieties raised by making power relations visible. Third, reflective practices contribute towards democracy in the organization. I continue by describing four reflective practices. These are: peer consultancy groups, role analysis and role analysis groups, action learning, and group relations conferences. I explain and explore each of these and define their impact at different levels of organizing. Collectively, the four reflective practices constitute an approach to reflection that represents one way of organizing for learning and change. I am therefore addressing the question, what are the various reflective practices that might stimulate strategic learning?

I have already outlined the importance of the relationship between politics and emotion to strategic learning. An analysis of the interaction between emotion and politics reveals how employees relate to and construct organizational practices, and therefore makes plain the structural features that tend to locate people in positions of inequality or impotence. This perspective invites 'critical reflection' (Reynolds, 1998) on what managers think they know and how they come to know it within an organizational context. Again, I use examples from Hyder plc to illustrate my thinking. I talk about the understanding and practice of reflection in Hyder, what this meant to members of organizations, and the organizational dynamics that had an impact on reflection. My aim is also to look ahead, and to make suggestions about what reflection can mean and involve for organizations in order to support and to develop strategic learning.

Briefly, to summarize the situation in Hyder, I have shown it to be a company where learning and change were feared as well as desired. The particular interplay between behaviour and structure that constituted Hyder as a company contributed to an idea of learning that was focused on the individual (on the reflective practitioner). Hyder did not suffer from a lack of individual learning but from a lack of organizing processes that could help members of organizations to understand better the entrenched organizational dynamics and established power relations that limited learning. In addition to the organizational dynamics I have already described, the focus on learning as an individual rather than strategic process arose in part from managers' individual perceptions of reflection and the ways in which such perceptions were created and reinforced.

The individual opinions of managers about what reflection involved in practice included: *standing back* from what is happening, *thinking back* about what has been done, and *examining personal thinking and/or performance*. The emphasis was on evaluating something past, rather than on reflection as an active process within the present ('reflection-in-action' – Schön, 1983). In addition, the imperative in Hyder for rapid and large-scale commercial development put managers under considerable pressure to deliver growth. While in theory the usefulness of reflective practices is high at such a time, in practice the anxiety that was generated by the need for commercial development meant that such practices were easily ignored and abandoned. For example, the opinion of one director was as follows:

> You find yourself in a scenario where it is all happening around you and you have a problem that you have got to solve and you are so bloody happy to accept the first logical explanation that comes into your mind that of course you apply it, if it works then it is fine, then you get on and face the next thing you have to do. It is just not part of the culture that says, you take time out now and examine and understand how we did it and could it have been done better.

Reflection in Hyder was understood and practised as an individual responsibility, something that the manager does, when they have the time, in order to solve or think back about a problem or issue, and the way they dealt with it. Such practices were produced through broader organizational dynamics where anxieties about growth and change were also constructed as an individual responsibility. It was the individual's success in growing the company that was rewarded or criticized, and this was a considerable burden for the individual to manage. Of course, individuals in all organizations do manage such expectations with varying degrees of stress and overwork. The consequence in Hyder was that managers were 'happy to accept the first logical explanation'. What the organization lost as a result of such dynamics was the ability to create organizing processes of reflection that could contribute to a shift from the individual to an organizational responsibility for growth, placing limitations both on the ability to grow and on the potential to learn. Breaking free of such limitations involves the development of a capacity for reflection at an organizational level of analysis.

From the reflective individual to organizing reflection

Experience in a variety of different organizations has shown me that Hyder was not alone in understanding the practice of reflection as primarily the function of individuals. Theoretical understanding within management learning supports this experience. Reynolds (1998: 186) has pointed out that the meaning of reflection 'has been limited by the individualized perspective which the theory promotes' and that reflection is seen 'primarily as a key element of problem solving', rather than as an organizing process. Reynolds (1998, 1999a, b), building on the work of theorists in adult education and critical management studies, adds the word 'critical' to reflection, and thereby describes a particular understanding of what reflection involves beyond both 'the individual' and 'the problem'. Critical reflection has the following characteristics (see Reynolds, 1998, 1999b):

- It is concerned with questioning assumptions.
- Its focus is the social rather than the individual.
- It pays particular attention to the analysis of power relations.
- It is concerned with democracy.

This frame forms the basis of my understanding of reflection as an organizing process and underpins the combination of reflective practices I summarize below. However, before moving into outlining the reflective practices I am proposing, I want to add some further thoughts about reflection.

Some thoughts on reflection

I came across the following quote in the business magazine *Fortune*, from two of the key exponents of business re-engineering. 'Although successful organizations fail in many different ways, all these failures share one underlying cause: a failure to reflect' (Hammer and Stanton, 1997: 291). The various prescriptions the authors offered to address such failure were dependent on a notion they called 'assumption breaking':

> Assumption breaking is the most arduous of all the steps in the reflection process, because identifying and questioning assumptions goes against the organizational grain.
>
> (Hammer and Stanton, 1997: 296)

The authors mainly locate assumption breaking as something that happens to individuals within an organization. However, whatever the practical difficulties of questioning collective assumptions, their paper also represents the fact that questioning assumptions has become part of a mainstream discourse about organizing and how to do it successfully. Of course, like all prescriptive messages (including the ones either hiding or on view in this book), it makes the process of assumption busting sound a lot easier than it actually is. Assumptions are the result of complex webs of relations and actions, built both quickly and gradually, and they represent what is entrenched about an organization's behaviour and structure, its *establishment*. As I said in the first chapter of this book, assumptions work both to constrain and to limit as well as to promote possibilities for action. An assumption that was institutionalized within Hyder, for example, was that it was unwise to fail. Managers therefore minimized risks and became very sensitive to expectations:

> Certainly I believe there are high expectations of me, and I have high expectations of myself to deliver it, but I have never actually tested that out and said, what happens if I don't? What happens if I demonstrate that I can't always be in control, that I can't always demonstrate that I am always right?
>
> (Hyder manager)

Such views have an impact on reflection by promoting defensiveness and self-justification in place of open decision-making and the questioning of assumptions. The questioning of assumptions does not just 'go against the organizational grain' it is a challenge to the rationality and stability that underpins organizing. Questioning assumptions therefore is more usefully conceptualized *as a part of how organizing is achieved* rather than a responsibility of aware or skilful individuals. In terms of reflection this implies a search for practices that contribute to the questioning of the strategic politics that underpin organizing. My view therefore is that the questioning of assumptions is a practice that needs to be thought of as integral to organizing rather than the province of individuals.

An acceptance that reflection is not primarily an individual process, but a collective capacity to question assumptions means that it implies an ongoing inquiry into the nature and consequences of strategic politics within organizations. Reflection (as collective action) is a key component in the politics of strategic learning, involving collective engagement with the ways in which thought and knowledge are being constructed (Kemmis, 1985). Through reflection, 'the unfolding relations of the group are seen as a microcosm of society, providing the means of understanding wider social and political processes' (Reynolds, 1998: 193). In practice, such a view promotes considerable anxiety for groups of managers and within the organization as a whole, where there is little preparation for the repercussions that can spill out from reflective practices (Marsick and O'Neil, 1999). Organizing reflection therefore involves helping to build experience of managing the anxieties that learning and change inevitably throw up (Obholzer, 1999).

A further danger with an individual focus on reflection is that it promotes detachment from both organizational politics (collective action) and the politics of organizing (the promotion or limitation of democracy). One reason why organizations are individualistically orientated is that it is easier to contain power relations from this position. Collective voice and movement is less amenable to control and can more easily undermine established organizational power relations. There is no conspiracy implied here, rather an acknowledge-ment that organizing takes place in the context of continuous tension between struggles for control and struggles for democracy. The push for control is driven by the idea that to make decisions individually is easier, particularly in terms of time and accountability. Added to this, modern organizations encourage participative approaches (like self-managed teams), as well as diversity and empowerment initiatives. In addition to the value that participative projects can add to organizational democracy, they are inevitably also processes of compliance to organizational norms. 'They communicate the limitations of organizational democracy at the same time as they encourage developments in it' (Vince, 2000: 40).

In order to inform strategic learning reflective practices will need to be informed by three interconnected strands. First, any reflective practices should contribute to the collective questioning of assumptions that underpin organ-izing, revealing the power relations that inform organizing, making them visible and therefore available for transformation. Second, making power relations visible gives rise to individual and collective anxiety, which promotes defensiveness and resistance to change (as well as providing the impetus for learning and change). Reflective practices need to offer opportunities for building experience and familiarity in containing anxiety. However, these need to have a social rather than individual focus. This then leads to my final point, which is that reflective practices need to contribute towards struggles for democracy, and that this is more likely to occur when they are perceived relationally rather than individually.

Reflective practices of organizing

How is it possible to organize reflection and what are the reflective practices that might underpin strategic learning? I try to answer these questions by linking various reflective practices of organizing with different levels of organizational analysis. In Table 7.1 I have outlined four specific approaches to reflective practice and looked at their impact on three different levels of organizational analysis in order to produce a matrix that describes one way of organizing reflection. In the section that follows I explain the parts of the matrix in more detail.

Table 7.1 Organizing reflection: examples of reflective practices for organizational learning and change

	Individual	Group	Organizational
Peer consultancy groups	Making connections for the self: review and reflection underpinned by friendship or mutuality.	Making connections with others: utilizing the impact of small groups as sites for interpersonal communication and dialogue.	Making connections with the organization: reflection on the ways in which the organization has been internalized.
Organizational Role Analysis	Organizational Role Analysis: understanding the connections between the person, the person in role, and the organization-in-the-mind.	Role Analysis Groups: the ways in which roles and understanding of roles interweave with the organizational dynamics enacted in a group.	Role is the medium through which person and organization meet.
Action learning	Involvement in learning with others: learning through focus on work-based project or problem.	Engagement between learning sets: 'the structure that reflects'.	Opportunities for connection to the whole organization: 'the structure that connects'.
Group Relations conferences	Experiencing and rethinking authority, and the consequences of leadership and followership.	Experience of defensive mechanisms, avoidance strategies, projective identification. Experience of organizing into sub-systems, belonging, representing, looking across boundaries.	Experiencing the ways in which institution becomes established through collective emotional experience, politics, leadership, authority and transformation.
	Relations between the person, the role and the organization-in-the-mind.	Relations across the boundaries of self/other and of sub-systems.	The relations between the internal and external establishment.

Reflective practices

1. Peer consultancy groups

Peer consultancy groups are non-managerial, self-governing groups of three managers or staff members. The thinking behind these groups has similarities to action learning in the sense that members share in the analysis and development of real work issues. Peer consultancy groups have a specific methodology involving one group member in presenting an issue, one consulting to this issue and one observing the process of consultation. The approach is often a powerful one for individuals, especially where the distinctive tasks associated with the different roles are rigidly adhered to.

However, it is the organizational impact that is of concern here. The value of such groups is twofold. First, they establish the legitimacy of reflection that is underpinned by relational patterns of friendship and mutuality. They create sites for interpersonal alliances, spaces in the organization where it is possible to say the things that organizational politics makes unsafe. It is important to have spaces *in* the organization (as opposed to down the pub, with my mates or in the therapy room), to have a legitimate organizational space where it is possible to speak the truth about experience. Second, the role of a third person, an observer of the process, adds an organizational dimension. The focus of observation is not so much the content of the interaction, but the process that informs it. There is a broader meaning to be had from such dialogue if the participants in peer consultancy groups can ask how the (spoken and unspoken) dialogue *reflects* the organization. In other words, what are the characteristic organizational patterns and issues that are being enacted and reflected in the dialogues between individual members of the organization? Such questioning leads towards an understanding of the 'organization-in-the-mind' (Shapiro and Carr, 1991; Bazelgette, Hutton and Reed, 1997).

Managers are often surprised by the additional insights that are generated by the peer consultant (intentionally or unintentionally). Her or his role is essentially to observe the interaction between two people, one of whom is listening and consulting to the other – to watch the interaction for clues about the *organization* that surrounds the pair. The peer consultant does not require any particular training or skill for this role since distinctive organizational characteristics infuse most interactions between members, and when one starts to look for them, these organizational dynamics often appear to be obvious. Communication of what is observed, however, may involve some tact or sensitivity. Peer consultancy groups are particularly good reflective practices for developing an appreciation of the organizing processes that accompany everyday experience in organizations, for revealing the ways in which behaviour and structures are linked, as well as how they might limit action or make it possible.

2. *Organizational Role Analysis and Role Analysis groups*

Organizational Role Analysis (Reed, 1976) is a method for in-depth, one to one reflection. The emphasis of this method is to encourage the individual to make links between themself as a person, the organizational role she or he occupies, and the organization both imagined and real. The process is designed to help individuals to reflect on the transformation of the organization within which her or his role is embedded. The focus, therefore, is not reflection on what an individual might feel, experience or encounter in their role, but on imagining how the organization might have to be transformed in order that a role can be transformed. In analysing this, the individual may not only have to consider the relations between their formal role within an organization. The situation is made more complex by informal roles that an individual might adopt as a result of their experience, as well as past roles that may be consciously or unconsciously mobilized. Role Analysis groups (Triest, 1999) have a similar emphasis on the interrelations between person, role and organization, but their focus is also on the dynamics that are constructed within the group and how these confirm or challenge distinctive organizational patterns.

Both of these situations are aimed at encouraging reflection and understanding of the organization-in-the-mind.

> [An organization] is composed of the diverse fantasies and projections of its members. Everyone who is aware of an organization, whether a member of it or not, has a mental image of how it works. Though these diverse ideas are not often consciously negotiated or agreed upon among participants, they exist. In this sense, all institutions exist in the mind, and it is in interaction with these in-the-mind entities that we live. Of course, all organizations also consist of certain real factors, such as other people, profits, buildings, resources and products. But the meaning of these factors derives from the context established by the institution-in-the-mind. These mental images are not static; they are the products of dynamic interchanges, chiefly projections and transferences.
>
> (Shapiro and Carr, 1991: 69–70)

Reflection on the transformation of the organization-in-the-mind implies engagement with more than the rational problems that organizing creates. It implies attempts at understanding what is emotional, relational and political about organizing. One of the ways in which organizational assumptions can be challenged is through reflection on the unconscious at work (Obholzer and Roberts, 1994; Neumann and Hirschhorn, 1999), and the impact that individual and collective emotional experience has on the enactment of roles. We have already seen, for example, in Chapter 4, how emotional experience (in this case caution and blame) impacts on organizing, how such emotions contribute to the creation of organizational processes that inhibit reflection and minimize communication. The importance of reflective practices that encourage identification of the organization-in-the-mind is that this analytical device helps to reveal how organizational roles are consciously and unconsciously connected to organizing assumptions, and how these assumptions are then put into practice.

3. Action learning

Action learning has proved to be an extraordinarily persistent and useful approach to learning in organizations, and over the fifty years of its development by Reg Revans, it has become a worldwide process promoting reflection and action. The idea that underpins much action learning is that it can provide the means through which the individual finds ways to learn 'about oneself by resolving a work-focused project, and reflecting on that action – and on oneself – in the company of others similarly engaged' (Weinstein, 2002: 6). In addition, action learning has been developed as a 'business-driven' process that can make a contribution to business success (Boshyk, 2000) at the same time as ensuring that 'organizational and individual learning is always *greater* than the rate of change' (Boshyk, 2002: 39). There is some recognition of the politics of organizing in this approach, which presents an important distinction between action learning as tactics and action learning as strategy. However, such shifts still focus on individuals, OD or HR professionals, who are 'not averse to risk-taking because they realize that implementing business-driven action learning is a far more challenging and demanding initiative than the usual . . . route for executive education' (Boshyk, 2002: 40). The risk-taking of the 'HRD professional' is located within the political support of other key players, particularly senior managers, and especially the Chief Executive. Whether the focus is on the development of individuals in their role, or the development initiatives of individuals with an HRD/OD role, or the senior individuals who are meant to legitimize learning initiatives, the focal point is on the behaviour of significant individuals, not on the politics that shape their experience in a role.

Reflecting back on his work with organizations, Edgar Schein remarked that 'the hardest part of learning to work with organizations was to see beyond individual dynamics into group and systemic dynamics' (Schein, 2000: 18). Recently, there have been attempts to extend and develop the practice of action learning so that it goes beyond a focus on individual members of the organization, and engages with the issues of power and politics that any attempt at learning and change inevitably mobilizes. There have been several voices raised in critique of the individualistic focus of action learning (Willmott, 1994; Pedler, 1997, 2002) that 'limits the growth of collective understanding and competence in organizations' (Pedler, 1997: 251). The broader political issue here is that it is actually very difficult in organizations for middle and senior managers (individually or collectively) to shift organizational assumptions. As Pedler (2002), in his reflections on action learning and organizational learning in Walsall Borough Council points out, something different is needed for organizational learning to take place. Action learning can generate important 'intelligence' for strategic managers and support and enable 'voice' from other staff, but it is addressing the emotions and politics within a specific context that makes the difference to shifts in assumptions. In Walsall, for example, learning occurred not 'as a matter of course nor was it achieved without effort. Courage and persistence, humility and commitment were needed.' The political problem was in 'finding a leadership prepared to be visible and take part in the public learning intended by these processes' (both quotes from Pedler, 2002: 534). There is much that remains to be said about how action learning (as a process of organizing) reveals and mirrors organizational dynamics, as well as the part that the approach might be able to play in questioning established assumptions and transforming the political processes associated with assumptions (Vince, 2004).

Action learning has an important role to play in changing repeated patterns of organizing, if the approach includes reflection and action on the organizational dynamics that are acted out in the set. The clues to this are in the emotions and politics that inform and result from action. To better comprehend the relationship between action learning and organizational learning does not require a new approach. It is only necessary to shift the focus from the actions of individuals towards the broader dynamics of organizing.

A recent paper integrating action learning and critical reflection has further developed organizational reflection practices, in this instance within a UK health authority (Nicolini et al., forthcoming). The authors investigate the extent to which reflection can be a stable and self-sustaining feature of organizing, exploring what a 'reflecting organization' might involve and how it becomes established. They also focus on a particular problem, of addressing 'the power conditions that would allow the result of reflection to be implemented to produce organizational effects'. To do this they link action learning and whole-system change conferences. Their intervention project, based on action learning sets for middle managers, emphasized two levels on which organizing reflection needs to be addressed. First, in addition to setting up Reflection Action Learning Sets (RALS) for managers to reflect on ongoing changes in their organizations, they also built in the ability to mobilize dialogue between sets. They call this interaction between sets 'a structure that reflects'. Such a structure is aimed at helping changes to take root in the organization by encouraging RALS to focus collectively on questions including, how can we work together and how can we make a difference? Second, this organizing structure of reflection provided the basis from which to create a space for suitable forms of engagement with key decision-makers within three large change conferences. They refer to this as 'a structure that connects'.

To summarize and emphasize this, the space in which dialogue between RALS occurred constituted *a structure that reflects* (collective engagement between sets), and also provided a space where reflective practices could be linked to power conditions that might support the implementation of the results of reflection – *a structure that connects*. The study highlights some interesting and important dynamics and conclusions. It develops a model of reflection that emphasizes learning from real-life issues, but also one that is situated overtly in the context of real-life power relations. First, the authors acknowledge the shift in organizational dynamics that is integral to bringing RALS together into a structure that reflects:

> A set of Sets cannot reproduce the same mechanisms that glue small Sets together because large groups behave and perform in very different ways. They are much less efficient as 'holding environments' . . . and are, in fact, anxiety-producing situations. Participants will have to be convinced to turn their primary attention, responsibility and caring concerns away from their initial focus, themselves and their 'comrades in adversity' in the Sets, and redirect them outwards to their organizations.

Second, the attempt to move from 'a structure that reflects' towards 'a structure that connects' was inhibited by the fact that most of the 'key decision-makers' did not turn up to the second large change conference.

> The overall failure of key decision-makers to show up was a powerful demotivator. The signal they sent was a painful reminder of the difficulties and high level of resources necessary to accomplish anything in the organization. The lesson of the key decision-makers' non-attendance was a harsh reality check.

Third, critique of their own intervention generated an insight that added to the potency of their approach. Their intervention was built on an assumption that other members of organizations, not directly involved in RALS, were also part of a learning experience. They interpreted the non-attendance of key decision-makers as a problem of their own making, and came to the conclusion that all participants should have endorsed the reflective practices used in the RALS from the beginning.

> Herein, lies a powerful practical lesson. Designing organizational reflection activities and promoting them in such a way that exempts the sponsors from being part of the reflective practices, deprives them of the experience of learning, and exposes a paradox of reflection being promoted at one level and denied at another. Inevitably, this will have practical repercussions and will be played out by the participants as they pick up and enact this inner contradiction.

This is both a distinctive and a welcome study. Not only does it extend reflection beyond the usual confines of a reflective group into collective reflection and attempt to link collective reflection with emotion and power and the organizational dynamics they created, but it also shows how an intervention to create collective reflection colluded with organizational assumptions about learning that inhibited organizational reflective practices.

As this example suggests, in the further development of action learning it will be useful to shift attention from questioning the impact of action learning on the organization towards asking additionally what is the impact of organization on action learning? Action learning is a developmental tool for a different type of reflection – not just the considered reflection of individuals, but also for 'social reflection-in-action'. Reflection that has a focus on organizing is undertaken in order to appreciate and to criticize the institutional dynamics that both make learning possible and restrict learning. This is not an abstract concept since it finds daily expression in the ways in which authority and leadership, strategy and decision-making are expressed and enacted. As such it is linked to questions of performance and practice.

I want to clarify what I have been saying about the ways in which politics, emotion, learning and organizing interact in the context of action learning by adding an additional component to the original formula ($L = P + Q$, where L is learning, P is programme knowledge and Q is questioning insight). If action learning is a developmental process that can have an impact on organizing as well as on experience then this needs to be reflected in the thinking or the model that underpins action. Learning, therefore, is a combination of pro-grammed knowledge, questioning insight *and* organizing insight ($L = P + Q + O$). Organizing insight is added in order to suggest that action learning is not only a learning process through which to comprehend individuals' experiences of action (learning from experience), but is also a reflection of existing organizational dynamics created in action (learning from organizing).

Asking the question – what is the impact of organization on action learning? – implies a willingness to try to understand how established assumptions constrain and contain action. The focus here is not on how individuals' behavi-our or options for action are themselves contained by assumptions, rather it is on what organizing has been and is being done to create and recreate the container that maintains and fosters particular assumptions. Action learning has the potential to transform organizing assumptions as well as being restricted by them. Organizing insight is a necessary aspect of the formula for action learning if organizational learning is seen as a reason for using the approach or as a desired outcome. Organizing insight becomes possible when there is an examination of the politics that surround and inform organizing. In addition, to comprehend these politics it is often necessary to question the emotions that drive political choices and decisions, both consciously and unconsciously.

Let me situate these thoughts in practice. At present there is an increased impetus in organizations towards informal learning, particularly the learning that is generated through projects and project teams. This is one reason why action learning continues to gain in popularity – it is an approach that is often project-based or business-driven. In other words, action learning is focused on real organizational demands and issues for delivery both of service and of growth. The approach is pragmatic – it is based on getting things done (action and reflection on action), rather than on organizational learning and change (social reflection-in-action). Getting things done is a different agenda from learning, learning is a possible by-product of projects but it is not the main issue or reason for action. Strategic learning therefore requires more than a focus on projects, it requires a focus on the politics and emotions that drive *projective* relations between people within and outside of projects as well as the unconscious and conscious designs and structures that emerge from such relations.

To illustrate this I will suggest one possible learning cycle relating to the generation of organizing insight. This is consistent with what I have been arguing about the nature of strategic learning – that it can be approached from inquiry into the emotions and politics driving the possibilities and limitations of learning, rather than as the impact of individuals' learning in practice. I use the same visual representation I used in Figure 4.2. Unlike that figure, which comes from the study in Fairness BC, Figure 7.1 is a speculative image or working hypothesis, not a model that has been developed from action research.

In this cycle (Figure 7.1), project-focused action learning has given rise to collective knowledge about the project itself and the politics and emotions generated or mobilized through action. The collective focus on a specific business project produces knowledge that is situated within the group. No other grouping has this knowledge in quite this way, which gives the group a particular type of provisional authority (the authority that comes from in-depth experience and inquiry). The fact that a group has engaged with a project has made its members authorities on the particular project, and also on the organizational relations (for convenience I call these *projections*) that may be mobilized around the project, whether they are aware of these or not. If, for example, this is a project that the senior managers see as a high priority, then the group members are likely to be aware of this even if such expectations have not been made explicit. This potency of the knowledge that makes up this situated authority can be lost because the group members are afraid to communicate what they have learned outside of their own group boundaries. They may even think that their knowledge is irrelevant or unimportant. However, in this example we can assume that they are willing to reflect 'out-loud' in the

Situated
authority

Action-based work generates knowledge
of projects and projections.

Organizing
insight

'Learning from organizing' as
well as learning from experience.

Public
reflection

Reflection is 'out loud' within the
organizational and political domain.

Collective
engagement

Moving beyond competition between different
groups to embed knowledge in other parts of
the organization.

Figure 7.1 Organizing insight (from Vince, 2004).

organization, through presentations of their knowledge and its implications. Of course, such presentations can easily mobilize competition and envy between different groups and sub-systems, thereby creating defences against the impact of project knowledge on other parts of the organization. Assume again that any such differences are worked through so that the knowledge emerging from the project has an impact on what is known and done elsewhere in the organization. It is not just the experience of the project group that has developed insight in and about the organization. This insight also comes from the broader decision or willingness to reflect in public on knowledge and to work through differences that inevitably emerge from other parts of the organization that have dissimilar perspectives and agendas.

There are many barriers to learning that could undermine the different types of knowledge that are generated through action and thereby weaken organizing insight. Discussion of the politics and emotions that surround projects may be seen as irrelevant or illegitimate by those in positions of power; the most controversial aspects of knowledge may be watered down or hidden to try to protect against conflict; it might seem like too high a risk to reflect publicly on organizational dynamics. In using the term 'organizing insight' and attaching it to action learning I am seeking to illustrate how action learning and strategic learning are potentially connected. Action learning in theory and in practice can reveal the complex relationship between organizing and learning, producing knowledge that informs business-driven issues of service or growth as well as information on the emotions and politics that give rise to specific organizational designs, habits and assumptions.

Action learning is a collective, situated (contextually specific) process that assists inquiry into actual and current organizational projects and projections. (I am using the word *projections* here to refer to general fantasies of imagined stability as well as unwanted aspects of experience that are defended against by making them belong to others.) Action learning therefore can provide an experiential framework within which to undertake and to reflect on projects, as well as the means to understanding organizational dynamics – particularly the fantasy, emotion, relations and politics that are mobilized through attempts to manage and to organize. Action learning contributes both to project-based (applied) learning and to the potential transformation of organizing practices (for example, whether and how processes of reflection are created, or understanding how to lead). In practice, the 'guiding idea' behind action learning is that it is focused both on real organizational projects (both short and long term) and imagined organizational projections. Projects and projections (reality and fantasy) are partners in the construction and reconstruction of organization. Fantasy is as much the output of organizing as profit or service. It is created through action and through the interaction of collective imagination and organization over time. As I have already said, an organization is a product of collective imagination, built as much on the strength of its own illusions of stability as on procedures that underpin established ways of working. Action learning – as an organizing process – is a container for emotions (unconscious and conscious), and for power relations that reveal assumptions underpinning organization and that influence the possibilities of and resistances to learning and change. This informs and links therefore to the application of action learning. In practice, action learning can be an inquiry process into strategic learning. That is: if sets work on projects that have a widely agreed organizational currency and legitimacy; if social reflection-in-action is mobilized in addition to individuals' reflective practices; and if set members can creatively reflect and act on the emotions and politics that are mobilized through experiences of organizing projects.

4. Group Relations conferences

One method that offers opportunities for individual learners to think about and to experience how organizational designs are generated by collective learning is the Group Relations approach (see Coleman and Geller, 1985; Miller, 1990; French and Vince, 1999). The approach was pioneered at the Tavistock Institute of Human Relations in London and has since been developed in many countries. Group Relations, or Institutional Transformation as it is called in some countries (see Gutmann, 2003), is an experiential learning method that reveals the complexities of emotions, interactions and politics that are integral to processes of organizing. Participants in Group Relations/Institutional Transformation conferences or workshops have the opportunity to engage with what is happening to them within the various conference events and how these relate to the organization that the participants are collectively creating around themselves. The general themes of such events are authority, leadership, political relatedness and transformation.

Group Relations conferences provide opportunities for reflection on organizational dynamics and their impact on individuals and groups. For individuals, they offer the possibility for review of how individuals and groups express authority and enact different roles, as well as experiencing the consequences of both leadership and followership. They offer opportunities for reflection on relational experience, inevitably surfacing individual and collective defensive mechanisms, avoidance strategies, and projective identification. They offer chances to explore organizing into sub-systems, the experience of belonging or not belonging, what it means to represent a group, and the issues that occur across the boundaries of sub-systems. More generally they provide opportunities for reflection and insight on the ways in which an institution becomes established through collective emotional experience, politics, patterns of leadership, authority and transformation.

Group Relations events, therefore, are designed to emphasize the exploration of learning within a collective context. 'It is the group that is the focus, not the personality characteristics of the people present' (Lawrence, 2000). Generally speaking, this would be an unusual starting point for those people within organizations who are responsible for development. The utilization of Group Relations as a method for development implies not only an interest in the ability of members of organizations to engage in learning from experience, but also a commitment to understanding the emotional and political contexts within which the (individual and collective) experience of learning is contained and constructed. The emotions and politics that are created in collectives as they evolve over time are necessarily the starting point for developing actions orientated towards strategic learning.

When people meet in such events, emotions, fantasies, histories and politics immediately have an effect on both behaviour and structure. These effects contribute to the creation of the 'organization' that conference members find themselves in, and to the subsequent difficulties that they have in changing the behaviours and structures that they have consciously and unconsciously created. A Group Relations event is a collective process of learning from organizing. The extent to which individuals can reflect, act and learn is important, but this is not undertaken in isolation from comprehension of the system and subsystems that are being collectively imagined and implemented. An individual involved in Group Relations might improve his or her ability as a 'reflective practitioner'; however, Group Relations events are concerned with social reflection-in-action and with understanding both the conscious and unconscious processes that impact on organizing. The educational value of the method is that it offers opportunities to experience and review how an institution is created and sustained. Within inter-system and institutional events participants can simultaneously explore both collective organizing and the consequences of individual or shared attempts to manage. The importance of the method is that it affords reflection on the relationship between learning and organizing at an individual, collective and organizational level. Group Relations conferences are designed to provide an environment within which to inquire into individual and collective emotional experience, to think about the power relations that are being collectively created, and the politics that are constructed through organizing, and to explore ways in which such relations can be transformed.

This approach provides safe (if somewhat confusing) environments for people to learn about the institutionalizing effects of behaviour and interaction outside of the organization to which they belong. Such events have also been transferred into specific organizational contexts (Gutmann, Ternier-David and Verrier, 1999) but it is not always easy or politic to set up educational processes that engage so directly with emotions and politics within an organization. The methodology can be employed alongside other, more usual, approaches, for example within an MBA (see Daunton et al., 2000) and assist in a more gradual transformation of the relationship between role and organization.

Levels of organizational analysis

All of these reflective practices have an impact on organizing at different levels of organizational analysis. They contribute to an understanding of individuals in the organization, groups (sub-systems) within the organization, and the organization as a whole.

At the level of the individual in the organization, the aim of reflection is to explore and understand the person in a role, and the organization-in-the-mind that governs the expression of that role. The focus on role offers opportunities for managers to comprehend the ways in which their authority is constructed and constrained within an organization. A role provides the framework in which person and organization meet, 'thus, although interpretation of personal experience affirms the uniqueness of the individual, placing that experience in the context of a role affirms the connection to the organization' (Shapiro and Carr, 1991: 77). It is unlikely that reflection on individual experience in itself will produce learning and change. Only when reflection is undertaken on the basis of connecting the person, his or her role and the organization-in-the-mind does it seem likely to call assumptions or power relations into question.

At the level of the group or sub-system, the aim of reflection is to explore and understand relations across the boundaries of self and other, and across the boundaries of sub-systems. The focus is on the political process of belonging and representing, on struggles with democracy, and the difficulties involved in moving across the boundaries of different organizational groups. This offers opportunities for managers to experience political action created out of mutual engagement or disengagement, through partnership and competition, and across organizational networks or 'empires'. Reflection on sub-system dynamics is usually done within separate sub-systems. More collective, inter-group processes of reflection are more likely to provide experience of the sub-system dynamics that undermine communication across different parts of an organization.

At the level of the whole organization, the aim of reflection is to explore and understand relations between the internal and external establishment. This refers to the organizational dynamics created through individual and collective emotional experiences and power relations. The focus is on the institutional-ization process, the way in which an organization becomes established. At this level the function of reflection is to offer opportunities for managers to examine conscious and unconscious emotional and political processes that inform organizing and that come to characterize the organization. Processes for reflection on the whole organization are rare, yet they provide an important source of information for the strategic direction of an organization and for recognising the need to loosen the assumptions behind established organizing processes.

Further discussion and conclusions

So far I have constructed a definition of the nature of reflection as an organizing process in an attempt to outline what is involved in the practice of reflection for strategic learning. I have argued that organizing reflection involves question-ing established assumptions, bringing power relations into view, contributing to a shift from individual to collective reflection, and helping to create more democratic modes of managing and organizing. I have suggested four, inter-linked activities (reflective practices) that can promote strategic learning.

Taking these reflective practices, which emerged from a critique of their approach to reflection, and trying to implement them in Hyder, was a challenge for and to the organization (a challenge that the takeover cut short). The absence of a critical form of reflection, over time, led to entrenched organizational dynamics and established power relations, which became normal aspects of organizing. To summarize these briefly, senior managers espoused collegiality but were very controlling in practice. Power was focused on the individual manager, not collective management. The emphasis on individual responsibility, accountability and development undermined and limited forms of collective authority. There were considerable expectations on individuals, and this reinforced controlling approaches to management. In this climate, managers tended to create separate empires within the company (to protect themselves), leading to poor or non-existent communication across the boundaries of sub-systems, which undermined corporate strategic thinking and action. The discourse of reflection as 'examining personal thinking' emerged directly from these organizational dynamics.

In addition, reflection is not always seen as something that is politically desirable. For example:

> If the objectives have been set, you don't want people to question them too much. The reflection embodied in that may be time badly spent because it's diverting you from what you have been told to do.
>
> (Chief Executive, Fairness Borough Council)

Senior managers are often aware that reflection can be a detrimental process as well as a productive one. Reflection that is wider than individual reflection is likely to undermine the efforts that have been put into communicating a consistent vision or direction. Certainly, interventions that aim to challenge assumptions are likely to bring about unwanted as well as desired consequences. These are not easy choices for overstretched managers. However, my view is that there are advantages to collective reflection, as an important additional process of knowledge generation, that have been too readily avoided or ignored.

The intent behind my critique of individualized forms of reflection is to propose an approach that challenges established assumptions, brings social power relations into view and promotes democracy and learning. However, in practice, it is equally possible that any approach can be utilized to serve or reinforce assumptions and power relations, and to limit democracy and learning. Inevitably, managers will find it easier to associate with the reflective practices I have suggested in terms of their individual value, and to construe them more as individual 'learning' opportunities than organizational interventions. The challenge here is to encourage members of organizations to find ways of continually rethinking authority, promoting interaction across company boundaries as well as collective reflection on existing power relations, in order to reveal the establishment that is behind the company's ways of organizing.

I would suggest that internal Group Relations events are particularly useful in this respect.

There is a powerful pull in organizations towards retrospective reflection and this is often reinforced by the view that there are actually very few opportunities to practise reflection as an integral aspect of everyday management (reflection-in-action). This position is fuelled by pragmatic concerns: high levels of anxiety and uncertainty within organizations concerning the future, job losses, poor management, commercial growth, being taken over, covering debts. It is genuinely difficult for managers to feel free to 'slow down the pace of action' (Ixer, 1999), when they are working somewhat frantically in order to survive. However, the challenge is for managers to start to see this as a reflection of the organization, rather than a constraint on the organization of reflection. Primarily, it is not the individual, the reflective practitioner, who is responsible for reflecting on his or her own performance. The organizational dynamics that inhibit strategic learning are transformed not through individual reflection but through reflective processes and practices, built into the organizational framework that underpins how decisions are made, how leadership is enacted, and how change is sustained and promoted. A focus on individual reflection causes managers to be detached from involvement in the strategic thinking that influences decision-making in the organization.

The four reflective practices I suggest constitute an organization level approach to strategic learning. The emphasis is on trying to increase collective reflection and engagement across the boundaries of sub-systems, and on increasing opportunities for management in organizations like Hyder to be underpinned by the collegiality that is espoused. Peer consultancy groups provide a basis for reflecting on the ways in which the controlling organization has been internalized, and sites of conversation on how a more collegial organization might be enacted. Role Analysis adds depth to managers' understanding of how the organization shapes and constrains their role, as well as providing a base from which to think about transforming the organization within which their role is embedded. Action learning can encourage reflective action and communication across the divides created by existing power relations, providing both 'a structure that reflects' and 'a structure that connects' (Nicolini et al., forthcoming). Group Relations conferences constitute a comprehensive reflection on the processes that underpin organizing. Within such conferences managers' attempts to organize differently inevitably lead to the recreation of the same designs, structures and behaviours that characterize their organization. Reflection on this opens up assumptions and power relations to the possibility of change.

I want to illustrate what I have been saying by introducing a fictional company that represents an ideal approach to organizing reflection. I call this company *ReflectWell plc*, in order to demonstrate what an organizational approach to reflection might look like. The focal point of organizational processes for reflection in ReflectWell is attempts to identify and to question established assumptions; they have re-framed the questioning of assumptions as an organizational imperative rather than a responsibility of aware or skilful individuals. Managers support this in practice by looking at whether their usual responses to situations (both individual and collective) are likely to be appropriate to the task or project they are working on. An integral aspect of doing project-based work in ReflectWell plc is that it might produce knowledge that is important outside of a specific project and relate to new insights or ways of working within the organization as a whole. Managers have learned to acknowledge the extent to which their role is to inquire into innovative possibilities for doing things differently at the same time as ensuring that tasks and projects are done effectively.

ReflectWell's approach to reflection has already made a contribution to a revised understanding of the nature of managerial authority. In Reflect Well, managers' authority is based on their ability to lead and make decisions in public. Authority therefore is in the act of creating processes of inquiry involving other stakeholders. In ReflectWell, managers' role is not about having responsibility for making decisions, but about creating shared responsibility for decision-making. Management is not an individual skill but an organizing process, one that involves making the thinking and politics behind decisions public, as well as involving others in processes of reflection on and about decisions. This in turn has contributed to a shift in understanding of the role of manager.

ReflectWell managers now have an organizational environment within which strategic learning is possible. Participation and involvement have become an integral part of the way in which management is thought about and undertaken. As a result, managers have a new idea of leadership, which involves the creation of critical processes of reflection, exploration and inquiry. The resentments that were previously created through entrenched politics, ways of behaving and habitual responses have become the starting point of attempts to learn and change, not the consequence of them. ReflectWell managers' approaches to learning and change are now based on how the organization is reflected and enacted within their own practice, and what this means in terms of transforming the particular organizational context that surrounds them. Managers have learned that the current power structures that characterize an organization are an integral part of their own thinking and ways of working. At the very centre of the understanding that has evolved in ReflectWell, has been the conscious construction of learning spaces for common reflection on activities, and which allow for developing awareness of the organization. They have constructed various different types of learning spaces, including role analysis groups, peer consultancy groups, action learning sets and Group Relations events. These spaces are inter-disciplinary and cross-departmental, they encourage a broad ownership of organizational projects as well as collective approaches to leadership, they promote individual, group, organizational interdependence.

Of course, it would be wrong to imagine that their efforts to organize reflection have been comfortable for members of the organization. In fact, the result of the learning that takes place within and about the organization is often uncomfortable. However, ReflectWell managers have learned: that they need not to be afraid of being uncomfortable, that they do not have to be in control, that they can take the risk to learn, that they contribute to the patterns of organizing that limit their ability to learn, and that there is no position or policy in the organization that cannot be reflected upon or questioned. Their very understanding of their authority as a manager comes from creating opportunities for learning and change. In the next chapter I further explore how this is done through a discussion of leadership.

8   Redefining leadership

There's a snowball's chance in hell of redefining leadership in this day
and age.

(Senge, 1999: 81)

In this chapter I am going to argue for a shift of focus, from an individualized
conceptualization of leadership, towards leadership as a product of human community: the collective capacity to create something of value. This definition of
leadership is a paraphrase of an idea of Peter Senge (Senge, Heifetz and Torbert,
2000), and his contrasting views about redefining leadership represent an
interesting paradox, which I think can inform our understanding of leadership, as well as providing ideas for practice. There is little doubt about the
central and continuing importance of leadership both as an organizational issue
and as an organizing process. Leadership is seen as 'the number one business
issue – higher even than determining customer needs' (Career Innovation
Group, 2002); as the primary competency that organizations are seeking to
develop (Brown and Posner, 2001); and changes in the understanding and
practice of leadership constitute an important challenge for both governments
and organizations in the future.

In my discussions of leadership I am going to take two unusual steps. First,
I am highlighting a single definition of leadership. The fact that I am deciding
on a single definition is unusual because I also think of leadership as a complex
and much-contested notion, for both academics and practitioners. In academic
writing, 'some writers argue that it does not exist; others suggest that it exists
but doesn't make a difference to organizational performance; still others say
that it exists, can make a difference, but is complex, ambiguous and paradoxical'
(Palmer and Hardy, 2000: 256). In the minds of practitioners, ways of understanding leadership are equally contested. For example, 'understanding that
learning is both study and practice has brought us great insight into our
leadership' (Steve Gibbons, Principal Financial Group, Des Moines, USA, in
Gibbons, 1999) contrasts with 'you don't have time to plan. Try a bunch of
things see if they work. If they don't, stop doing them. If they do, feed them'
(Paul Hogan, Fleet Boston Corporation, Boston, USA, quoted in Bennis, 2001).
Given the complexity and contested nature of leadership, common definitions

usually say very little. 'A common definition of leadership is not practically possible, would not be very helpful if it was, does not hit the target and may also obstruct new ideas and interesting ways of thinking' (Alvesson, 1996: 460). It may be useful, however, to propose an *uncommon* definition of leadership. An uncommon definition (leadership as the product of human community: the collective capacity to create something of value) might challenge how we think about leadership at least until it becomes an integral part of mainstream understanding. An uncommon definition is both a critique of mainstream views and, as speculative thinking, invites critique onto itself.

Second, I am going to argue against conventional ideas about leadership that construct it as an individual process and responsibility. The reason why there is 'a snowball's chance in hell of redefining leadership' is not because it is impossible to imagine how leadership could be redefined in theory, or how it might be newly understood. For example, it is clear that learning about individual team-building skills and behaviour covers only a part of what is important to understand about leadership in teams, which is that teams build the behaviour and approach of the leader as much as that the leader builds the team. Difficulties of redefinition relate to leadership in practice, which, in a great many institutions, organizations and enterprises, recreates itself through the idea that the leader is the boss and the boss is the leader. Teachers of leadership, role models, coaches, mentors, often reinforce this view, even when they do not overtly espouse it. In practice, managers and other members of organizations are wedded to the idea that leadership is the function of an individual leader. The most prevalent assumption about leadership is that it is something that is done by individuals. It is seen as 'a solo act – a one person undertaking' (O'Toole, Galbraith and Lawler, 2002). 'We cling to the myth of the Lone Ranger, that great things are accomplished by a larger than life individual shouting commands, giving direction, inspiring the troops, sounding the tocsin, decreeing the compelling vision, leading the way and changing paradigms with brio and shimmer' (Bennis 1999: 73). Ideas about the relationship between leadership and individual skills, style, personality and behaviour remain popular despite studies that show that the same person who exercises leadership effectively in one context can fail to do so in a different context even though he or she is utilizing the same range of skills and knowledge (Senge, Heifetz and Torbert, 2000).

We have become profoundly dependent on the individual leader and therefore on an individualized understanding of leadership. For working groups, it is always easier to let an individual take responsibility and therefore also to be available as a focal point for blame if things don't work out. Sometimes it is difficult to stop an individual from jumping into the leadership role. In any group there always seems to be at least one individual who is willing to rise to this challenge either for purposes that are to do with control, the desire to help move things forward (which may be another way of saying control), competition, self-importance, the avoidance of embarrassing silences, or all the other varieties of emotions and politics that can drive the individual initiative to lead and/or the collective energy to avoid leading. It is sometimes difficult to disentangle such motivations from other impulses to lead, like having a good idea, possessing and creating knowledge or experience that might make a difference, identifying contradictions, and making challenges to established behaviour or ways of thinking.

Looking at this from another direction, the idea that leadership is the task of the leader implies that the individual's role is to intervene. Any action is better than no action; leading scholars of leadership seem to agree on the importance of acting in order to think (what Henry Mintzberg has called 'emergent strategy'). However, interventions are enacted from a wide variety of roles and assumptions. For example, the leader may assume that his or her seniority or experience implies an expertise relevant to leadership. She or he may prefer to facilitate as an expression of a leadership role, inviting others to participate in a process of control within poorly defined boundaries and with questionable long-term effectiveness. Either way, intervention or the withholding of intervention in the role of leader focuses back on the responsibilities of the individual, often reaffirming existing power relations between the individual in her or his role and other members of organizations. Words like 'followership' have been coined to avoid explaining the different types of power relations that may have to be enacted in organizations to sustain individualized perspectives of leadership.

In this chapter I explore two examples that help to situate leadership in a broader context than the individual leader within an organization. This includes an example of the way in which leadership development is tied to the economic development of the principality of Wales, and I examine one aspect of the leadership dynamics in Hyder plc, where managers reverted to a high degree of control in order to try to lead change. Both of these examples help me to explain and develop my uncommon definition of leadership in more detail. Before this, however, I briefly review some of the thinking that currently informs our understanding of leadership.

Ways of thinking about leadership

Leadership thinking has been dominated by three interconnected approaches: a focus on the personal qualities and characteristics of leaders (traits); a focus on the identification of the features of effective leadership behaviour (style); and contingency thinking about leadership that can be characterized in the phrase 'it all depends on the situation' – in this type of situation, that approach is probably the best. Contingency theories of leadership have sought to identify the characteristics of situations in which different cognitive traits and leadership styles are found to be most effective. The situational variables which moderate the effectiveness of different leadership approaches are therefore placed towards the centre of understanding leadership. Whether leadership is seen in terms of specific characteristics, effective behaviour, or the situations within which leadership is enacted, these approaches are all concerned with the development of individual leadership skills and knowledge. Leadership skills and knowledge are applied through the ability of the individual to *influence* others by inducing them to behave in a certain way. Influence often takes place in a group context and the influence on the behaviour of the group is towards the fulfilment of group tasks or goals (Bryman, 1996). There is much to criticize in these approaches, whether this is the limited explanatory power and 'artificial rigour' inherent in the identification of traits, or the detachment of style from the social and structural dimensions of leadership processes (Knights and Willmott, 1992).

In the last decade, the development of a 'new' approach to leadership emphasized the individual leader in the company of others or followers, and in relation to the creation of corporate culture. The new leader is a charismatic individual, someone who defines organizational reality through the articulation of a vision, which is a reflection of how he or she defines the organization's mission, and the values that will support it. Leaders therefore have an integrative role: they can create and change organizational culture through the transmission of cultural values. Leaders do not directly influence, rather they are managers of meaning (Bryman, 1996), and the focus is on empowering the troops in order to command them. The role of the leader therefore is to 'discern what puts others into motion' (Avery, 1999) rather than to attempt to influence. Various competencies that relate to the management of meaning and determine the success of the new leader have been outlined (Bennis, 1999: 39). First, the leader understands and practises the 'power of appreciation' or the overt acknowledgement of the efforts of others. Second, she or he keeps reminding people of what's important – because 'a powerful enough vision can transform what would otherwise be routine and drudgery into collectively focused energy'. Third, the leader generates and sustains trust. This involves distinctive behaviours – constancy, caring, fairness, candour and authenticity. Finally, leader and followers are 'intimate allies', and this is made possible when the leader is 'not the loudest voice but the most attentive ear'.

The leader has been seen as 'a facilitator who cultivates the group and its members. As a result leadership is dispersed throughout the team' (Katzenbach and Smith, 1993). Leaders therefore 'develop capacity in others . . . they turn their constituents into leaders' (Kouzes and Posner, 1993). This particular definition of 'dispersed' leadership emphasizes participation – employees share in decision-making and take responsibility for their own work, thereby building the capacity for self-leadership throughout the organization. This has led to the growth of 'self-managed' teams in organizations. Increased autonomy to influence projects, products and decisions within a self-managed workforce is seen to create greater internal entrepreneurship, productivity and job satisfaction. The extent to which teams are self-managed is debatable, however, the emphasis of new leadership is less on overt command and control and more on the entrepreneurial, action-focused team leader. In theory, self-managed teams should have no dominant leadership style, but will contain a range of styles matched to particular tasks and projects. Bryman (1996: 286) has noted that 'there is a kind of optimism in the view that people are able to carve out spheres of interpretive autonomy which distance them from the mind-games of leaders who attempt to control what others think and feel'.

A more critical perspective on the leader's role in relation to organizational culture is not that the leader is a source of consensus and integration, but of differentiation. Leaders are dispersed through the organization and may engineer particular sub-cultures. Dispersed leadership can (also) be viewed as a political technique for achieving greater employee output (Palmer and Hardy, 2000). Dispersed leadership does not necessarily dissolve hierarchy, but allows it to evolve, becoming less overt, obscuring the boundaries of expectations and power relations, and promoting 're-centralization' under a smaller group of powerful individuals. Despite the notions of fairness that are explicit in the discourse of dispersed leadership, underlying structures of power can inhibit its implementation. The desire to collaborate cannot be uncoupled in organizations from the compulsion to dominate.

Theories of leadership have not reflected very deeply on the relations of power through which leadership knowledge and action are continuously expressed, limited and developed. Critical perspectives on leadership therefore see mainstream views as 'implicit in political bias' and, as a result, they exercise a conservative influence on the field (Knights and Willmott, 1992). For example, the consent of followers is integral to the enactment of a leadership role. However, the consent of followers can be precarious and is often accomplished through the exercise of power. As Knights and Willmott (1992) point out, consensus is often the product of force. They prefer to inquire into leadership as a practical accomplishment, studied as a core phenomenon, with a focus on leadership action. The particular emphasis is to highlight aspects of social processes and relations and the actions of subjects, which may be interpreted as leadership. Such an approach acknowledges organizations as arenas of confusion and ambiguity. One of the ways in which leadership might be understood, therefore, is as a source of ambiguity: leaders send contradictory and confusing signals through the organization, undermining stability as well as contributing to it.

From a psychodynamic perspective, 'leaders first and foremost spin dreams' (Gabriel, 1999). Ideally, the leader stands at the boundary between rational and non-rational decision-making, between realities and fantasies, helping to assess obstacles and to produce the necessary plans to overcome them. To understand leadership, therefore, it is important to understand fantasy: how fantasies provide hope or discourage action, as well as how they are communicated, for example, through projection onto others. The leader is never alone; he or she is also a product of the fantasies of followers. Such fantasies inevitably impact on the emotional and political dynamics and experiences surrounding attempts at leadership. The leader may be seen as someone who cares, can read my mind, is indifferent, accessible, aloof, omnipotent, unafraid, hopeless, externally driven, the one, or a fraud. All of these projections contribute to the complexity of leadership relations and reinforce the sense in which leadership is a product of the dynamics between self and other. One particular problem for leaders is that it is impossible to remain dreamers; and necessity requires that vision be turned into reality, something that inevitably requires the assistance of others. Emotions, both conscious and unconscious, which are individually felt and collectively produced and performed, interweave with political problems of leadership (e.g. that consensus often requires force). The fact that leadership is an ambiguous process within a social and political context mobilizes anxiety and self-doubt, encourages insecurity, gives rise to defensive behaviour, fosters the development of avoidance strategies, and leads to detachment from reflection and from criticism. An interest in psychodynamic theory adds emotional and relational complexity to an understanding of leadership.

There are perspectives on leadership that do not emphasize the role of the individual leader, instead framing leadership as a shared, social process (Yukl, 1998). Ideas about shared and collaborative leadership have developed in order to replace the emphasis on individual leadership. This can be illustrated briefly with a quotation from Richard Olsen, CEO of Champion Paper: 'none of us is as smart as all of us' (quoted in O'Toole, Galbraith and Lawler, 2002). Research into notions of shared leadership within UK schools points to the dilemma that leaders (in this case head teachers) have about collaborative leadership processes. 'Their greater dependence on colleagues disposes them towards sharing leadership. In a context of unprecedented accountability however, they may be inhibited from sharing because it could backfire' (Wallace, 2002: 157). In this study the author notes that shared leadership approaches fail to take into account two features of the politics of school management. First, the risk that sharing may result in ineffective leadership (with a consequent negative impact on both education and institution) and, second, the strict hierarchy of accountability, where the head teacher will have to answer when things go wrong. The conclusion is that shared leadership is likely to involve 'an occasional regression to hierarchy' (Wallace, 2002: 166). The importance of this insight is that such actions are acknowledged as regression. In practice, shared leadership (or at least the focus on team leadership) within the secondary-school sector in the United Kingdom has produced a clear perspective on the direction of current and future practice. 'Schools in difficulties aren't turned around by Superheads; they are turned around by teams of teachers working together' (John Dunsford, General Secretary of the Secondary Head Teachers' Association, quoted in the *Guardian* newspaper).

To summarize these ideas about leadership: common definitions of leadership emphasize the individual's role as having an influence on others. There may be specific traits and styles that make this possible as well as situations where specific styles are likely to be successful. The leader may have a 'new' or more general task, the creation of corporate vision or culture, which is achieved by influential and charismatic individuals who have discerned what puts others into motion. Such individuals may have engineered consensus or initiated dispersed leadership, but both are political techniques for achieving greater employee output through making hierarchies seem less overt. Looking at this emotionally as well as politically, the leader spins dreams – and is also subject to fantasies, which might stimulate defensive as much as charismatic behaviour. The leader's desire is also to share authority, to collaborate in a social context where 'none of us is as smart as all of us'. The reality of individual accountability for outcomes, however, implies a broader politics, where 'occasional regression to hierarchy' may be a necessary compromise.

I can also summarize, from this brief exploration of ways of thinking about leadership, why it is that we need to think differently about leadership:

- Leadership thinking is too connected to individuals, and their capacity to influence others.
- Leaders send contradictory and confusing signals through the organization, undermining stability as well as contributing to it. (The desire to collaborate can't be uncoupled in organizations from the compulsion to dominate.)
- Leadership is an ambiguous process within a social and political context. It mobilizes anxiety and self-doubt, encourages insecurity, gives rise to defensive behaviour, fosters the development of avoidance strategies, and leads to detachment from reflection and from criticism.
- Even shared leadership is likely to involve 'an occasional regression to hierarchy'.

Examples: leadership in context

What is the point of an uncommon definition of leadership in practice? First, an uncommon definition of leadership contrasts with current assumptions about leadership, thereby calling into question key assumptions that drive leadership in action (for example, that leadership is done by an individual). Second, the process of disbelief, contestation and critique that is levelled at an uncommon (or even unlikely) definition is inevitably a collective one. It is difficult to build a definition without the experience and opinion of those who fundamentally disagree with it. An uncommon definition of leadership has one key advantage over other definitions in that it is very obviously experimental – it does not pretend to be truth. This collective potential, built from difference, is one possible starting point for understanding how leadership in practice might be transformed. I use two examples to explain in greater detail what I mean.

Leadership development in Wales

Wales is a country, like many other small countries and regions in Europe, where the economic profile has changed considerably over the past two decades. There are no longer large coal and steel industries, and the character of the economy is defined now in terms of individual entrepreneurship, small and medium-sized businesses. This economic shift has motivated an increased interest in leadership, since leadership is recognized as a skill and process that relates to a much larger proportion of the community than it used to. The political impetus to redefine leadership in Wales is driven by the National Economic Development Strategy of the Welsh Assembly Government, for 'A Winning Wales' (published in January 2002). The vision of the Assembly Government is to achieve a prosperous and dynamic economy in Wales, one that is inclusive and sustainable, based on successful, innovative businesses with highly skilled, well-motivated people. The three specific and interlinked objectives at present are to encourage innovation, encourage entrepreneurship, and make Wales 'a learning country'. Specifically, the idea of a learning country involves increasing the skills of the workforce, removing existing barriers to learning and education, strengthening links between learning and business, creating new opportunities for work-based learning, and providing lifelong learning opportunities for all. There is a focus on improving mechanisms of workforce development, especially the identification of skill needs, as well as translating these into learning programmes and job creation.

The implementation of a national learning strategy is the task of Education and Learning Wales (ELWa), which comprises two Assembly-sponsored public organizations that together are responsible for all post-16 education and training in Wales. These are the National Council for Education and Training for Wales and the Higher Education Funding Council for Wales. National Council ELWa's mission is 'to promote lifelong learning and provide world-class learning opportunities for all in Wales to fulfil their potential' (National Council, Education and Learning Wales, 2002: 6). Applied to businesses, this means that every business in Wales 'will value the benefits of learning, continually invest in developing its workforce and access the training it needs to move forward'. By March 2005, ELWa intends to have 'developed a new and simplified range of skills support which meets the needs of all business; increased private sector investment in learning; developed and implemented an effective all-Wales management development programme; and raised demand for and investment in workplace learning'.

The organization that has specifically considered management and leadership training and development in Wales is the Wales Management Council (WMC). WMC has recently produced a provisional report or 'agenda for action' on leadership development (WMC, 2002). The WMC is an employer-led body supported by the Welsh Assembly government with a mission 'to help managers in Wales to lead and manage successfully'. The focus is on management and leadership in small to medium-sized enterprises (SMEs), as SMEs now make up 98% of all businesses in Wales. The following statistics from the WMC report elaborate on this:

- 98% of businesses in Wales have less than 20 employees, employ 46% of the workforce and produce 36% of total turnover.
- More than 1% of the businesses in Wales have between 20 and 250 employees, employ 20% of the workforce and produce 21% of total turnover.
- Less than 1% of businesses in Wales has more than 250 employees, employ 34% of the workforce and produce 43% of total turnover.

The WMC view of leadership is a rational and pragmatic one: 'our approach focuses strongly upon the achievement of quantifiable results . . . our ultimate benchmark is a major increase in the efficiency and profitability of businesses and organizations, leading to significant economic growth for Wales' (WMC, 2002). The competencies and skills necessary to make businesses and organizations grow are the stated priority. For the WMC, 'a pre-requisite of any management and leadership agenda for action is a description of management and leadership skills. Not only do these help to define roles, but they also provide an essential framework for management and leadership abilities.' They base these skills on a survey of management and leadership literature over the last 50 years, which produced a list of 'building blocks of leadership' (CEML, 2002). These are:

- communication and social skills
- personal drive, sense of purpose and motivation
- dependability, conscientiousness and persistence
- ability to motivate
- innovation, vision, long-range view and originator
- honesty and integrity
- self-confidence, accept challenge and risk, and emotional maturity
- inspiring trust
- intelligence and cognitive ability
- knowledge of the business
- genuine interest in others and valuing them
- team orientation.

Of course, a survey of management literature offers no guarantee that acquiring any or all of these core skills will make any difference to the growth of an enterprise. The different interpretations and enactments of these skills in theory and in practice within different organizational settings transform most of the above list into (at best) helpful generalizations. Some of these skills can be in direct contradiction in the context of business growth. Honesty and integrity, for example, do not always fit with personal drive, sense of purpose and motivation.

In addition to leadership skills, it is the idea of best practice that provides a broader context for (individuals') leadership development in the WMC model. However, a focus on best practice may ultimately undermine as much as it inspires local innovation. While the idea of best practice reassures managers that the wheel does not have to be reinvented, it can also detract from the need to analyse and understand the specific context within which leadership is applied. The same practices have different effects or are interpreted differently in one organization compared to another, and there are many recipes available which claim to be best, so it is sometimes difficult to know which 'best' one to follow:

> What works in one department or one organization may not work in another, not simply because the context is different, but also because the

best practice template which is transferred cannot capture all of the knowledge involved in actually making it effective. Thus, templates and practices presented as best will be interpreted differently in each context of application. Indeed, in many cases, what is considered to be best practice in one context may be deemed unworkable in another.

(Newell et al., 2002: 182)

Focus on best practice can be a diversion from the firm's own knowledge. Best practice can be, in part, an avoidance of asking about the state of knowledge within this organization – the knowledge there is, as well as the lack of it. The identification of existing knowledge also raises anxieties about what is not known, and this is an organizational dynamic that is often ignored. A focus on the best practices of others provides opportunities to externalize both problems and knowledge, to generalize what is known by detaching it from the emotional and political context within which its specific meaning resides. The most important knowledge in SMEs is likely to be local, and this is not simply internal knowledge but also the knowledge that resides in the various networks of close relations between individuals and enterprises. Individual leadership style, approach and behaviour, as well as skill development, are important, but they are not necessarily the most important factor in SME growth. The most important factors are likely to be situated in the community that surrounds an enterprise, in the wider patterns of relations that support innovation within specific business contexts. The community that surrounds SMEs has been represented by Gibb (1997), see Figure 8.1.

The WMC agenda explains the relationship between leadership and economic growth, but does not provide an adequate process for the development of

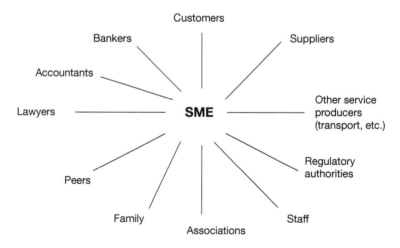

Figure 8.1 The SME transactional and business relationship network (from Gibb, 1997).

leadership that is allied to growth. Leadership is seen as individual style and behaviour and development relates to individual ability and effectiveness in a role. Mentoring, multi-disciplinary teams and leadership for dispersed staff are added in, but they are not central. One key problem in Wales is not only the creation of new business, which in key areas already attracts funding and support, but also sustaining and developing existing businesses to provide local growth. The individually situated managerial and entrepreneurial skills that often drive the creation of business will at some stage need to be transformed into different, more collectively orientated approaches to leadership. This is not an easy transition for managers and entrepreneurs to make. Individual entrepreneurs understandably have a very high emotional attachment to the company they have created. It is here that an uncommon definition of leadership might be able to make a difference. The problem with the WMC approach (and this mirrors a broader problem in understanding leadership development) is that it is unlikely to lead to significant growth because it does not address one of the key leadership issues that underpin growth. In order to do this, resources will also need to be deployed towards leadership development based on collective leadership.

There is a great deal riding on successful leadership development as an important component in the development of the Welsh economy, as well as the business knowledge that drives this success. A 'prosperous and dynamic economy' may well be the result of improved leadership, but leadership is not necessarily improved through a focus on individual development. What is the knowledge that is important for business development? The WMC, for example, has focused on dissemination (of a set of prescribed skills for individual leaders) and imitation (best practice across firms). The emphasis is to 'help *managers* in Wales' not organization, and this identifies an underlying assumption, which is that learning, innovation and entrepreneurship are the province of (developed) individuals, albeit individuals working together with others.

The WMC has emphasized the development of entrepreneurial skills, which is not the same as the knowledge that helps to sustain growth. While the leadership skills of an individual entrepreneur are a significant factor in the initial development of SMEs, this is not necessarily the approach to leadership that will help the SME to grow. The leadership dynamics that help to create enterprises are probably not the same ones needed to sustain them. Traditional approaches to the development of individual leaders (even in the context of self-managed teams or leading dispersed groups) will be insufficient in the context of a broader objective and strategy for innovation and economic growth. The Welsh Assembly government perspective is clear that leadership development needs to be understood as a key organizing process in Wales, particularly linking learning with innovation and entrepreneurship. It is unfortunate therefore that the current 'agenda for action' itself lacks innovation and is unlikely to give rise to development processes that can support strategic learning and innovation.

Perceptions of leadership in Hyder

The issues and perceptions about leadership and leadership development in Welsh SMEs are not dissimilar to issues and perceptions of leadership encountered in Hyder. As I have already outlined in earlier chapters, organizational dynamics in Hyder militated against reflection and communication, reinforcing groupings with impermeable boundaries and over-emphasizing individual responsibilities and expectations. Emerging and established processes of organizing tacitly supported members of organizations' fears of stepping forward or working to sustain significant forces for learning and change. These dynamics underpinned and informed an approach to leadership with obvious limitations. As one of the senior managers in Hyder said: 'if leadership is seen as maintaining, developing and representing, then we are kind of taking the imagination out of it, aren't we?' Another manager put it this way: 'we are not going to create anything special by carrying on the practices of the past'.

Leadership in Hyder was continually reconstructed and enacted in the context of past practices, relationships and expectations, which were seen to arise from the organization's public-sector history and were particularly characterized by control.

> The present style does come out of the old way of doing things, where you did have a high degree of control. I think that a lot of people might see themselves as not having given up the reins in the old tradition to a large extent, and you would probably be surprised at how strong they really still are.

> I think that part of the reluctance to debate and discuss is if you have got a preconceived idea of the result you want. If you know all the bloody answers you are hardly likely to seek advice, are you?

Somewhat inevitably, as the company moved slowly towards its demise, the focal point for much of the dissatisfaction about leadership in Hyder was with the Chief Executive (CE). The most senior management role in any company is likely to attract a wide variety of feelings, fantasies and opinions. The CE was seen as isolating himself, avoiding conflict, he was stressed and tired (so he could not lead in the way he 'needed' to), he was unsure of his role, detached from his successors, and cautious (both in the management of his team and financially). Some senior managers thought that the CE was a poor role model and that they were not offered the opportunity to test and develop their own leadership skills and knowledge at the highest level of the company. The lack of opportunity for engagement with the strategic direction underpinned an idea that strategy was to be delivered from above rather than be a collaborative and emergent process. Without a wider involvement in corporate strategy some senior managers have come to feel that 'there isn't really a strategy to tackle the way the work has changed' and that 'the long-term strategy looks like indecision'. Not only was the CE seen as problematic but also the Chief Executive's Committee (CEC – the senior management team) had 'stopped being receptive to ideas'. It was 'too distant and remote from the real business'. It lacked an understanding of what was happening and would not be influenced. It was not making strategic decisions; it was too closed, afraid of losing control and 'status-driven'. It was seen as a group of strong individuals, not as a team ('there is a lot of ego in the CEC'). It was seen to operate 'almost as a sort of a discrete entity' detached from what was going on 'down here' and unable to influence development.

These projections and opinions provide a description of the organizational dynamics in Hyder concerning leadership. Whatever the feelings were about the CE's leadership or the workings of the CEC, none of the senior managers seemed to be able to mobilize the imaginative leadership they desired. In interviewing the members of a team belonging to one of the senior managers who had been most critical of the CE's approach to leadership, it was clear that he had adopted many of the same ways, and was subject to many of the same criticisms as the CE. The comments levelled at the CE may or may not have been a reflection on the performance of that individual in his role, but they did communicate a great deal about the experience and enactment of leadership within the organization. The example in Hyder illustrates how difficult it is in complex organizations to create and sustain the imaginative leadership we desire. The tendency is to revert to 'a high degree of control' in order to try to lead change, which undermines communication across internal boundaries and limits ways in which authority might be enacted both from above and from below.

Redefining leadership

The two examples I have provided are intended to illustrate that, if we think of leadership mainly or exclusively as the function of an individual and not also as a product of community, then opportunities to comprehend the nature and practice of strategic learning will be lost. In the example of leadership development in Welsh SMEs, the Welsh Assembly government's agenda for significant economic growth is unlikely to be fully supported by a perspective on leadership development that focuses only on the skills and behaviours of individual leaders. Such a perspective does not represent two dynamics associated with the situation, and that are important in linking learning, innovation and growth. First, there may come a point in the development of a company where the leadership skills and behaviours of an individual entrepreneur or even a small group of directors are insufficient to manage the company towards growth. Skills, traits and style of leadership make little difference here since this is more about, for example, individuals' emotional and political attachment to ownership, the desire to retain absolute control over decision-making, or even the idea that the company is mine and I am the only one who really understands it. The ability of lead managers and entrepreneurs to make the emotional transition from individual to collective responsibility for decisions about the future is just as much an aspect of the difficulties that are involved in growth. Second, leadership development that is orientated only towards the skills of individuals undermines strategic learning. Strategic learning is built from collective leadership, whichever individual may ultimately come to represent or lay claim to responsibility for future direction.

In Hyder, leadership was in part enacted as individual attempts to control change. Individuals' tight rein on change stifled the desire and willingness to act in interdependent ways across organizational roles and boundaries. Several key managers in Hyder were committed to the idea of the participation and involvement of all staff in learning and change initiatives. However, they saw involvement as happening through discrete events rather than as an integral part of the everyday role and responsibilities of those in leadership positions. As a result of this thinking, 'involvement' was seen as something separate from leadership, and the senior managers had little or no sense of being directly involved in the learning processes developed within the organization. They were isolated from collective perspectives on organizational issues and did not relate directly to inquiry, reflection and critique on existing ways of organizing.

In both examples, there are limitations to leadership in practice driven by common ideas and assumptions about leadership as individual skill and behaviour. These limitations can be addressed (at least partially) through a definition of leadership aimed at generating appropriate knowledge for collective action. Like all knowledge, the knowledge that relates to leadership is rooted in practice, action and social relationships; it is dynamic (the process of knowing is as important as the knowledge); and it exists in the interplay between the individual and the collective. Leadership therefore, is not so much linked to individual knowledge as to the collective inquiry from which knowledge is generated. Leadership is not static, not something that is well represented by lists of behaviours or examples of good practice. It is more realistically represented as a variety of approaches to practice linked to the situated and shifting nature of knowledge within communities.

> Leadership is both normative and collective because it is the whole process by which valued social/organizational aims are articulated and by which social strategies are designed, enacted and tested to see whether the aims have been achieved.
>
> (Senge, Heifetz and Torbert, 2000: 59)

One paradox of attempting to redefine leadership is that redefinition is both impossible and essential. There's 'a snowball's chance in hell' of shifting the focus from individuals, but at the same time leadership that is redefined in a 'mutually inclusive way, can help to solve many of the problems encountered in work life today' (Raelin, 2003). The focus on individuals that dominates approaches to leadership serves an organizational purpose, to detach ideas about leadership and leadership development from the emotions and politics that construct and drive them in practice. One of the emotions driving leadership in Hyder, for example, was fear of failure and the perceived need to protect oneself from criticism. To link this to politics, it was about trying to maintain or undermine an image of connection to a whole, while at the same time securing the viability of personal positions. Both of these dynamics help to construct the practice of leadership as an individual rather than a collective process. I see little value in an approach to understanding leadership that ignores these dynamics.

Research into collective leadership is not well developed, despite the well-established understanding that leadership is likely to involve many individuals (Pettigrew and Whipp, 1991). However, one recent study (Denis, Lamothe and Langley, 2001) has looked at how leaders might achieve strategic change in organizations 'where strategic leadership roles are shared, objectives are divergent and power is diffuse' (p. 809). The authors note that this is a more and more common description of modern organizational designs given the increased incidence of collaborative arrangements, the diversification of the workforce, and the growth of internal markets, matrixes and networks. They conclude that collective leadership is a fragile concept in a context of diffuse power and multiple objectives, and that the impact of members' individual or collective actions on their political positions is what sustains or undermines the implementation of collective leadership in practice. They also note that collective leadership implies the support and management of relationships outside of the organization, within a broader network. This is because demands and opportunities within such networks evolve over time and impact on collective leadership roles within individual organizations.

In order to understand better in practical terms what might be meant by the idea that leadership is a product of human community, the collective capacity to create something of value, I refer to an example provided by Peter Senge. I have quoted him in detail.

> Xerox . . . launched a very interesting product, the Document System 265. It is Xerox's first fully digitized product, a copier that is doing extremely well in the marketplace. This product is also 97% recyclable. It has 200 parts; it replaced a product with over a thousand parts. The parts primarily clip together or are screwed together without welds. It is an extraordinary breakthrough and has won many engineering awards.
>
> What we need to understand is how the heck they did this and see it as an example of the extraordinary breakthroughs in thinking and practice that are necessary to build environmentally sustainable businesses. Within about a year of forming, the team that produced this came up with an overarching image of what they were trying to do. When we walked into the facility where this machine is manufactured, one of the first things we noticed was a huge banner hanging from a 20-foot ceiling that said 'Zero-to-Landfill'. They wanted to build a product where nothing would ever go into landfill. Within a year after coming up with that guiding image,

the team decided they couldn't do it unless they had a zero-to-landfill manufacturing environment. And they needed to have zero-to-landfill commitments from their suppliers.

Is this not leadership? By any sense of what the phenomenon of leadership is really all about, is this not an extraordinary example of leadership? These are people creating a whole new reality of what's possible. There was a boss . . . so there was a hierarchy. But you couldn't spend more than five minutes talking to those engineers and not come away quite inspired. There were no CEOs although there was support from the CEO. So I will leave you with the question, is that not leadership?

(Senge, Heifetz and Torbert, 2000: 58)

This example provides two insights about leadership as collective capacity. First, the realization of the team's goal was only possible if it crossed boundaries between their idea and the environment within which it was situated. This included the commitment of other stakeholders (their suppliers) to the idea. The behaviour of the Xerox team would seem unusual to Hyder managers, for example, because there, ideas and actions were often only fully discussed and understood within the boundaries of the sub-system within which they were generated. Containing ideas and actions in this way provided the means to control and sell them, although this was not necessarily a conscious decision, or an effective one. In Xerox, the idea of 'zero-to-landfill' became public with a wider constituency, not solely in terms of information exchanged or knowledge shared, but in relation to the whole process of organizing that determined the successful reconstruction of the product.

The second insight concerns the phrase 'people creating a whole new reality of what is possible'. This is to a certain extent the conclusion that has been reached by many organizational thinkers and consultants since whenever. Thinking outside of the box, assumption-busting, reframing, learning to learn and so on all represent and express the permanent learning agenda within Human Resource and Organization Development – creating a whole new reality of what is possible. What is the insight then? It is that established ways of leading do not generally encourage organizing processes and outcomes that are transformational. For all the leaders who have successfully implemented radical processes that transformed their organizations, there are many, many others whose management education, role models and experiential learning all point them in a direction that militates against negotiating new realities of what is possible.

Organizing is individualistically orientated in part because this makes it easier to contain emotions and politics that might be capable of undermining organizational stability and create the potential for learning and change. The collective capacity to inquire, learn, intervene and change is often problematic for individuals in positions of power (in Hyder, for example). A potent fantasy has developed to support individuals' ambivalence about learning and change, which is that making decisions individually is easier, particularly in terms of time and accountability. The desire for change as an idea, and the knowledge of change as it emerges in an organization, are often two different experiences. Such organizational dynamics imply that different assumptions and experiences might need to inform the development of any collective capacity for leadership. I want to argue, therefore, that a key assumption underpinning leadership as a collective capacity is that leadership is a public process.

When I say that leadership is a public process, I do not mean that individuals need to be more open or say what we think. Organizations are hierarchical and therefore political environments where it is sometimes at least unwise, if not dangerous, for individuals to say what they think in public. At times, as a consequence of 'speaking the truth to power', individuals have become the victims of processes, both political and psychological, scapegoats for problems within the wider political and social system. When I say that leadership is a public process I am referring to two things in particular. First, the way in which leadership is done is likely to be the result not only of the person who leads, but also of how the organizational context has shaped that leadership. For example, team building is seen as an individual skill that can be taught on management and leadership development courses. However, it may also be useful to recognize that the team builds the individual or individuals who represent and lead them. A team produces the behaviour of the leader, as well as the leadership decisions and choices that are voiced, through their conscious and unconscious actions and inactions, through the various ways in which emotions and politics in a team impact on organizing. Second, leadership involves creating opportunities for more public debate, dialogue and decision-making, thereby moving beyond procedures that might undermine individuals for the risks that they take. There is as much to be understood from the emotions and politics that inhibit collective approaches to leadership as there is from the experience of making decisions collectively and in public. For individuals this may involve a less fearful and protective take on their leadership role, since such fears inhibit the development of wider involvement and shared responsibilities. Within organizations, the leadership role can be the starting point for a broader public accountability, to create the 'structure that connects' learning with strategy (Nicolini et al., forthcoming).

Redefining leadership as collective capacity provides opportunities to comprehend the nature and practice of strategic learning. I have identified three components to this. First, collective leadership is a 'fragile' concept in practice, it is more difficult to hold in mind and it provides less tangible objects to identify with than an individual with a vivid personality or vision. This is also its strength, because it implies no clear assumptions about how to lead and therefore emphasizes the collective inquiry and broad knowledge-generation process that is likely to be integral to the development of strategy. Second, collective leadership is about crossing boundaries – between individuals in a group, between collections of groups, and between networks and organizations. It is by crossing boundaries that strategy is given wider legitimacy and critique – the opportunities for disagreement and dialogue are increased. This is seen as an important aspect in the generation of knowledge about existing organizational dynamics and future practice. Finally, collective leadership is a public process, at best it evolves with others within a social and political context, providing opportunities for authority and representation that are located in several or all of the members of a team, project or group rather than with one individual.

I have argued that current thinking about leadership is too individualistic, too connected to individuals' capacity to influence others, and that such a perspective does not contribute to the further development of strategic learning, which is increased through collective and public approaches to reflection and leadership. Leaders inevitably send contradictory and confusing signals through the organization, undermining stability as well as contributing to it. This is a paradox that informs strategic learning because it does not pretend that an individual can control future outcomes, but it does suggest that the ability to mobilize critique and inquiry is likely to be of profound use in generating the collective knowledge that informs future strategy. I have already said in this chapter that leadership is an ambiguous process within a social and political context. It mobilizes anxiety and self-doubt, encourages insecurity, gives rise to defensive behaviour, fosters the development of avoidance strategies, and leads to detachment from reflection and from criticism. This is what makes it such an important organizing process; there are likely to be considerable opportunities for strategic learning if these everyday aspects of organizational behaviour and design can be the subjects of public reflection.

One intention in this chapter on leadership has been to raise questions about collective leadership, to start to suggest why this perspective on leadership is as important as one that seeks to identify individual traits, styles or competencies. There are several questions that require additional investigation and research. The most obvious of these is the further clarification of what 'leadership as a product of human community' means. Of particular interest here is a more developed understanding of the ways in which the leadership approaches of individuals are influenced by the communities they lead; in other words, how does a community build the individual or individuals that represent or lead them? An opposite and connected way of looking at this will involve further investigation of the leadership approach and behaviour of an individual, and how this reflects the characteristics, opinions or perceived needs of the collective that he or she belongs to and represents. Both of these questions are necessarily situated in understanding the ways in which a community is constructed and contained by emotion and politics.

Further research in this area will also need to consider different questions implied by different interpretations of community. If community is defined in terms of interaction within a project group or team of people engaged in practice, then an important question concerns how a collective reaches the idea that direction or leadership is required. Is this idea the result of experience within a community, for example, when things feel too uncomfortable or too complicated, and to what extent does this reflect dynamics that are external to the team? In addition, how does a community accept an individual or minority voice as a leading voice – by design, by imposition, by choice, by accident, through habit, through laziness (responding unquestioningly to the first good idea expressed), or by thorough evaluation? Investigation of these possibilities will afford insights about authority, legitimacy, accountability and responsibility that are not solely based on leadership as the function of individuals. Such questions will provide opportunities for a further critique of what we know about leadership.

I am emphasizing an *uncommon* definition of leadership as both a critical and a practical suggestion. An uncommon definition of leadership is useful, not so much because it is a definition, but because it is uncommon. One aim in redefining leadership is to shift the focus away from established assumptions about leadership, both what it is and how it is done. To define leadership as a product of human community: the collective capacity to create something of value is to critique the idea of individual influence and how it is achieved. Similarly, it is not necessary to pursue further the quest for appropriate traits, behaviours, styles or competencies for individual leaders – even though this may well be useful information. The personal charisma and force of personality of individuals will always have an impact on other members of organizations – but not necessarily the desired or imagined impact. My definition is, to some extent, recognition that leadership is a subject dominated by an intense search for certainty at the same time as being 'one of the most confused and confusing areas in the whole field of management' (Thomas, 2003: 162). In a way, the fact that it is a confused and confusing notion is useful because it means that anything we discover about leadership is likely to be highly debatable. Making things highly debatable is one way of describing the impact of leadership as both a collective and public capability.

9 The point of intervention

Critique is an activity engaged in by the wise scholar and the wise man or woman of action equally.

(Watson, 2001)

Critique (Greek, *kritikē*): the art of criticism.
(*The New Shorter Oxford English Dictionary*, 1993)

The ideas that I have brought together under the theme of *strategic learning* provide a bridge between academic studies of organizational learning, and learning and organizing in action. From an academic point of view, I have used the phrase to highlight a variety of insights that emerge from studying the relationship between emotions, politics, learning and organizing. From the point of view of practice, my inquiries into the relationship between emotions, politics, learning and organizing have provided a basis from which to rethink the organization of reflection, ideas and actions related to leadership, and in this chapter, issues concerning intervention from a development role.

Human resource development is a practice of organizing that is explicit in its focus on learning and change. A consistent part of my argument has been that this focus should not solely involve the development of skills and abilities for the individual within a role. It also concerns the relationship between the enactment of a role and the establishment within which roles are situated. HRD can be understood as a critical practice of development, one that might make a distinctive contribution to organizing, especially where there is recognition that all development is intervention within a political system. This final chapter includes thoughts about the future practice of HRD. These come from my interpretation of the transcripts of the conference I organized for a small group of academics and practitioners, and that formed the basis for my critique of HRD in Chapter 2. My reflections on HRD are followed by a review of some issues raised by attempts to intervene in organizations to create opportunities for learning and change. I am asking, what is the point of intervention? This question refers to *reasons* for intervention and to the *roles* that are taken and given by individuals and collectives with responsibility for intervention. I finish with some reflections on how I am beginning to move beyond the writing of this book.

Six thoughts on future practice

The future of HRD will benefit from less superficial approaches to training, learning and development processes. HRD needs to be understood less as a set of skills and techniques, and more as *inquiry* into knowledge and lack of knowledge, into fears and frustrations, and into power relations both social and strategic. A good inquiry process is likely to discover things that we both want and don't want to know, and it is this that will provide the material from which strategic learning can be developed. The double-edged and complex nature of such intervention is highlighted in the following example from the conference referred to in Chapter 2.

'Any inquiry process is likely to lead us into trouble'

The trouble that I get into all the time with my practice is first of all getting Action Learning started under the right conditions, but having got it started then getting into trouble with the rest of the organization. Any inquiry process is likely to lead us into trouble. I've got this [Action Learning] set at the moment who've been meeting for two years, every two months for a day, all second tier managers. They consider themselves to be excluded from the power of the organization, and they are severely demoralized. They formed a set, eight of them, and now the set is the most corporate thing about the organization. They still have few resources but they have started talking collectively, when they go to meetings they have started representing the collective. This has been noticed. The organization has an Executive Team that is not corporate, individual team members compete for resources among themselves. The Executive have commissioned an Organization Development (OD) programme, which means that they have brought a consultant in, everyone is going to be turned into super-teams and it's all going to be about empowerment. As a result, the action learning process has got to fold because it's not part of the overall OD scheme. Here we see OD being used to stop something happening, to resolve a problem created by a maverick process. It is not the only reason for the OD programme, which they do need, particularly at the Executive level, but they don't want to have a conversation with the regional managers. Members of the Executive are not capable of having a conversation because they are not a collective. They would need to be able to understand what they wanted as a team in order to have a conversation with a group who are saying – we have an argument about the way we should be doing things here. So that's the sort of thing I find really difficult, and I don't feel I have any power or mandate with the Executive. What is easy to say in the set is not easy to say in the organization.

There are a number of ways of thinking about HRD that help to define future practice. First, it is the role of HRD practitioners to ask risky questions, to get further into the emotions and politics that surround attempts at learning and change. For example:

In working with a group of people who had just agreed to participate in an activity I said – 'I know that when we get out of this room a number of you won't do what you just said you would, so can you tell me why now?' To raise such questions is to start getting into hidden agendas – there's a lot of danger in discussing and exploring these and risk, but you can overcome this and it can be very powerful.

The HRD practitioner has to juggle the twin pressures of safety and risk, creating processes and 'spaces' within which the personal and political risks that underpin development can be taken. There are several dilemmas. Much HRD is concerned more with filling spaces rather than creating them, learning environments always contain anxiety (in both senses of the word 'contain'), what seems to be safe sometimes is not, public and open discussion is often avoided. Creating learning spaces means running risks, not least the risk that they will be taken over by the usual people who take them over. To create learning environments that are free from anxiety and risk creates the danger of making them invisible or self-indulgent. Participants might well be happy with that but they will not change the organization. HRD is therefore about *what might be*, creating a space in the hope that something will happen.

Second, the HRD role involves process consulting in its widest sense, which suggests, for example, that one function of the HRD role may be in disseminating an alternative picture of what managing can be. HRD practitioners have responsibility for the identification of possibilities and problems located in processes, practices and roles – including the roles of manager and leader. The HRD role is the focal point for the development of projects and projections within the organization. Projects inspire business-related knowledge and learning (which can be shared or ignored) and projections represent the barriers to learning that are integral to any attempts to learn. All individuals to some degree defend against unwanted ideas or images of the self by projecting them onto others. Similarly, any collective efforts to mobilize learning within organizations is likely to involve attempts to exclude what is unwanted, undesirable or uncomfortable about strategic learning.

A dilemma about future practice is that HRD can be very prescriptive, based on attempts to devise systems and processes and to rationalize action. The emphasis of HRD, therefore, needs to be development not prescription, and while the starting point may be the same for many organizations, the actual journey is likely to be very different. The third point, therefore, is that HRD has to move away from prescribed competencies, both in relation to the HRD profession and to the managers and leaders that practitioners serve. In moving away from prescribed competencies for individuals, HRD practitioners are also necessarily abandoning the idea of 'good practice', since practice (as I argued in the previous chapter) is always situated within different organizational or inter-organizational contexts. HRD is reductive when it seeks to identify practice that works in one context and apply it in a different context. Part of the HRD role, therefore, is to help to reinvent the wheel of practice in the search for innovation. The discipline

for HRD practitioners involves looking at practice as it is changing and developing, trying to make sense of and to transform the various processes and practices
that emerge.

A fourth point involves HRD practitioners in leading the idea that changes
can be determined lower down in the organization, that there are likely to be
benefits from decentralization and democracy. Leading such a political change
can be a frightening thought, and it requires a good understanding of key power
relationships, as well as what the politics are and how one might work with
and through those politics. HRD practitioners from their experience are likely
to know what other leaders need to know regarding development, that 'you
can only create the context, you can't actually control it'. In my discussions of
leadership in this book I have defined it as a product of human community. I
argue that leadership is more about creating the conditions and enabling them
to be put into place than it is trying to control a process once it has been set in
motion. Leadership involves the creation of processes and procedures for collective or public reflection and action (rather than individual reflection and action).
Future practice will require a more developed perspective on reflection and the
impact that reflection can have on organizing.

Fifth, the design and delivery of HRD is increasingly likely to change both
in terms of approaches to delivery and in relation to the organizational forms
that it serves. New technologies will have more and more impact, involving
both e-learning and 'blended learning' (a mixture of e-learning and face-to-face
learning). E-learning has already proved useful, for example, for basic skills
training:

> E-learning allows us to do fire safety training very effectively. People no
> longer have to sit in a room for an hour being bored out of their minds; they
> can sit in front of a computer for ten minutes and have the same, probably
> a better outcome. It allows us to use that time more productively.

HRD has to adapt to new and emerging organizational forms. The traditional
curriculum of HRD is a big company curriculum. However, increasingly HRD
has to position itself within different organizational designs and forms, most
notably in relation to the growth of small and medium-sized enterprises (SMEs).
SMEs represent the growth potential in the economy, yet they are often too
small to have an HR function and HRD capacity on their own. SMEs are much
more likely to frame learning in terms of informal, on-the-job learning and
knowledge sharing. In a small company the chances of learning leading to
action are very high and the link between learning and business performance
is much easier to see and to make. Many SMEs, however, do not have a development (or growth) agenda, nor are they necessarily aware of development
in the same way as HRD practitioners in larger organizations might be. At the
same time, managers in SMEs have to operate with high-level skills across and
between organizations, to be adaptive and contextually focused in what they do.
Development occurs, but not with the sorts of labels we might traditionally

attach to it. There are both optimistic and a pessimistic perspectives on learning and SMEs. The optimistic view says that learning is more likely to happen because organizations are small and highly focused. The pessimistic view is that SMEs just about cling to survival and that they don't have time to learn.

These issues are not exclusive to SMEs, many larger organizations don't have HRD *per se*, and if they do it is the first thing to be cut back when times are hard. Whatever the forms and designs that characterize the overall context of HRD, practitioners will be delivering HRD more and more to business clusters, and this requires different provision than to a single unified organization. Part of the HRD role may be to encourage clusters and to devise approaches to HRD that are appropriate to such designs. Increasingly the agenda for HRD is not development in general, but a high-performance, work-based approach to business development. My sixth point is that, there are likely to be many assumptions about what HRD is and why HRD is an important activity, as well as concerns about the processes and practices associated with HRD. My own assumption is that HRD is a pivotal process in organizing for the future since its primary concern is change. HRD therefore has implications for future ways of behaving, structuring and organizing, across organizations and organizational domains. It is the future practice of HRD that is the point of HRD. HRD can be characterized as evolving practice, as activity that inspires critique in order to create possibilities for learning, as attempts at organization and organizing that seek to create the ways we will be thinking and acting.

Back to the future of HRD – a reality check

I can highlight a number of potential problems and criticisms with the perspective on HRD that I have been building, and I am sure that there are more that I do not mention. My view may well be 'a minority vision' and it is possible that the ideas outlined here would be completely alien to many practitioners. Perhaps few practitioners would look at HRD as this complex, seeing it as focused on *effective development practice within organizations* – which is to say how involved people are in development processes. I could be 'romancing the exciting frontiers of HRD while ignoring a solid core' or devising 'wonderful schemes' about how HRD is going to be, while being aware that in practice HRD is not going to change much from its current emphasis. Difficulties in changing how HRD is understood and implemented have been reinforced by the general lack of debate about HRD at key professional conferences. Many of the people who attend the annual conference of the Chartered Institute of Personnel and Development (CIPD is the main UK professional body in this area) are there to buy products and pick up techniques and tricks for their HRD toolkit, not to enter debate about *why* HRD is being done, or the politics and emotions that inform it. Therefore, it would seem that the majority of practitioners are not seeking new ideas about future practice, but rather a couple of tricks to get them through their next instructional session. I hope that I am wrong about this.

I would certainly acknowledge that the mainstream work of HRD comprises a lot of basic but important development work, such as health and safety training, which is often required by law, is important that it is done well, and matters that it is done on a big enough scale. It is possible that this 'core' training work of HRD is the most important in terms of reaching the bulk of staff, particularly support or front-line workers who make a big difference to the way services are delivered. Perhaps in general I have not thought enough about the value of basic training of a kind that actually helps the widest constituency of people. My views may recognize 'core' training as part of an overall 'value chain', but also contribute to how such training is devalued in organizations:

> Why would I want to work with a group of support workers and domestics on a Thursday afternoon in a broom cupboard when I've got the opportunity to work with the Chief Executive and the board? The danger here is in the lack of investment at the grassroots level, which actually means that all the stuff we do at the top is not affecting the number of patients we can get through so that they can have their surgery and a better quality of life; it is about improving the overall value of the organization.

Mainstream practitioner views of HRD adopt a more or less apolitical stance, based on the idea that development is everyone's business and everyone's right. The function of HRD is to support the development of all the people in the organization, and development is about widening access to learning opportunities in whatever form that takes. Practitioners are interested in learning and development wherever it occurs, whether this is the broom cupboard or the boardroom, because both venues raise equally interesting questions about learning and how it works. There are even occasions where the broom cupboard may be a more attractive place to be than the boardroom:

> Working with the board isn't necessarily that attractive to me; working with support workers is a little less dangerous.

> You don't see it from the inside; the excitement of working with some Chief Executives is excitement you can live without.

As these thoughts suggest, HRD practitioners are likely to be only too aware of the politics of development, and the choices that have to be made about intervention or the lack of it.

It seems that, whatever view is taken about how and why HRD adds value, both academics and practitioners agree that the general emphasis of HRD is organizational learning and change. This suggests that all involved in HRD and its associated disciplines, ideas and practices are interested in how, why and when to intervene within organizations in order to try to make learning and/or change happen. It is to this aspect of my argument that I now turn, in order to explore questions concerning the point of intervention.

The point of intervention

In this section of the chapter, I begin by looking at what intervention means and involves, as well as the individual and collective role that both internal and external change agents have as a focal point of intervention. I am therefore exploring the point of intervention, both in terms of reasons for intervention and the roles that are taken and given by individuals and collectives with responsibility for intervention. My focus on role does not mean that I am primarily interested in, for example, the skills and knowledge of the individual. I am more interested in the roles of HRD practitioners or external consultants as one of the focal points for intervention in a system, as well as the institutional dynamics that are likely to be mobilized, experienced and created by the HRD practitioner or consultant as he or she engages with or disengages from the system within which intervention is made.

Reasons for intervention are reflected in a cacophony of many and varied consultant voices that say that the point of intervention is: managing change for the better; promoting greater performance, efficiency and effectiveness; to develop the individual and the organization; to explore and exploit knowledge; to solve a problem and to take necessary action; down-sizing, right-sizing and re-engineering; to ensure competitive advantage; to deliver growth; to create value for shareholders; to provide people with greater insight into their behaviour and actions. These are just a small selection of the possible answers, but they do represent a common assumption: that the point of intervention is mostly seen as something rational, problem- and solution-related, clear, individually focused, and, on the whole, apolitical. As I have indicated throughout the book, this is not my view of intervention.

Intervention always has an institutional impact, often a different impact from the one first imagined by the HRD practitioner, the external consultant or the managers who are supporting and legitimizing change initiatives. Sometimes intervention helps to mobilize fears and anxieties that promote resistance to learning and change, sometimes the techniques and approaches used, or the emotions that underpin their use, will obscure the real change needs within organizations. At times, transformation occurs, through insight or accident, or both. Every individual who has an organizational role can be said to intervene, through his or her actions or inactions, within the system of which she or he is a part. However, taking up an HRD, OD or consultant role, whether internal or external, means taking on something specific within an organization, it means taking up the authority to mobilize transformation. These roles are therefore an explicit point of intervention precisely because implicit within them is the legitimization of action that is at least by intention orientated towards learning and change. Another way to express this authority is to say that, for example, HRD managers are given the legitimacy to engage with existing organizational dynamics, and through this engagement either to try to make change happen (and perhaps also to take the rap for whatever else transpires). The complexity of the situation surrounding various organizational roles explicitly aimed at intervention is intensified when one realizes that the organizational dynamics informing them are often unconscious in nature.

Before I explore this further, there are two issues of terminology that I want to clarify. First, I intend to keep the term 'intervention' in a relatively undefined state, so that it can carry a variety of meanings. The phrase *the point of intervention* describes my reflections on the various reasons for intervening and the experiences that can arise from it. In addition, the phrase describes the role of the HRD practitioner or consultant within a system, a focal point for the potential transformation of both organization and role. Second, persons occupying this role may be bought into an organization as external consultants; they may be internal – a member of staff with a specific HRD or OD department, or a manager as action-researcher, trying to mobilize inquiry into everyday behaviour, decisions and actions. I am therefore using the term 'consultant' in a very general way, to include all such individuals, internal or external who are contributing to attempts at learning and change.

Although the term 'consultant' is often used to describe the intentions and actions of individuals, it is useful to remember that such a role is never separated from, is always constructed by, and generally represents, relations between self and others. Indeed, what makes the role of consultant so important and interesting in terms of strategic learning and change is that it is a magnet for the projections and fantasies of others, stimulating emotions that impact on self but do not necessarily belong there. For example, the leader of a team invited intervention into the team on the basis that it was not working well. The consultant discovered that, as far as the team members were concerned, they were working well together, they were just unhappy with the lack of leadership. In this example, the function of the consultant was to receive the different versions of the truth that could not be communicated directly between the leader and his team. This example expresses one of the main ways in which the role and the intervention are joined, through a continuous attempt to associate with, interpret and possibly to understand the complex emotions and politics that organizing creates and that in turn influence and legitimize particular ways of behaving and organizing. Experience in the role of consultant within one part of a system is often a reflection of the broader organizational dynamics within which intervention is undertaken.

For example, recently I happened to be talking to the Chief Executive of an insurance company, who had had a bad experience with consultants who 'came in and ripped us apart, leaving us to pick up the pieces. They gave us a lot of pain and grief.' This is a common enough story, and the Chief Executive was still angry as he talked about the experience. Clearly, many individuals have had experiences with consultants, both internal and external, where they felt unhappy, that did not meet expectations and that gave rise to feelings of anger, pain or grief. In addition to the idea that consultants in their various guises cause feelings of anger, pain or grief, there is an idea that they are paid too much, that they sell products which have a very short sell-by date and are square packages in round organizations. On the other hand, consultants are used as a scapegoat for the enactment of agendas that managers themselves do not want to be responsible for. The brief they are given is sometimes designed to avoid the real organizational issues and senior managers often shy away from the results of intervention because they are in danger of making change happen. It seems sometimes as if the consultant just has to expect to be positioned either as the expert to be lauded or the devil to be expelled – neither of which is helpful to the task. The jargon-soaked language of intervention is also unhelpful – re-engineering, assumption-busting, total quality, six-sigma, the learning company. It has meant that intervention has had to be sold on the basis of constantly reinventing new packages, a whole wardrobe of new clothes for the emperor.

The view put forward by the insurance company Chief Executive that the result of intervention was pain and grief is an interesting one. While I have little sympathy for the idea that 'there is no gain without pain', I do know that grief is likely to be an integral aspect of intervention since implicit within the notion of grief is a powerful connection to a process of change (Marris, 1974). Grief is full of powerful emotions – fear and anger among them – that ultimately drive changes that derive from loss. All change implies loss, as well as feelings generated about loss, that has to be worked through and transformed. Intervention therefore should not be about pain, but it might well be about grief and loss. All of us in enacting our organizational roles become attached to ways of working that are comfortable and habitual, and that would feel like a loss were they to be confronted. Yet they have to be confronted and transformed in order for the self, the group and the organization to move forward, for learning to take place.

As I have mentioned previously, in my studies of Hyder plc I found that, despite a consistent and powerful discourse concerning change, there was an equally powerful underlying desire for the company to stay the same. The transition from Welsh Water to Hyder was meant to be a transformation into new territory and identity, yet the most powerful dynamic in the company concerned contested ideas about what was important in the business – the core task of being a Welsh water company, or the growth agenda towards being a global infrastructure management company. The inability to acknowledge the importance of paradoxical tensions and self-limiting processes in the company, the competition between the desire for and resistance to change, undermined the ability of key managers to develop strategic learning.

Intervention is not only about the mobilization of rational procedures for solving problems or improving performance, although clearly these are useful reasons that underpin attempts to intervene. Intervention is crucial to transformation because it touches the emotions that underpin organization, the fantasies on which organizations are constructed. One way to think about the point of intervention, therefore, is to say that whereas a traditional assumption might be that intervention is about trying to find rational solutions to problems, an equally useful assumption could be that intervention is about *problematizing the rational*, which implies acceptance that not everything can be planned, worked out, adhered to and managed. Intervention that is about more than rational approaches is likely to show an interest in what is unknown, undiscussable and uncomfortable.

Inevitably, all members of organizations struggle with the relationship between what is known and what is unknown. The everyday tasks of managing and organizing mean that it is always difficult for the known and the unknown to be held together. The known is often, although not always, comfortable and comforting. It is expressed in our attachment to past ways of working, letting old solutions suffice for new problems. The unknown can be difficult and disturbing – exploring it might involve using too much of our time and energy, often without any clear indication of positive results. The unknown generates fear as it half-informs our experience. It is difficult to accept, for example, that at times we are acting out other people's wishes and preferences, or to believe quite how or why we are suffering from other people's helpfulness. This is not just uncomfortable but unwanted knowledge, and sometimes it may be better to stay with the idea, for example, that we are a friendly bunch of people who get on well with each other, than to investigate the actual relations and dynamics that characterize the 'team'.

The fact that there are times when intervention cannot be planned, produces unwanted outcomes, does not work, and times when it is best avoided, does not undermine the need for intervention. Attempts to intervene in organizations have helped to reveal a delightful and important fact, that however competent we are as individuals we cannot hope to guess, understand or manage the complex and shifting dynamics of the social systems that surround and fashion us. To put this in the context of strategic learning – individual knowledge, however broad and developed it may be, is of itself insufficient for institutional transformation. If, in the role of HRD practitioner or consultant, individuals are to engage fully with the responsibilities implied in interventions that aim to generate learning and change then it is important to address dynamics that exist in addition to the development of individuals' learning.

In this book, I have emphasized the relationship between emotion and politics, as well as the importance of this relationship to the creation of organizational dynamics that then legitimize emotional and political responses. I have argued that HRD practitioners can be responsible for finding ways of learning through collective experience, of reflecting and acting on the conscious and unconscious structures that are inevitably created through attempts to learn, and on the reflexive relationship between collective experience and the politics that both construct and constrain learning. To put this simply, we must learn to perceive and to act together in relation to that of which we are a part. This is inevitably and always a journey of becoming and one that is likely to produce the unexpected.

To summarize my thoughts about intervention, I have argued that it is too often aimed at the individual – whether this is the recipient or the agent of intervention. This focus has perpetuated a tendency to ignore emotions and politics that are integral to the relationship between an organizational role and organizing. In order to intervene in ways that support learning and change, it is necessary to mobilize and understand much more than rational capabilities and knowledge. All organizational actors are situated within, and are a part of, the complex and shifting dynamics of the social system that surrounds and fashions us, and that 'we' (through our relatedness) contribute to fashioning. Change is always a journey of becoming, yet we relate to it through 'an excessive preoccupation with planned change' (Tsoukas and Chia, 2002). These ideas have a profound impact on the ways in which intervention is imagined and undertaken, whether this involves an internal role, part of the responsibility of manager or leader, or whether it is an external role, the invited and temporary manager of attempts at learning and change.

Transforming the organizational processes within which roles such as leader, manager or consultant are embedded involves the development of approaches to intervention that encourage the questioning of those assumptions that organizing has created. The questioning of assumptions is a challenge to the rationality and stability that underpins organizing – it implies but rarely results in transformation. Questioning assumptions is an organizational imperative rather than a responsibility for individuals; it involves continuous inquiry into what the organization may become. It can prove very difficult for both individuals and collectives to perceive the importance of this definition of strategy. Such a perspective on strategy and learning suggests new imperatives for the delivery of HRD, and the potential of the role of the practitioner in the success of interventions aimed at learning and change. Personal appraisal, individual development, mentoring, self-managed learning – the current tools through which organizing is individualized – can be supplemented with new ideas and emerging techniques that recognize the importance of collective leadership and public reflection.

The result of engaging with characteristic emotions, politics and assumptions are often uncomfortable and unpredictable. However, I am suggesting that it is possible for all who intervene in organizations to actively speculate on how these dynamics contribute to the creation of patterns of organizing that limit our own and others' ability to learn. Through such speculation collective knowledge and action will be built. The potential impact of the HRD practitioner or consultant role has been diminished by our inability and unwillingness to engage with the unknown and the uncomfortable, as well as our difficulties in comprehending the organizational dynamics that emerge from everyday emotions and politics like expectations, caution and blame. Roles that have an emphasis on intervention and development are likely to be focal points where expectations, anxieties and fears are placed. As such, individuals or groups that have these roles will internalize limitations and enact them in strategies and practices for learning and change.

Intervention is important because it is not simply about rational techniques and plans for change. Problematizing the rational provides a broader picture of the point of intervention. In addition to the reasoning that underpins strategic learning, intervention is also an attempt to *realize* how little we know about the emotions and politics that drive and inform the ways we manage and organize. I have emphasized the word 'realize' here because it provides the ambiguity of language and meaning necessary to characterize intervention as a journey of becoming. There are two senses here to this word. First, realize means to understand (to appreciate/to apprehend) and, second, to make happen (to accomplish/to attain). In addition to its descriptive potential, the ambiguity in the word 'realize' also expresses and represents the two main components of any process of experiential learning – reflection and action; and two crucial components in processes of scholarship and inquiry – theory and practice. Therefore, the point of intervention is to make our individual and collective lack of knowledge visible and to allow it to disturb and to realign what we think we know. The point of intervention is to disturb our individual theories in use and our collective assumptions; it is to participate continuously in the struggle for learning and for transformation; it involves creating the space in our minds and in our organizations for the shock and delight that new and uncomfortable knowledge often brings.

Final reflections

To finish this chapter I want to outline briefly some thoughts that I am taking with me as I start to move beyond the actual writing of this book. The practical aspects of my argument about the impact of emotions and politics on learning and organizing are not difficult to explain. There are thoughts and feelings, emotions and expectations behind all actions that are taken from the roles of manager and/or leader. These thoughts and feelings are complicated because they are conscious and unconscious, as well as being situated within various interpersonal and organizational power relations. A way forward in terms of implementation is to make the various emotional and political processes that are at work behind actions as visible as possible, to open them up for discussion and critique, and therefore for transformation. This implies willingness from practitioners both individually and collectively to imagine that, at least in part, their roles concern the continuous generation of contextually specific learning and knowledge, as well as processes for sharing and rethinking such knowledge. Strategic learning is not likely to interest those leaders and managers who want to ignore or underplay emotions and politics generated by attempts at learning, or what they have to say about the organization as a system in context.

However, the emotions and politics experienced at work also undermine the desire to open up processes to critique. Equally, individuals sometimes delight in not sharing knowledge, and are content with the advantages of position or opportunity that are mobilized by withholding information or avoiding decisions. There are inevitably many attempts in everyday organizational experience to protect oneself against other people's political manoeuvres or simply to reinforce the advantages of a quiet life or the illusion of control. This is the paradox of development: that the desire for learning sits alongside the avoidance of learning. Using comments from two different reviewers who read my first draft, I can illustrate how the anxiety that is integral to this paradox is likely to make an impact on strategic learning in practice, either to promote learning or to avoid it. The comments are as follows:

> I must admit to ending up wondering what the non-academic can make of it . . . I get the workaday impression that organizational intervention is really too deep to enter. It should have a health warning: 'organizational learning is dangerous. You may open a can of worms – or bury it unopened, which is equally perilous.'

> Sometimes I felt I needed to work hard (harder than I wanted to) to understand what you meant . . . At one point I felt a bit despondent, it all seemed so difficult and a bit hopeless – for a few moments.

I think that these two perspectives suggest wider fears and/or anxieties that are going to accompany any practitioners with responsibilities for transformation. Actions that attempt to promote learning and change draw attention to themselves, they attract expectations and assumptions that do not necessarily belong to them, and they are transformed along the way by political agendas as well as broader organizing processes and relations. In one sense, therefore, the HRD practitioner cannot win – to open up or to bury learning may well produce either desired or undesired outcomes, or both. The role is potentially uncomfortable and annoyingly difficult, as well as being fascinating and rewarding. My own view is that the emotional experience and political processes that surround strategic learning are inevitably difficult to contain, but actions that encourage learning are often worth the risks. The HRD role in organizations is fundamentally important for the evolution of my perspective on strategic learning, and I think that the benefits of it are immense.

I have argued that there are many insights to be generated through inquiry into social, emotional and political processes that impact on learning and organizing, as well as the links between these and system psychodynamics. I have also described organizing as a process of *establishment*, a politics of imagined stability that is created through individual and collective action and inaction. Understanding the ways in which establishment has been and is being constructed is a key element in understanding the possibilities for human resource development within any specific organizational (or inter-organizational) context. However, these insights do extend the practice of HRD into the realms of strategic leadership and learning (rather than, for example, the training and development processes that accompany strategic leadership). This perspective asks the HRD practitioner to recognize his or her role as explicitly political, and one that has a strong connection both to the promotion and the avoidance of learning. I hope that this book will encourage continuing debate about how awareness of underlying emotional and political processes is useful to practitioners in their attempts to promote or to avoid learning and change. I can provide one example of *why* it is important.

I am currently involved with a company that wants to change the way they review their bids for contracts, both successful and failed. The institutional knowledge that inspired this decision is that existing bid reviews invariably ignore or avoid the emotions that are generated both throughout and after the bidding process (especially with failed bids); the power relations within the teams that have the responsibility to put the bid together; and the broader organizational politics and expectations that impact on bids. For the organization development team there are two broad questions that are particularly important. First, how are they to share learning across four international regions when there is a predisposition not to share information or to promote mutual learning? Second, how are they to create a reflective process that generates the openness necessary to raise and deal with all the organizational (e.g. emotions, power and leadership) as well as technical issues that the bidding process reveals? In effect, what they want to know is how to increase the effectiveness and ownership of the bidding process within the regions and how to share knowledge about bidding across their regions. Their aim is to increase the success rate of bids; however, (because their role is organization development) they also want to increase the impact that reviews make on openness, thereby improving the quality of communication and the depth of issues addressed.

This is one example of an organizational process that, because it is explicitly about success and failure, would benefit from inquiry into the emotions and politics that define how reviews are done, as well as how they might be done differently. It is my strong contention that the further consideration of such dynamics is an important part of the actions of individuals who occupy development roles as well as teams with development responsibilities. There is a very clear business case for *organizing reflection* here; it is going to improve the ability of company managers to win contracts. Given the wider agenda of the organization development team it might also make an impact on the quality of communication across regional boundaries, as well as on established organizational assumptions and their consequences.

One of my academic reviewers identified an assumption that he saw in my argument, which was that collectively is the *right* way to organize, that groups left to their own devices will collectively learn to do the right thing. This reviewer makes the point that 'collective learning will be bedevilled by its own politics and the right thing may have to be defined and held for the collective – by a leader?' He questions whether I am unnecessarily privileging the collective over the individual. The problem he identifies concerns both collective learning and collective reflection. For example, 'how is it possible to have collective reflection-in-action?' The reviewer's specific argument goes as follows:

> Reflection *on* action takes place outside the moments of action and can be anticipatory in advance of practice . . . Reflection *in* action takes place in the midst of and during action. That leads me to consider how possible is it to have collective reflection in action. The whole point about reflection in action is that it is contemporaneous with action, so it is not possible to

articulate reflections in action . . . because in the process of articulation, the moment of action has gone. Do you need to have another term that captures and represents what you are presently seeing as collective reflection in action, to create a new place for the idea which links to, but is separate from, Schön's individual reflection in action?

It is this latter question that I want to explain further, and at the same time illustrate how this issue of collective reflection in action can be raised as management education, as well as how it impacts on human resource development.

One thing I have learned from the experience of group relations approaches to human resource development is that there is 'collective' reflection-in-action (although I have referred to this as 'social reflection-in-action'). In the management courses I teach, I sometimes run an experiential exercise designed to show how quickly institutionalizing forces impact on behaviour. I ask the whole group of students to arrange themselves into small groups and stipulate only that each group gives themselves a name and that they start to discuss their distinctive identity. After twenty minutes, the small groups can interact with other groups if they want to, within a designated space that is provided for that purpose. Often, in the midst of their identity construction, the small groups not only create telling and extraordinary names and identities for themselves but also elaborate assumptions about other small groups, assumptions that influence how they feel about what is happening to their own group as well as what they say to and about other groups. It never fails to amaze me how quickly tacit rules, assumptions and fantasies are mobilized in the service of a group identity, and how quickly individuals adjust to the need to justify or protect that identity in the face of others' inquiries. Sometimes group members reach this point even before they have communicated directly with any of the other groups. I see this process as reflection-in-action because it can be addressed as an integral aspect of strategic relations with others, even as they are being negotiated. To be aware of the institutionalizing effects of organizing is not the same as being able to manage or even to understand them. However, in the midst of action it is important to carry an idea of the self-limiting effects of action.

Both of these examples describe my future engagement with strategic learning, working alongside practitioners and within my academic role. I hope to contribute to rethinking organizing processes so that they can include the emotions and politics that impact on them. Within a broader organizational context I intend to inquire into ways of sharing such knowledge, and further into the various structures and designs that might connect learning and organizing. I will continue to take for granted that management education can challenge assumptions about management and leadership as well as teaching about it, and that human resource development has a pivotal role to play in transforming both leadership and learning.

References

Alvesson, M. (1996) Leadership studies: from procedure and abstraction to reflexivity and situation. *Leadership Quarterly* 7/4: 455–485.

Antonacopoulou, E. and Gabriel, Y. (2001) Emotion, learning and organizational change: towards an integration of psychoanalytic and other perspectives. *Journal of Organizational Change Management* 14/5: 435–451.

Argyris, C. (1982) *Reasoning, Learning and Action*. San Francisco: Jossey-Bass.

Argyris, C. (1990) *Overcoming Organizational Defenses*. Needham Heights, MA: Allyn and Bacon.

Argyris, C. and Schön, D. (1996) *Organizational Learning II: Theory, Method, and Practice*. Reading, MA: Addison-Wesley.

Armstrong, D. (1991) *The 'Institution in the Mind'*. London: The Grubb Institute.

Armstrong, D. (2000) Emotions in organizations: disturbance or intelligence? *International Society for the Psychoanalytic Study of Organizations Annual Symposium*, London, June.

Avery, C. (1999) All power to you: collaborative leadership works. *Journal for Quality and Participation*, March/April.

Bain, A. (1998) Social defenses against organizational learning. *Human Relations* 51/3: 413–429.

Baum, H. S. (1993) Organizational politics against organizational culture: a psycho-analytic perspective. In L. Hirschhorn and C.K. Barnett (eds) *The Psychodynamics of Organizations*. Philadelphia: Temple University Press.

Bazelgette, J., Hutton, J. and Reed, B. (1997) Organisation-in-the-mind. In J. E. Neumann, K. Kellner and A. Dawson-Shepherd (eds) *Developing Organisational Consultancy*. London: Routledge.

Bennis, W. (1999) The end of leadership: exemplary leadership is possible without full inclusion, initiatives and cooperation of followers. *Organizational Dynamics* 28/1: 71–80.

Bennis, W. (2001) Leadership in unnerving times. *Sloan Management Review*, Winter: 97–103.

Bion, W. R. (1962) *Learning from Experience*. London: William Heinemann.

Bion, W. R. (1985) Container and contained. In A. D. Coleman and M. H. Geller (eds) *Group Relations Reader 2*. Washington DC: A. K. Rice Institute.

Bontis, N., Crossan, M. and Hulland, J. (2002) Managing an organizational learning system by aligning stocks and flows. *Journal of Management Studies* 39/4: 437–470.

Boshyk, Y. (ed.) (2000) *Business Driven Action Learning: Global Best Practices*. London: Macmillan.

Boshyk, Y. (2002) Why business driven action learning? In Y. Boshyk (ed.) *Action Learning Worldwide: Experiences of Leadership and Organizational Development*. Basingstoke: Palgrave Macmillan.

Brown, A. D. and Starkey, K. (2000) Organizational identity and learning: a psychodynamic perspective. *Academy of Management Review* 25/1: 102–120.

Brown, L. M. and Posner, B. Z. (2001) Exploring the relationship between learning and leadership. *Leadership and Organization Development Journal* 22/6: 274–280.

Bryman, A. (1996) Leadership in organizations. In S. R. Clegg, C. Hardy and W. Nord (eds) *The Handbook of Organization Studies*. London: Sage, pp. 276–292.

Callahan, J. L. and McCollum, E. E. (2002) Conceptualizations of emotion research in organizational contexts. *Advances in Developing Human Resources* 4/1: 4–21.

Cardona, F. (1999) The team as a sponge: how the nature of the task affects the behaviour and mental life of a team. In R. French and R. Vince (eds) *Group Relations, Management and Organization*. Oxford: Oxford University Press.

CEML (2002) Managers and leaders – raising our game. London: Council for Excellence in Management and Leadership, April.

Career Innovations Group (2002) Today's leadership challenge. *Strategic HR Review* 1/5: 16–18.

Clegg, S., Hardy, C. and Nord, W. (1996) *The Handbook of Organization Studies*. London: Sage.

Cohen, M. D. and Sproull, L. S. (eds) (1996) *Organizational Learning*. London: Sage.

Coleman, A. D. and Geller, M. H. (1985) *Group Relations Reader 2*. Washington, DC: A. K. Rice Institute.

Cooper, A. (1998) Psychoanalysis and the politics of organizational theory. *Group Analysis* 31/3: 283–296.

Coopey, J. (1995) The learning organization, power, politics and ideology. *Management Learning* 26/2, 193–213.

Coopey, J. and Burgoyne, J. (1999) Politics and learning. In M. Easterby-Smith, L. Araujo and J. Burgoyne (eds) *Organizational Learning: 3rd International Conference*, Volume 1, pp. 275–298. Lancaster University.

Coopey, J. and Burgoyne, J. (2000) Politics and organizational learning. *Journal of Management Studies* 37/6: 869–886.

Coutu, D. (2002) The anxiety of learning: the HBR interview (with Edgar Schein). *Harvard Business Review*, March: 100–106.

Crossan, M. (2003) Chris Argyris and Donald Schön's 'organizational learning': there is no silver bullet. *Academy of Management Executive* 17/2: 38–39.

Crossan, M., Lane, H. W. and White, R. E. (1999) An organizational learning framework: from intuition to institution. *Academy of Management Review* 24/3: 522–537.

Daunton, L., Hole, C., James, C. and Vince, R. (2000) The development and evaluation of experiential learning methods on the Masters in Business Administration (MBA), 'Pont Dysgu' Papers Series, University of Glamorgan.

Denis, J.-L., Lamothe, L. and Langley, A. (2001) The dynamics of collective leadership and strategic change in pluralistic organizations. *Academy of Management Journal* 44/4: 809–837.

Diamond, M. A. (1990) Psychoanalytic phenomenology and organizational analysis. *Public Administration Quarterly* 14/1: 32–42.

Dierkes, M., Berthoin Antal, A., Child, J. and Nonaka, I. (2001) *The Handbook of Organizational Learning and Knowledge*. Oxford: Oxford University Press.

Domagalski, T.A. (1999) Emotion in organizations: main currents. *Human Relations* 52/6: 833–852.

Easterby-Smith, M. (1997) Disciplines of organizational learning: contributions and critiques. *Human Relations* 50/9: 1085–1113.

Easterby-Smith, M. and Araujo, L. (1999) Organizational learning: current debates and opportunities. In M. Easterby-Smith, J. Burgoyne and L. Araujo (eds) *Organizational Learning and the Learning Organization*. London: Sage.

Easterby-Smith, M., Araujo, L. and Burgoyne, J. (1999) *Organizational Learning: 3rd International Conference* (2 volumes). Lancaster University.

Easterby-Smith, M., Snell, R. and Gherardi, S. (1998) Organizational learning: diverging communities of practice? *Management Learning* 29/3: 259–273.

Easterby-Smith, M., Crossan, M. and Nicolini, D. (eds) (2000) Organizational learning: past, present and future. *Journal of Management Studies* 37/6: Special Issue.

Elkjaer, B. (1999) In search of a social learning theory. In M. Easterby-Smith, J. Burgoyne and L. Araujo (eds) *Organizational Learning and the Learning Organization*. London: Sage.

Ellinger, A. D., Watkins, K. E. and Bostrom, R. P. (1999) Managers as facilitators of learning in learning organizations. *Human Resource Development Quarterly* 10/2: 105–125.

Erlich-Ginor, M. and Erlich, S. (1999) Mental health under fire: organizational intervention in a wounded service. In R. French and R. Vince (eds) *Group Relations, Management and Organization*. Oxford: Oxford University Press.

Fanning, D. (2000) Hyder's power failure. *Business Age*, May: 31–32.

Fineman, S. (1993) *Emotion in Organizations*. London: Sage

Fineman, S. (1996) Emotion and organizing. In S. Clegg, C. Hardy and W. Nord (eds) *Handbook of Organization Studies*. London: Sage.

Fineman, S. (1997) Emotion and management learning. *Management Learning* 28/1: 13–25.

Fineman, S. (2001) Managing emotions at work: some political reflections. Paper presented at the *Academy of Management Conference*, Washington, DC.

Fineman, S. and Sturdy, A. (1999) The emotions of control: a qualitative exploration of environmental regulation. *Human Relations* 52/5: 631–663.

Freire, P. (1972) *Pedagogy of the Oppressed*. Harmondsworth: Penguin.

Freire, P. (1974) *Education as the Practice of Freedom*. London: Readers and Writers Publishing Co-operative.

French, R. and Grey, C. (1996) *Rethinking Management Education*. London: Sage.

French, R. and Vince, R. (eds) (1999) *Group Relations, Management and Organization*. Oxford: Oxford University Press.

Gabriel, Y. (1999) *Organizations in Depth*. London: Sage.

Gabriel, Y. (2000) Psychoanalytic contributions to the study of the emotional life of organizations. *Administration and Society* 30/3: 291–314.

Garvin, D. A. (1993) Building a learning organization. *Harvard Business Review* 71/4: 78–91.

Gherardi, S. (1999) Learning as problem-driven or learning in the face of mystery? *Organization Studies* 20/1: 101–124.

Gherardi, S. (2003) Knowing as desiring: mythic knowledge and the knowledge journey in communities of practitioners. Paper presented to the *Organizational Learning and Knowledge 5th International Conference*, Lancaster University, May/June.

Gherardi, S. and Nicolini, D. (2001) The sociological foundations of organizational learning. In M. Dierkes et al., *The Handbook of Organizational Learning and Knowledge*. Oxford: Oxford University Press.

Gherardi, S., Nicolini, D. and Odella, F. (1998) Toward a social understanding of how people learn in organizations: the notion of situated curriculum. *Management Learning* 29/3: 273–297.

Gibb, A. A. (1997) Small firms' training and competitiveness: building upon the small business as a learning organization. *International Small Business Journal* 15/3: 13–29.

Gibbons, S. (1999) Learning teams: action learning for leaders. *Journal of Quality and Participation*, July/August: 26–29.

Greenwood, R. and Hinings, C. R. (1996) Understanding radical organizational change: bringing together the old and the new institutionalism. *Academy of Management Review* 21/4: 1022–1054.

Gutmann, D. (2003) *Psychoanalysis and Management*. London: Karnac Books.

Gutmann, D., Ternier-David, J. and Verrier, C. (1999) From envy to desire: witnessing the transformation. In R. French and R. Vince (eds) *Group Relations, Management and Organization*. Oxford: Oxford University Press.

Hammer, M. and Stanton, S. A. (1997) The power of reflection. *Fortune Magazine*, 24 November: 291–296.

Hinshelwood, R. D. (1998) Creatures of each other. In A. Foster and V. Zagier Roberts (eds) *Managing Mental Health in the Community: Chaos and Containment*. London: Routledge.

Hirschhorn, L. (1988) *The Workplace Within: Psychodynamics of Organizational Life*. Cambridge, MA: MIT Press.

Hochschild, A. R. (1979) Emotion work, feeling rules and social structure. *American Journal of Sociology* 85/3, 551–575.

Hochschild, A. R. (1983) *The Managed Heart*. Berkeley: University of California Press.

Hoggett, P. (1992) *Partisans in an Uncertain World: The Psychoanalysis of Engagement*. London: Free Association Books.

Hopfl, H. and Linstead, S. (1997) Introduction: learning to feel and feeling to learn: emotion and learning in organizations. *Management Learning* 28/1: 5–12.

Hosking, D. and Fineman, S. (1990) Organising processes. *Journal of Management Studies* 27/6: 583–604.

Hurlow, S., James, C. and Lenz, P. (1998) Creating learning partnerships: a case study of a higher education institution and a commercial organisation. Paper delivered to the *Emergent Fields in Management: Connecting Learning and Critique Conference*, University of Leeds, UK, 15–17 July.

Isaacs, W. (1999) *Dialogue and the Art of Thinking Together*. New York: Currency/Doubleday.

Ixer, G. (1999) There's no such thing as reflection. *British Journal of Social Work* 29: 513–527.

Jacobs, R. L. (1997) HRD partnerships for integrating HRD research and practice. In R. Swanson and E. Holton III (eds) *Human Resource Development Handbook: Linking Research and Practice*, San Francisco: Berrett-Koehler, pp. 47–61.

Katzenbach, J. R. and Smith, D. K. (1993) *The Wisdom of Teams: Creating the High Performance Organization*. Boston, MA: Harvard Business School.

Kemmis, S. (1985) Action research and the politics of reflection. In D. Boud, R. Keogh and D. Walker (eds) *Reflection: Turning Experience into Learning.* London: Kogan Page.

Kets de Vries, M. F. R. and Miller, D. (1985) *The Neurotic Organization.* London: Jossey-Bass.

Knights, D. and McCabe, D. (1998) When 'life is but a dream': obliterating politics through business process re-engineering. *Human Relations* 51/6: 761–798.

Knights, D. and McCabe, D. (1999) 'Are there no limits to authority?': TQM and organizational power. *Organization Studies* 20/2: 197–224.

Knights, D. and Willmott, H. (1992) Conceptualising leadership processes: a study of senior managers in a financial services company. *Journal of Management Studies* 29/6: 761–782.

Kofman, F. and Senge, P. M. (1993) Communities of commitment: the heart of learning organizations. *Organizational Dynamics* 22/2: 5–23.

Kolb, D. (1984) *Experiential Learning.* Englewood Cliffs, NJ: Prentice-Hall.

Kouzes, J. M. and Posner, B. Z. (1993) *Credibility: How Leaders Gain and Lose It, Why People Demand It.* San Francisco: Jossey-Bass.

Kuwada, K. (1998) Strategic learning: the continuous side of discontinuous strategic change. *Organization Science* 9/6: 719–736.

Lawrence, W. G. (2000) *Tongued with Fire: Groups in Experience.* London: Karnac Books.

Lee, M. (2001) A refusal to define HRD. *Human Resource Development International* 4/3: 327–341.

Lei, D., Slocum, J. W. and Pitts, R. A. (1999) Designing organizations for competitive advantage: the power of learning and unlearning *Organizational Dynamics* 27/3: 24–39.

Lipshitz, R. and Popper, M. (2000) Organizational learning in a hospital. *Journal of Applied Behavioural Science* 36/3: 345–361.

McGoldrick, J., Stewart, J. and Watson, S. (2002) *Understanding HRD.* London: Routledge.

March, J. G. (1996) Exploration and exploitation in organizational learning. In M. D. Cohen and L. S. Sproull (eds) *Organizational Learning.* Thousand Oaks, CA: Sage, pp. 101–123.

Marris, P. (1974) *Loss and Change.* London: Routledge and Kegan Paul.

Marsick, V. J. and O'Neil, J. (1999) The many faces of action learning. *Management Learning* 30/2: 159–176.

Menzies-Lyth, I. (1990) Social systems as a defence against anxiety. In E. Trist and H. Murray (eds) *The Social Engagement of Social Science, Vol. 1.* London: Free Association Books.

Miller, E. J. (1990) Experiential Learning 1: The development of the Leicester model. In E. Trist and H. Murray (eds) *The Social Engagement of Social Science, Vol. 1.* London: Free Association Books.

Miller, E. J. and Rice, A. K. (1967) *Systems of Organisation.* London: Tavistock.

National Council, Education and Learning Wales (2002) *ELWa Corporate Strategy,* Online. Available HTTP: <http://www.elwa.ac.uk/elwa.asp?pageid=1134> (accessed December 2002).

Neumann, J. (1999) Systems psychodynamics in the service of political organizational change. In R. French and R. Vince (eds) *Group Relations, Management and Organization.* Oxford: Oxford University Press.

Neumann, J. and Hirschhorn, L. (1999) The challenge of integrating psychodynamic and organizational theory. *Human Relations* 52/6: 683–695.

Newell, S., Robertson, M., Scarborough, H. and Swan, J. (2002) *Managing Knowledge Work.* London: Palgrave.

Nicolini, D., Sher, M., Childerstone, S. and Gorli, M (forthcoming) In search of the 'structure that reflects': promoting organizational reflection practices in a UK health authority. In M. Reynolds and R. Vince (eds) *Organizing Reflection.* London: Ashgate.

Obholzer, A. (1994) Managing social anxieties in public sector organizations. In A. Obholzer and V. Zagier Roberts (eds) *The Unconscious at Work.* London: Routledge.

Obholzer, A. (1999) Managing the unconscious at work. In R. French and R. Vince (eds) *Group Relations, Management and Organization.* Oxford: Oxford University Press.

Obholzer, A. and Roberts, V. Z. (1994) *The Unconscious at Work.* London: Routledge.

Organizational and Social Dynamics (2001) Editors' introduction: values, and the journal's guiding perspectives. *Organizational and Social Dynamics* 1/1: 1–7.

Orlikowski, W. J. and Hofman, J. D. (1997) An improvisational model for change management: the case of groupware technologies. *Sloan Management Review* 38/2: 11–21.

O'Toole, J., Galbraith, J. and Lawler, E. E. (2002) When two (or more) heads are better than one: the promise and pitfalls of shared leadership. *California Management Review* 44/4: 65–83.

Palmer, B. (1979) Learning and the group experience. In G. Lawrence (ed.), *Exploring Individual and Organisational Boundaries.* Chichester: Wiley, pp. 169–92.

Palmer, I. and Hardy, C. (2000) *Thinking about Management.* London: Sage.

Pedler, M. (1997) Interpreting action learning. In J. Burgoyne and M. Reynolds (eds) *Management Learning: Integrating Perspectives in Theory and Practice.* London: Sage.

Pedler, M. (2002) Accessing local knowledge: action learning and organizational learning in Walsall. *Human Resource Development International* 5/4: 523–540.

Pedler, M. and Aspinwall, K. (1998) *A Concise Guide to the Learning Organization.* London: Lemos and Crane.

Pedler, M., Burgoyne, J. G. and Boydell, T. (1991) *The Learning Company.* Maidenhead: McGraw-Hill.

Pettigrew, A. M. and Whipp, R. (1991) *Managing Change for Corporate Success.* Oxford: Blackwell.

Pfeffer, J. (1981) *Power in Organisations.* Cambridge, MA: Ballinger.

Prange, C. (1999) Organizational learning: desperately seeking theory? In M. Easterby-Smith, J. Burgoyne and L. Araujo (eds) *Organizational Learning and the Learning Organization.* London: Sage.

Raelin, J. A. (1999) Preface to the Special Issue: The action dimension in management: diverse approaches to research, teaching and development. *Management Learning* 30/2: 115–126.

Raelin, J. A. (2001) Public reflection as the basis of learning, *Management Learning* 32/1: 11–30.

Raelin, J. A. (2003) *Creating Leaderful Organizations: How to Bring Out Leadership in Everyone.* Williston, VT: Berrett-Koehler.

Reason, P. (1988) *Human Inquiry in Action*, London: Sage.

Reed, B. (1976) Organisational role analysis. In C. L. Cooper (ed.) *Developing Social Skills in Managers.* London: Macmillan.

Revans, R. (1983) *The ABC of Action Learning*, Bromley, Kent: Chartwell Bratt.

Reynolds, M. (1998) Reflection and critical reflection in management learning. *Management Learning* 29/2: 183–200.

Reynolds, M. (1999a) Grasping the nettle: possibilities and pitfalls of a critical management pedagogy. *British Journal of Management* 9/3: 171–184.

Reynolds, M. (1999b) Critical reflection and management education: rehabilitating less hierarchical approaches. *Journal of Management Education* 23/5: 537–553.

Reynolds, M. and Vince, R. (forthcoming) *Organizing Reflection*, London: Ashgate.

Schein, E. H. (1993) How can organizations learn faster? The challenge of entering the green room. *Sloan Management Review*, Winter.

Schein, E. (2000) Comments by Edgar Schein (on 'The clinical paradigm: Manfred Kets de Vries's reflections on organizational therapy'). *European Management Journal* 18/1: 17–18.

Schneider, S. C. and Dunbar, R. L. M. (1992) A psychoanalytic reading of hostile takeover events. *Academy of Management Review* 17/3: 537–567.

Schön, D. (1983) *The Reflective Practitioner: How Professionals Think in Action*. New York: Basic Books.

Senge, P. M. (1990) *The Fifth Discipline: The Art and Practice of the Learning Organization*. London: Century Business.

Senge, P. (1999) The gurus speak (panel discussion): complexity and organizations. *Emergence* 1/1: 73–91.

Senge, P., Heifetz, R. A. and Torbert, B. (2000) A conversation on leadership. *Reflections* 2/1: 57–68.

Shapiro, E. R. and Carr, A. W. (1991) *Lost in Familiar Places: Creating New Connections between the Individual and Society*. New Haven, CT: Yale University Press.

Sievers, B. (2001) 'I will not let thee go, except thou bless me!' (Genesis 32:26): some considerations regarding the constitution of authority, inheritance and succession. *Human Resource Development International* 4/3: 357–381.

Statt, D. A. (1994) *Psychology and the World of Work*. London: Macmillan.

Stein, M. (1996) Unconscious phenomena in work groups. In M. A. West (ed.) *The Handbook of Work Group Psychology*. Chichester: Wiley.

Sun, H.-C. (2003) Conceptual clarifications for 'organizational learning', 'learning organization' and 'a learning organization'. *Human Resource Development International* 6/2: 153–166.

Swanson, R. (1997) HRD research: don't go to work without it. In R. Swanson and E. Holton III (eds) *Human Resource Development Handbook: Linking Research and Practice*. San Francisco: Berrett-Koehler, pp. 47–61.

Thomas, A. B. (2003) *Controversies in Management* (2nd edition). London: Routledge.

Thomas, J. B., Watts-Sussman, S. and Henderson, J. C. (2001) Understanding strategic learning: linking organizational learning, knowledge management and sense-making. *Organization Science* 12/3: 331–345.

Triest, J. (1999) The inner drama of role taking in an organization. In R. French and R. Vince (eds) *Group Relations, Management and Organization*. Oxford: Oxford University Press.

Trist, E. and Murray, H. (1990) *The Social Engagement of Social Science, Vol. 1*. London: Free Association Books.

Tsoukas, H. and Chia, R. (2002) On organizational becoming: rethinking organizational change. *Organization Science* 13/5: 567–582.

Turnbull, S. (2002) The planned and unintended emotions generated by a corporate change program. *Advances in Developing Human Resources* 4/1: 22–38.

Ulrich, D., von Glinow, M.A. and Jick, T. (1993) High-impact learning: building and diffusing learning capability. *Organizational Dynamics*, Autumn: 52–66.

Vince, R. (1996) *Managing Change: Reflections on Equality and Management Learning*. Bristol: The Policy Press.

Vince, R. (1998) Behind and beyond Kolb's Learning cycle. *Journal of Management Education* 22/3: 304–319.

Vince, R. (2000) Learning in public organizations in 2010. *Public Money and Management* 20/1: 39–44.

Vince, R. (2001) Power and emotion in organizational learning. *Human Relations* 54/10: 1325–1351.

Vince, R. (2002) Organizing reflection. *Management Learning* 33/1: 63–78.

Vince, R. (2004) Action learning and organizational learning: power, politics and emotion in organizations. *Action Learning: Research and Practice* 1/1 (in press).

Vince, R. and Broussine, M. (1996) Paradox, defense and attachment: accessing and working with emotions and relations underlying organisational change. *Organization Studies* 17/1: 1–21.

Vince, R. and Broussine, M. (2000) Rethinking organisational learning in local government. *Local Government Studies* 26/1: 15–30.

Vince, R. and Martin, L. (1993) Inside action learning: an exploration of the psychology and politics of the action learning model. *Management Education and Development* 24/3: 205–215.

Vince, R., Sutcliffe, K. and Olivera, F. (2002) Organizational learning: new directions. *British Journal of Management* 13: Special Issue, September.

Wales Management Council (2002) *Leadership Development: 'Agenda for Action'*, November draft, online. Available HTTP: <http://www.crc-wmc.org.uk/welcome/Agenda_for_Action.htm> (accessed December 2002)

Wallace, M. (2002) Sharing leadership of schools through teamwork: a justifiable risk? *Education Management and Administration* 29/2: 153–167.

Watson, T. J. (2001) Beyond managism: negotiated narratives and critical management education in practice. *British Journal of Management* 12/4: 385–396.

Weick, K. E. (1995) *Sensemaking in Organizations*. London: Sage.

Weick, K. E. (2002) Puzzles in organizational learning: an exercise in disciplined imagination. *British Journal of Management* 13 (special issue): S7–S16.

Weick, K. E. and Westley, F. (1996) Organizational learning: affirming an oxymoron. In S. Clegg, C. Hardy and W. Nord (eds) *The Handbook of Organization Studies*. London: Sage.

Weinstein, K. (2002) Action learning: the classic approach. In Y. Boshyk (ed.) *Action Learning Worldwide: Experiences of Leadership and Organizational Development*. Basingstoke: Palgrave Macmillan.

Welsh Assembly (2002) *A Winning Wales*. Online. Available HTTP: <http://www.wales.gov.uk/keypubpublicationslists/index.htm> (accessed December 2002).

Western Mail (1999) Can Hyder clear the next hurdles? Leader comment, Friday, 10 December.

Willmott, H. (1994) Management education: provocations to a debate. *Management Learning* 25/1: 105–136.

Willmott, H. (1997) Critical management learning. In J. Burgoyne and M. Reynolds (eds) *Management Learning: Integrating Perspectives in Theory and Practice*. London: Sage.

Winter, R. (1989) *Learning from Experience: Principles and Practice in Action-research*. London: Falmer Press.

Woodall, J. (2003) Editorial: Saying Hello. *Human Resource Development International* 6/1: 1–4.

Yukl, G. A. (1998) *Leadership in Organizations* (4th edition). Hemel Hempstead: Prentice-Hall.

Index

Lightning Source UK Ltd.
Milton Keynes UK
UKHW021953120219
337149UK00006B/64/P